Katherine Howard

CONOR BYRNE

Katherine Howard

HENRY VIII's SLANDERED QUEEN

Front Cover: Portrait of a Lady, perhaps Katherine Howard (1520–42),
Royal Collection Trust / © Her Majesty Queen Elizabeth II, 2018

First published 2019

The History Press
The Mill, Brimscombe Port
Stroud, Gloucestershire, GL5 2QG
www.thehistorypress.co.uk

British Library Cataloguing in Publication Data.
A catalogue record for this book is available from the British Library.

ISBN 978 0 7509 9060 8

Typesetting and origination by The History Press
Printed and bound in Great Britain by TJ International Ltd

CONTENTS

ACKNOWLEDGEMENTS

THIS BOOK IS THE culmination of over five years of research into the life of one of England's most defamed queens consort. When I began researching Katherine Howard's brief life in 2012–13, very little had been written about her. Popular evaluations of her usually repeated sordid rumours of her sexual misdemeanours and the scandalous reasons for her execution after less than two years of marriage to Henry VIII. *Katherine Howard: A New History* (2014) aimed to redress these shortcomings in the extant writing about her; since then, two further biographies of Katherine have been published. Some of the theories I put forward in the 2014 biography have subsequently been adopted by other historians, including my agreement with Susan James that the portrait dated *c.* 1540–45 housed at the Metropolitan Museum of Art (reproduced in the images section of this book) may well be a likeness of Katherine painted during her brief period as queen.

This biography provides further insights into Katherine's life and queenship, while responding to the latest scholarship concerning her. It stresses my initial conclusions that Katherine was neither adulterous nor a 'juvenile delinquent' who was solely responsible for, or deserved, her execution in 1542. My interpretation draws on and is informed by early modern perceptions of sexuality, fertility and gender, while providing additional evidence for her date of birth and portraiture. The present volume also offers a discussion of how Katherine has been represented in the medium of film and television. Essentially, republishing this biography has offered me a welcome opportunity of revisiting my earlier conclusions about Katherine's brief life in the context of early modern gender relations. As this book indicates, I have long been fascinated by how Katherine has been represented, both during her lifetime and posthumously, by her contemporaries and by those living in the twentieth and twenty-first centuries. This book is as much a study of Katherine's historiography and how she has been represented as it is a narrative and analysis of her life.

There are a number of libraries and archives that I wish to thank: in particular the University of Exeter Library, the National Archives at Kew, the Surrey History Centre, Cheshire Record Archive and Fleet Library. I want to thank the team at The History Press, especially Mark Beynon, for agreeing to take on my project and for providing invaluable support during the research and writing of this book. A number of individuals have encouraged my research and writing over the years: in particular my sixth-form teachers, Diana Laffin and Jo Chambers, who subsequently invited me to return to speak to A-level students about my experiences. I am immensely grateful for the opportunities that they have afforded me.

I must thank the lecturers, professors and teachers at the universities I attended who inspired me with their passion and knowledge of the past, especially those who specialised in early modern history and fuelled my fascination with the period. My research into Katherine Howard's tragic life began in 2012, and I am very grateful to St Hugh's College, Oxford, for responding so warmly to my initial research for their essay competition. I wish also to thank those who have encouraged me to write for their websites and publications over the years, including Natalie Grueninger (On The Tudor Trail), Susan Bordo (*The Creation of Anne Boleyn*), Olga Hughes (Nerdalicious), Moniek (History of Royal Women), Janet Wertman (*Jane the Quene*) and Debra Bayani (*Jasper Tudor*).

I would also like to thank my colleagues at the Universities of Exeter and St Andrews for publishing my research in their undergraduate academic journals and for working with me on the respective committees, whether as a writer or co-editor. I must also pay tribute to the many historians who corresponded with me over the years, with whom I discussed theories and whose work I continue to respect and enjoy, including among others Retha Warnicke, Alison Weir, Gareth Russell and Suzannah Lipscomb. Retha Warnicke, in particular, was very helpful in sharing her thoughts and research with me about Katherine.

And finally, thanks to those historians and researchers who have provided friendship and support in varying circumstances, including Melanie V. Taylor for providing both advice and editorial assistance, but also to my close friends and family outside of history who have been there for me when I have needed it.

THE HISTORIOGRAPHY OF QUEEN KATHERINE HOWARD

In histories that treat men as three-dimensional and complex personalities, the women shine forth in universal stereotypes: the shrew, the whore, the shy virgin, or the blessed mother.

Retha M. Warnicke, *The Rise and Fall of Anne Boleyn: Family Politics at the Court of Henry VIII* (Cambridge, 1989).

It is not yet said who will be Queen; but the common voice is that this King will not be long without a wife, for the great desire he has to have further issue.

French ambassador Marillac writing to François I of France on 13 February 1542, the day of Katherine Howard's execution.

FOLLOWING HER EXECUTION ON charges of high treason in February 1542, as the second of Henry VIII's queens to be beheaded in less than six years, Katherine Howard was consigned to history as a flirtatious and irresponsible teenager who courted disaster through her reckless behaviour and adulterous liaisons with a succession of lovers under her ageing husband's nose. Unlike Anne Boleyn or Katherine of Aragon, she has not proved to be a particularly popular subject among historians, almost certainly due to the briefness of her reign and the scarcity of wide-ranging source material. Despite this relative lack of interest, the historiography relating to Katherine is significant in offering insights into how the specific political and social context has informed interpretations of the career of Henry's fifth queen. Exploring the historiography of Henry's fifth queen is relevant, from the perspective of this biography, in indicating how problems of evidence and a lack of cultural awareness have often obscured understandings of Katherine's story.

To many, she remains the vain and unintelligent 'bad girl' who deceived her doting husband firstly by concealing her pre-marital past and secondly by actually cuckolding him after their marriage. It is worth emphasising, as Holly Kizewski noted, that 'both detractors and defenders usually reduce Katherine to her sexuality'.[1]

The first contemporary writer to explore Katherine's career in detail was the unknown author of *The Chronicle of Henry VIII of England*, more usually known as the *Spanish Chronicle*, which was probably composed ten years or more after the events it describes, by an unknown Spaniard living in London.[2] Characterising Katherine as 'more graceful and beautiful than any lady in the Court' when she first met the king aged around 15, the chronicler created a sympathetic tale of true love, passion and premature death.[3] This writer emphasised the queen's youth, explaining that it created difficulties in her relationship with her elder stepdaughter Mary Tudor, before recounting how her 'giddy' nature guided her infatuation with Thomas Culpeper, who had been in love with Katherine before her marriage to the king.[4] Downcast with his poor fortune, Culpeper supposedly wrote a letter to the queen which he passed to her while dancing with her, leading the queen to reply in encouragement. Revealing her secret love for Culpeper to a lady-in-waiting named Jane (perhaps inspired by Lady Jane Rochford), the queen was eventually arrested and charged with treason when that lady informed Edward Seymour about the relationship.[5] Later, both the queen and Culpeper were beheaded, professing their love for one another on the scaffold.[6] In this chronicle, no mention was made of Francis Dereham, Henry Manox or Jane Rochford, all of whom were implicated in the queen's downfall and, with the exception of Manox, were executed alongside Katherine and Culpeper.

Other contemporary sources found Katherine a less interesting subject. Lord Herbert, writer of *The Life and Raigne of King Henry the Eighth*,[7] spent at most four pages (in a work comprising over 600) on the brief queenship of Katherine, which was overwhelmingly focused on her downfall in 1541. Herbert concluded his brief account with the detail of Katherine's execution alongside Lady Rochford.[8] Nicholas Harpsfield, an English historian and Catholic apologist and priest writing during the reign of Katherine's step-daughter Mary I, scarcely mentioned Henry VIII's fifth queen but recounted her 'pain and shame' at being found 'an harlot before he [Henry] married her, and an adulteress after he married her'.[9] Perhaps Harpsfield was aware of Katherine's alleged conflict with her stepdaughter, whom Harpsfield surely admired as the restorer of what he perceived as true religion. George Cavendish, writing during the 1550s, similarly emphasised, as had the writer of *The Chronicle of Henry VIII*, Katherine's 'floryshyng ... youthe with beawtie freshe and pure'. Cavendish made mention of Katherine's youth several times in his narrative, while indicating that the queen's 'blazing beautie' brought her 'myschefe'. Believing, like the Spanish chronicler, that Katherine and Culpeper had indulged in a romantic or adulterous liaison, Cavendish wrote: 'Culpeper yong, and I, God wott, but fraylle, we bothe to feeble our lusts for to resist.' Culpeper allegedly 'folowed [his] pleasure' through his 'pride and viciousnes' in choosing to seduce Queen Katherine, which eventually resulted in his disgrace and execution.[10] Nicholas Sander, who wrote a treatise attacking Henry VIII and the annulment of his marriage to Katherine of Aragon, ignored Katherine Howard entirely but for his dismissive comment that 'but as the king was faithful neither to God nor to his first wife, so also his wives were not faithful to him', explaining that Katherine had sexually sinned with both Francis Dereham and Culpeper.[11] For Sander, Katherine's betrayal of Henry constituted a form of poetic justice.

The first modern historian to discuss Katherine's career in detail was Agnes Strickland, whose *Lives of the Queens of England* was published in twelve volumes between 1840 and 1848; her *Memoirs of the Queens of Henry VIII* followed in the 1850s. Undoubtedly influenced by pervading Victorian values, Strickland characterised Katherine's life as 'a grand moral lesson', in which she condemned 'the vanity of female ambition' and Katherine's personal 'guilt'.[12] Despite this judgemental analysis, Strickland seemed to view Katherine sympathetically, for she blamed the 'polluting influence' of individuals within the household of the dowager Duchess of Norfolk, who took 'a fiendish delight in perverting the principles and debasing the mind of the nobly born damsel [Katherine]'.[13] Strickland doubted that Katherine committed adultery with Culpeper, believing that the testimony of Katherine's ladies was 'unfavourable' to their mistress and prompted by the 'deadly malice' of the enemies of the Howards.[14] Strickland also remarked bitterly that 'Katharine Howard was led like a sheep to the slaughter, without being permitted to unclose her lips in her own defence'.[15]

Henry Herbert's short book on the queens of Henry VIII, published in 1860, similarly viewed Henry's fifth queen with sympathy, believing that 'history … has no sadder tale than this of the young, beautiful, unhappy Howard', and remarking that 'from the stones of the Tower yard, [her] blood still cries for vengeance'.[16] Martin Hume, who edited *The Chronicle of Henry VIII* in which, as has already been noted, Katherine was presented as a youthful beauty who was forced to marry an ageing monarch despite her affections for his courtier Thomas Culpeper, suggested in his biography of Henry's queens, published in 1905, that when she became queen Katherine was 'a very beautiful girl of about eighteen', who had participated in 'immoral liberties' with the musician Henry Manox 'while she was yet a child, certainly not more than thirteen', before she fell 'deeply in love' with Dereham. Hume concluded that Katherine 'had erred much for love … but taking a human view of the whole circumstances of her life, and of the personality of the man she married, she is surely more worthy of pity than condemnation'.[17]

Lacey Baldwin Smith's biography of Katherine in 1961, however, marked a watershed in the historiography of Henry VIII's fifth queen, for it was the first full-length study of her and the circumstances of her brief tenure as queen. Like Strickland, Baldwin Smith was undoubtedly influenced by the social and cultural values present in his own day, while adhering to traditional gender stereotypes in his characterisation of Katherine. Believing that Katherine was guilty of adultery with Culpeper and thus deserving of her eventual fate, Baldwin Smith concluded that her life was 'little more than a series of petty trivialities and wanton acts punctuated by sordid politics'.[18] As with Strickland in the Victorian age, Baldwin Smith believed that Katherine's life could be interpreted as 'a lesson in Tudor morality'.[19]

In suggesting that Katherine was a tool of her ambitious family, Baldwin Smith indicated that she was orthodox in her religion and 'naïvely credulous'.[20] He argued that Katherine willingly and knowingly engaged in sexual relations with both Henry Manox and Francis Dereham, accepting the details of the indictments in which Katherine was presented as the instigator in both relationships – 'That Catherine knew exactly what she was doing is undeniable'.[21] Baldwin Smith stated that, during her teenage years, Katherine 'was a bundle of contradictory passions and desires' who was attractive, passionate, mercurial and giddy, who sought to advance her family's fortunes at court.[22] Believing that Katherine rashly committed adultery with Culpeper with the aid of Lady Rochford, Baldwin Smith concluded his study of the queen's life with his pessimistic opinion of her:

> The end would have been the same, history would have been unchanged, had she never lived or died … the Queen never brought happiness or love, security or respect into the world in which she lived. She enacted a light-hearted dream in which juvenile delinquency, wanton selfishness and ephemeral hedonism were the abiding themes.[23]

Baldwin Smith's characterisation of the queen marked the beginning of a trend in which she was interpreted as a selfish hedonist who cared for nothing but her own pleasure.

Other modern historians have been similarly critical of Katherine's behaviour. Because he accepted that Katherine was involved in a love affair with

Culpeper, Eric Ives unfairly and incorrectly concluded that she had no respect for royal protocol.[24] Alison Plowden, in her book *Tudor Women: Queens and Commoners*, published in 2003, believed that Katherine 'possessed all the instincts of a natural tart who knew exactly what she was doing ... having discovered the delights of sex, [she] saw no reason to settle for the first man who'd bedded her'.[25] In 2010, Tracy Borman likewise argued that the 'empty-headed' Katherine 'was far from the corrupted innocent she is often portrayed as. The evidence suggests that she was as much a sexual predator as Dereham and knew exactly what she was doing.'[26] Alison Weir, in her 1991 biography of the six queens of Henry VIII, agreed with this interpretation of Katherine's life, believing that Katherine was 'certainly promiscuous' before her marriage while, during her adulterous affair with Culpeper, she 'had not only been playing with fire, but she had also been indiscreet about it, and incredibly stupid'.[27] Similarly, in her biography of Henry's wives, Antonia Fraser voiced some sympathy for Henry VIII's fifth wife in suggesting that 'a less moralistic age will feel more sympathy for girl whom the freak wave of the King's desire threw up so cruelly ill-prepared on the exposed shore of history', but nonetheless concluded that, in relation to Katherine's involvement with Culpeper, 'the repeated confessions and reports of clandestine meetings between a man notorious for his gallantry and a woman who was already sexually awakened really do not admit of any other explanation than adultery'.[28] So apparently widespread has acceptance of Katherine's love affair with Culpeper become that in his book *The Queen and the Heretic*, Derek Wilson indicated that Dereham and Culpeper were Katherine's 'bedfellows' and 'lovers'.[29]

These modern interpretations of her brief life and reign have been filtered through the prism of sexuality, leading to mostly negative conclusions about her character and actions. In his 2012 biography, David Loades proclaimed that 'a biography is inevitably largely a study of her sexuality and its consequences'.[30] Undoubtedly Loades had indicated that Katherine's sexuality shaped his views on her in earlier books; in 2009, he thundered that Katherine 'certainly behaved like a whore both before and after her marriage'.[31] Believing that Henry VIII's fifth consort 'was a stupid and oversexed adolescent',[32] Loades concluded that her sexuality 'was devious and manipulative' and 'fraudulent'.[33] Unlike her predecessors, Katherine 'had almost no redeeming feature'.[34] It is interesting that Loades contrasted Katherine negatively with her four predecessors, especially Jane Seymour, without once considering that Katherine was significantly younger and less experienced in court protocol than Henry's four previous queens were. Jane, for example, was at least 25 and possibly closer to 28 when she married the king in 1536. She and Anne Boleyn had resided at court for lengthy periods of time, while it hardly needs emphasising that Katherine of Aragon and Anne of Cleves were foreign princesses and were educated as such. Few historians have contextualised Katherine's actions at court with regard to her age, education and duration of service to Anne of Cleves prior to marrying the king. One exception was Anne Crawford, who noted that 'Katherine was not really in the same position as either her cousin Anne [Boleyn] or Jane Seymour ... Katherine ... was much younger, without experience, and with nobody to keep an eye on her'.[35] Unfortunately, despite showing this awareness of the queen's youth and inexperience in her analysis, Crawford concluded that Katherine was 'a spoilt child' and her downfall in 1541 'contained none of the tragedy or dignity of the end of Anne Boleyn'.[36] As might perhaps be expected from his excessively harsh judgements, Loades failed to interpret her career in the context of sixteenth-century gender relations and sexual mores, while omitting to consider the contemporary evidence for her age, especially with regard to how old she might have been when her relations with Manox and Dereham took place during the mid to late 1530s. Concluding that she 'may well have had others [lovers]',[37] for which there is no evidence whatsoever, Loades appears to have transferred the joint guilt of Katherine and her male admirers to her shoulders alone, without appreciating that she was 13 years old in 1536 and 15 in 1538, whereas Dereham was at least fourteen years her senior, as will become apparent. Her relations with Manox and Dereham took place in a social and cultural context that stressed female inferiority. Such misguided and one-sided perspectives on Henry's fifth queen, which mostly seem to be informed by the author's own attitudes to sexuality and gender, are thankfully no longer as prevalent in modern historiography.

Other historians have, for a variety of reasons and from a range of differing perspectives, interpreted Katherine's life more sympathetically. Joanna Denny, in her 2005 biography, characterised Katherine as a 'vulnerable and abused child of 11 or 12' during her affair with Manox and agreed with Strickland that Katherine was strongly influenced by the examples of her childhood companions within the household of the dowager duchess, since she was 'eager to be part of their inner circle and to be included in their romantic adventures'.[38] Later, as 'a precocious and knowing girl with an attractive figure', Katherine indulged in a sexual relationship with Dereham, in what could be termed 'persistent child abuse'.[39] At court, the Duke of Norfolk manipulated his niece Katherine 'to further his own political agenda', for she was 'the victim of a conspiracy between ... Thomas Howard, Duke of Norfolk, and Stephen Gardiner, Bishop of Winchester'.[40] As queen, Katherine engaged in an adulterous affair with Culpeper as a means of conceiving a child to pass off as the impotent king's: 'Katherine was urged to become pregnant as soon as possible, regardless of the paternity. Culpeper's bastard could be passed off as the King's legitimate son.'[41] One would assume that the subtitle of Denny's biography, *A Tudor Conspiracy*, alluded to this deceitful plan alleg-edly concocted by Katherine and Culpeper. Interestingly, Denny is the only biographer to actually suggest that Katherine attempted to cuckold the king by giving birth to another man's son, for which there is no contemporary evidence whatsoever.

David Starkey, in his 2004 study of the six queens of Henry VIII, disagreed with the prevailing view that Katherine committed adultery with Culpeper in the physical sense. Agreeing with other writers that 'she knew how to attract men with a skill beyond her teenage years', Starkey believed that Katherine did not allow Manox to have sexual intercourse with her, 'not out of virtue, but rather a fierce sense of Howard pride'.[42] He was appreciative of her personal qualities, believing that, during her childhood, 'she … displayed leadership, resourcefulness and independence' as 'a rebel without a cause'.[43] Characterising the queen as a 'love-sick Juliet' during her relationship with Culpeper, Starkey interpreted their affair as 'like a piece of romantic fiction'.[44] Concluding that, while Katherine and Culpeper were strongly attracted to one another, they never engaged in sexual intercourse, Starkey perceived Katherine to be 'a sympathetic figure'.[45]

Karen Lindsey's feminist reinterpretation of the careers of Henry's queens saw her agree with Starkey that a virtue can be discerned in 'promiscuity'. Viewing the events of Katherine Howard's life through a twentieth-century mindset of sexuality and femininity, Lindsey believed that 'a lot of pity has been wasted on Henry VIII over Kathryn's infidelity', arguing that Katherine was 'a woman who enjoyed both sex itself and the admiration she got from the men with whom she had her few sexual adventures'. Katherine 'was a woman who listened to her body's yearnings, and in spite of all she had been taught, understood that she had a right to answer those longings. She was willing to risk whatever it took to be true to herself.'[46] By contrast, Retha Warnicke characterised Katherine as 'a victim of sexual predators' from the age of 13, believing that 'in her short life, she had faced great adversity because of cul-tural attitudes toward human sexuality. Her male abusers seemed to assume that her reluctance to have sexual relations masked "interior consent".'[47] In 2016, Josephine Wilkinson similarly affirmed that Katherine was victimised by the 'many persuasions' of both Manox and Dereham, who took advantage of 'her relatively lowly position' in the household of the dowager Duchess of Norfolk. Both men 'pestered' Katherine 'relentlessly' and Dereham 'forced himself upon Katherine'.[48] Unlike Warnicke, who believed that Culpeper coerced the young queen, Wilkinson suggested that Katherine's relationship with Culpeper was that of friendship, in which she relied on him to 'provide ... information about her husband's health and his ever fluctuating moods'.[49] By contrast, Gareth Russell's 2017 biography, which disagreed with the arguments presented by Warnicke and later Wilkinson, offered a portrayal of Katherine's character and motives that was closer to that presented in Baldwin Smith's 1961 version of her life. While acknowledging that Katherine's queenship has been interpreted as 'shallow yet profane', Russell concluded that she 'probably did not commit physical adultery with Thomas Culpeper ... but ... adultery would have taken place had their liaison not been discovered in November 1541'.[50] Russell's conclusion is especially interesting in light of the extant evidence for Katherine's relationship with Culpeper and her recorded remarks about their interactions, especially her insistence that Lady Rochford chaperone the handful of meetings that took place between queen and courtier. It is recorded that Katherine herself explicitly instructed Lady Rochford 'bid him [Culpeper] desire no more to trouble me or send to me', and dismissed him as a 'little sweet fool'.

The extant historiography reveals, firstly, the emphasis that both contemporary authors and modern historians placed on Katherine's sexuality. This is unsurprising in the sense that she was convicted and executed for intending to commit adultery with Culpeper – the act itself was suspected, never proven – but it limits the insights that can be achieved with regard to her brief tenure as queen. Moreover, it has fuelled the popular and salacious perception of her as a 'bad girl' (as Starkey characterised her in his 2004 biography). In almost every account of Katherine's life, the author's interpretation of her pre-marital liaisons and her subsequent association with Culpeper was informed by their own sexual attitudes. Yet 'upon closer examination of the primary sources, Katherine appears to have been, at least outwardly, an almost "ideal" sixteenth-century Englishwoman, and the perfect queen to the aging king'.[51] The dominant perception of her as a 'bad girl' who recklessly committed adultery, or intended to, and thus in a sense 'deserved' her beheading in 1542 ignores two critical realities: firstly, the exact nature of her relations with Culpeper remains uncertain and it will be argued in this biography that adultery was not committed and was probably not intended or welcomed by Katherine, even if Culpeper pressured her for it. Secondly, Katherine's personal and political difficulties arose essentially because she failed to provide her husband with a male heir with which to secure the continuation of the Tudor dynasty. The unsavoury gossip that circulated about Katherine from early on in her marriage placed her in a difficult situation, especially when individuals from her youth, such as Dereham, arrived at court and openly boasted of their – often dubious –

acquaintances with her. But this unfavourable political context could have proven negligible had Katherine delivered the much longed-for second son. These two essential circumstances have usually been marginalised, if not ignored, in accounts of Katherine's brief life, in preference to representing her as a sexually immoral adulteress. Moreover, the extant historiography demonstrates that, while several historians have noted Katherine's youth, they have not always factored this awareness into their analyses of either her pre-marital liaisons or her actions as queen. As an illustration of how significant Katherine's youth is – or should be – in modern analyses of her life and queenship, she was the youngest woman to become Queen of England in almost 100 years.

Only in recent years have historians recognised the importance of analysing Katherine's life from the perspective of gender, which pays attention to how both her biological sex and sixteenth-century conceptions of womanhood influenced the nature of her career and her ultimate downfall. This study will interpret her life in the context of sixteenth-century social customs and cultural values, focusing on Katherine's experiences from a gendered per-spective, which focuses on attitudes to sexual relations, fertility customs and early modern gender mores. It will probe the mostly fragmentary surviving evidence for insights relating to fundamental questions which should be con-sidered: why was it, for instance, that highborn women within the Henrician court were readily expected to play critical roles in raising their family's for-tunes and prestige, yet were vulnerable to accusations of heinous crimes such as witchcraft or adultery by male contemporaries in unfavourable political and religious climates who may have feared these women's alleged power? Why were sexual relations often attributed to the licentiousness and moral failings of women rather than men? What led to women being frequently blamed and condemned for failures in pregnancy and childbirth, resulting in accusations of sorcery or witchcraft? And why have documents, including both letters and interrogations produced by the Crown, often been read transparently and uncritically, rather than situating them in the context of early modern legal, religious and social mores?

In asking such questions through analysis of contemporary evidence, this biography seeks to address lingering misconceptions and myths concern-ing Henry VIII's fifth queen, who was executed in 1542 for sexual crimes perceived to be treasonous to her husband and, by extension, to the state. Interpreting such sources from a gendered viewpoint illuminates the extent to which early modern men feared and mistrusted their female contemporar-ies, whom they associated with unrestrained, even deviant, sexuality and the ability to bewitch or inflict ill upon men. As a result, this study will conclude that not only Katherine but her four predecessors were at least partly victims of what will here be termed fertility politics: their ability, or in four cases inability, to provide a male heir to solve the paranoid if understandable issues surrounding the Tudor succession. From the moment that she married Henry VIII in July 1540 to her shocking downfall in November 1541, court rumours and gossip circulated about Katherine's alleged pregnancies, which indicates how her childbearing role as Henry's consort was perceived to be central to her queenship. It underpinned whether she was perceived to be a successful consort; ultimately her childlessness – the reasons for which are still not clear – placed her in a vulnerable position. The belief that she committed adultery with Culpeper in 1541 may have encouraged some court observers to conclude that she was attempting to pass off Culpeper's bastard as the king's legitimate child. Some historians, including Joanna Denny, have argued that this attempt to produce a child – irrespective of who the father was – accounts for Katherine's secret meetings with Culpeper.

With this political and cultural context in mind, it will be argued that the prevailing modern notion of Katherine Howard as an immoral young woman who recklessly took several lovers under her ageing husband's nose is unconvincing. While it is unlikely that her reputation will ever be fully restored, it is important to challenge the prevalent and ultimately sexualised interpretation of her as a 'juvenile delinquent' or 'empty-headed wanton'. These condemnatory opinions of Katherine mean that it is possible to regard her as Henry VIII's slandered queen, a woman whom Lacey Baldwin Smith argued lacked supporters 'because she was shallow and brittle, arrogant in success and servile in distress'.[52]

It is worth emphasising, however, that this biography does not pretend to offer a definitive account of Katherine Howard, mainly because the evidence is fragmentary and much of it is no longer extant. She remains one of the more shadowy of Henry VIII's queens, understandably so in view of the brevity of her tenure as consort and because of how young she was when she died in 1542. From their recorded actions, letters, personal possessions and patronage, we can know a great deal about Katherine of Aragon, Anne Boleyn and, to a certain extent, Katherine Parr. This is much less true in the case of Katherine Howard. The reader is warned, therefore, that much of Katherine's life and character remain unknown and may never be recovered from the lost fragments of history. This study is as much an examination of her historiography, that is, the ways in which she has been represented in modern analysis, as it is a straightforward biography of her life. The biography also makes no apologies for examining the tenures of Anne Boleyn, Jane Seymour and Anne of Cleves in the period 1533–40, for they have direct bearing on

Katherine's experiences as queen and the context in which she married the king, while also shedding light on the political fortunes of the Howard family in the years prior to her marriage. It is impossible to fully understand her life without this political and religious context.

Ultimately, Katherine only became Queen of England because of her husband's failed marriage to Anne of Cleves, and one could argue that the rejection of Katherine of Aragon, the downfall of Anne Boleyn and the unexpected death of Jane Seymour also, in the long term, paved the way for Katherine Howard to become the king's wife in 1540. Irrespective of the incomplete historical record, she remains one of England's most slandered queens, and this biography attempts to offer a fairer and more sympathetic version of her brief life.

1

HENRY VIII'S ACCESSION
AND THE HOWARDS

THE ACCESSION OF HENRY VIII to the throne of England in 1509 was
viewed positively by his expectant subjects, ushering in hopes of dynastic
stability following the devastation caused by the Wars of the Roses in the
previous century. Henry's accession was the first time in some eighty years
that the crown had passed directly from king to son without the challenge presented by a pretender, and, in an attempt to enhance his lineage and improve
his international standing, he decided to marry the Spanish princess Katherine
of Aragon, the widow of his elder brother Arthur. Indeed, 'great provision was
made for the … costly devices of the other [Henry VIII] with that virtuous
Queen Katherine, then the king's wife, newly married'.[1]

  Those present at court in the early years of Henry VIII's reign were unanimous in their praise of him. The Venetian ambassador Sebastian Guistinian
opined that 'nature could not have done more for him … He is much handsomer than any sovereign in Christendom; a great deal handsomer than the
King of France, very fair and his whole frame admirably proportioned'.[2]
That same ambassador went on to record in 1514:

> His Majesty is the handsomest potentate I ever set eyes upon: above the usual
> height, with an extremely fine calf to his leg, his complexion very fair and
> bright, with auburn hair combed straight and short in the French fashion,
> and a round face so very beautiful that it would become a pretty woman, his
> throat being rather long and thick.[3]

Such statements offer revealing insights into sixteenth-century perceptions
of masculinity and kingship, for they indicate that the ideal of early modern

kingship extolled virtuous masculinity, demonstrated through a rigorous phys-icality combined with an almost godly beauty, which Henry personified to foreign observers visiting court. The apparently unanimous praise of England's new king was at least partly influenced by the ambivalence, if not dislike, with which the English had viewed Henry's father, Henry VII, the first Tudor king. Although he has perhaps unfairly been represented as a miser, there is no doubt that Henry VII lacked the charisma and personal charm that endeared his son to his subjects.

Katherine of Aragon, Henry's queen, would have been well aware of her marital duties, for the expectation at the sixteenth-century English court was, as it would have been elsewhere in the courts of Europe, that she would pre-sent her husband with several sons in order to ensure the continuation of the ruling dynasty and prevent the dynastic bloodshed and civil war that would be caused by her failure to bear a son. Indeed, Katherine had no better example than her own family; her only brother, Juan, had died as a teenager, plunging the Spanish succession into turmoil. The repercussions of that in the long term were to prove problematic, with conflict occurring between Katherine's father, Ferdinand of Aragon, and her brother-in-law Philip, husband to her sister Juana, as to who had the stronger claim to the throne of Castile.[4] It was imperative that Queen Katherine present the new king with male heirs in order to preserve the stability of the Tudor lineage in England. Indeed, having been married to Henry VII's ill-fated heir Arthur for a period of five months in 1501–02, Katherine would have appreciated the concerns and fears of Henry VIII. Both of them were aware that a 'spare' male heir was always necessary in case the firstborn died, as had proved to be the case in 1502.

At the time of Henry VIII's succession, several English noble families could claim royal blood through their descent from Edward I. The most prominent was the Howard family, whom one author lyrically wrote of thus:

> What family pervades our national annals with achievements of such intense and brilliant interest as the Howards? As heroes, poets, politicians, courtiers, patrons of literature, state victims to tyranny and revenge, they have been constantly before us for four centuries … No story of romance or tragedy can exhibit more incidents to enchain attention or move the heart, than might be found in the records of this great historical family.[5]

At least to begin with, the Howard family were viewed with suspicion if not hostility by Henry VII and later his son, for the 1st Duke of Norfolk, father of the present Thomas Howard, Earl of Surrey, had died fighting for Richard III, the last Yorkist king, at Bosworth in 1485. Surrey, however, successfully placated the hostility of the Tudors directed towards the Howard dynasty by publicly demonstrating his loyalty and support of the ruling royal family. As a consequence, by 1501 – the date of Katherine of Aragon's first marriage to Arthur, Prince of Wales – Surrey's lands in East Anglia could be valued at £600 a year and he had risen to Lord Treasurer of England. Surrey conclusively proved his loyalty to the Tudors through his victory against the Scots at Flodden in 1513 at the age of 70.[6] Indeed, 'long before the Howards won back their ancient titles, the family had been systematically fortifying its political and social position through marital alliances with the most vigorous and distinguished families of the century'.[7] This was amply demonstrated in Surrey's achievement of a marriage alliance in 1495 between his heir and Anne of York, sister of Queen Elizabeth. As a demonstration of his intimacy with, and value to, the Tudor dynasty, Surrey was also closely involved in the marriage negotiations of Henry VIII's younger sister Mary Tudor to Charles of Castille in 1508 when that princess was aged 12.[8]

Surrey was to act as effective head and representative of the Howard family until his death in 1524, leading to the succession of his eldest son Thomas, Lord Treasurer since 1522, to the dukedom of Norfolk and estates worth over £4,000 per annum.[9] Thomas was one of three sons and two daughters born to Surrey and his second wife Elizabeth Tilney who lived to adulthood. Thomas Howard became Earl of Surrey in February 1514, with an annuity of £20 per annum, receiving two castles and eighteen manors in Lincolnshire in 'consideration of the timely assistance he rendered his father … at the Battle of Branxton, 9 Sept. last. This creation is made on surrender by the said Duke [of Norfolk] … of the title of Earl of Surrey.'[10] In 1513 Surrey's influence increased further through his marriage alliance with the 15-year-old Elizabeth Stafford, daughter of Edward, 3rd Duke of Buckingham, thus further glorifying the prestige of the Howard lineage through its alliance with this noble English family. The Howard–Stafford alliance proved short lived, however, for the 3rd duke was to be executed for treason against the king in 1521, with his own father-in-law, the Duke of Norfolk, presiding as Lord High Steward of England at his trial.[11]

Thomas Howard, Earl of Surrey and later 3rd Duke of Norfolk, remains a controversial figure, with one author emphatically describing him as a 'monster … ruthless in his cold-blooded use of those around him, including the members of his own family [who were] just pawns for his ambition'.[12] This is, however, to view the events in the mid Tudor period with hindsight and a lack of awareness of political and social norms among the English nobility in the sixteenth century. Indeed, one Venetian ambassador lauded Thomas's 'liberal, affable and astute' personality and his desire to associate with anyone regardless of social origins.[13] He was experienced and shrewd, as well as pragmatic in setting aside his Roman Catholic faith in order to achieve the will of the king through his 'versatile and inconstant humour', according to the Spanish ambassador.[14]

Thomas's younger brother Edmund, born around 1478, was comparatively less successful in his ability to equal, or surpass, his elder brother's achievements at court and his closeness to the king, on which much depended in the way of attaining political and financial prestige and preferment. Edmund had still managed to demonstrate his loyalty and usefulness to the English crown through commanding some 1,500 men from Cheshire, Yorkshire and Lancashire at Flodden in 1513, where he was knighted by his father as a reward for his courage.[15] One popular verse thereafter ran thus: 'And Edmund Howard's lion bright / Shall bear them bravely in the fight.'[16] Despite this martial achievement, Edmund never managed to gain the trust and support of Henry VIII that was readily, if intermittently, granted to his elder brother. He was, however, granted a pension of 3*s* 4*d* daily, terminated three years later.[17] Edmund had also fought in the jousts in 1511, held to celebrate the birth of Henry VIII's son by Katherine of Aragon. Starkey's dismissive view of Edmund as 'a man of no importance' is somewhat misguided, for it may not have been so much his personal characteristics as his relative state of economic poverty following the death of his father Norfolk in 1524 that limited Edmund's ability to live and perform as a successful nobleman at the Henrician court.[18]

However, Edmund's situation was somewhat improved by his appointment to the lucrative position of Comptroller of Calais in 1531, perhaps as a result of the intercession of his niece and Henry's wife-to-be Anne Boleyn, which he held until his death in 1539. Notwithstanding this, the king's disfavour for Edmund was demonstrated when he was elected mayor by the assembly of Calais in August 1537, when the Lord Privy Seal Thomas Cromwell quashed the election, since 'the King will in no wise that my lord Howard be admitted to the mayoralty'.[19] According to John Hussey, the agent of Lord Lisle at Calais, 'my Lord Comptroller [Edmund] is not contented because he was not admitted Mayor, your lordship shall right well abide his malice'.[20]

By 1515 Edmund had married Joyce Culpeper, born in 1480 to Sir Richard Culpeper of Oxenhoath, Kent. Married at the age of 12 to Ralph Legh, Joyce brought considerable assets to her marriage with Edmund for both the Legh and Culpeper families held substantial lands in Kent, Surrey and Sussex.[21] Notwithstanding this, the Legh family were well aware of Edmund Howard's financial difficulties and understandably viewed with concern his ability to successfully keep a wife in a lifestyle sufficient to her status and lineage. Unsurprisingly, in his will dated 16 June 1523, John Legh, stepfather of Joyce, wrote that 'if the Howards trouble the Executors they are to have nothing. If any others make trouble the difficulty to be expounded and ordered by Sir Richard Broke Knight of Kings Bench John Rooper the Kings attorney John Spylman Serjeant at law and Roger Legh.'[22] The birth date of the eldest son, Henry, probably named for the king, is unknown but seems to have been relatively early in the marriage, perhaps in 1515 or the year after, with two additional sons, Charles and George, following at some point before 1527.[23] These sons may have spent their childhoods residing in the households of their Howard relatives in East Anglia and perhaps within the household of their step-grandmother, Agnes Howard, the dowager Duchess of Norfolk.[24] The eldest daughter, Margaret, was born to Edmund and Joyce by 1518, probably earlier, for she is known to have married Sir Thomas Arundell of Wardour Castle in November 1530.[25] Legally, girls could marry at 12 years of age in sixteenth-century England, but it was unusual for them to do so. In view of this, one would expect Margaret to have been aged at least in her mid teens when she wed Arundell in 1530.

Thereafter, two younger daughters were born to Edmund and Joyce: Katherine and Mary, probably born in about 1523 and 1525 respectively, although without conclusive evidence it is impossible to be certain. The birth date of 1520–21 for Katherine was favoured by early historians, but this is almost certainly incorrect for it relies on the French ambassador Charles de Marillac's apparent suggestion that the queen was aged around 18 in 1539. However, since that same ambassador was certainly incorrect about the respective ages of both Anne of Cleves (believing her to be 30 when she was in fact 24) and Margaret Pole, countess of Salisbury (stating that she was 80 when she was only 67), his remarks on women's ages must be viewed with caution, if not scepticism, and cannot be uncritically relied on when considering Katherine's exact age when she attracted the attention of Henry VIII.[26] For an extended discussion of Katherine's date of birth, which draws on several years of research and includes a reinterpretation of the French ambassador's comments on Katherine's age, see Appendix II. The exact birth order of the six children born to Edmund and his wife is unknown, but since Katherine was appointed a maiden of honour to Queen Anne of Cleves in 1539, rather than her sister Mary, it would seem likely that she was the second of the three daughters. Where the children were born is a matter of mystery, though some sources indicate Lambeth in London, the seat of the Howard family.[27]

At an unknown date, Edmund's wife Joyce died, likely in her late forties, although she appears to have still been alive in 1527.[28] It has been surmised that she may have died in childbirth, especially since it is apparent that women living in the mid sixteenth century were able to bear children into their early fifties according to the Spanish ambassador Eustace Chapuys, although it cannot be known for certain whether this actually was the context in which Joyce died.[29] In 1527, Edmund's financial problems, compounded by the birth of six children by his wife, led him to complain to Cardinal Thomas Wolsey and assert that, were it not for his noble status, he would gladly 'dig and delve' in order to remedy his poverty.[30] By her first marriage Joyce had borne five children, which worsened Edmund's economic difficulties since he was expected to provide for them as well as for his own. By 1528 Edmund had married Dorothy, widow to Sir William Uvedale of Wickham, who was a landholder of some substance in Hampshire; this marriage may have perhaps led to Edmund's appointment to the commission of peace for that county in 1531.[31] It is possible, therefore, to interpret Edmund's regional influence as transferring from Kent, where his first wife's lands and wealth had been based, to Hampshire by virtue of his second marriage. Following Dorothy's death, Edmund married Margaret Jennings, daughter of Markeaton Hall in Derbyshire, by whom he had no further issue.

Before she was sent to the household of her step-grandmother, the dowager Duchess of Norfolk, it is reasonable to suppose without any other surviving evidence that Katherine was brought up in the household of her stepmother while her father performed his duties in Calais. According to Gerald Brenan and Edward Statham, following the death of her mother, Katherine lived with her maternal aunts: in Oxenhoath with Margaret or in Teston with Elizabeth Barham.[32] It is more likely, however, that Katherine grew up with her step-mothers Dorothy and Margaret respectively, for surely Edmund would have intended these women to act as mothers to his infant daughters. Following the death of a parent in the early modern period, and the subsequent remarriage of the surviving parent, children were accustomed to referring to their new step-parent as 'father' or 'mother' irrespective of their personal feelings on the matter. Henry VIII's daughter Elizabeth, for instance, addressed Katherine Parr in a 1545 letter as 'your hithnis humble doughter'. Katherine's own personal relations with her parents are impossible to ascertain, although whether or not they were similar to those recorded by a fifteenth-century Venetian in London as follows is possible, if ultimately unknown:

> The want of affection in the English is strongly manifested towards their children, for having kept them at home until they arrive at the age of seven or nine years at the utmost, they put them out, both males and females, to hard service in the houses of other people, binding them generally for another seven or nine years.[33]

An immediate difficulty apparent with analysing Katherine's childhood is the fact that, as has been stated, 'much of the evidence about them [women] … was compiled or invented by men and rests on male assumptions'.[34] It is essential to appreciate how Katherine, as a young aristocratic girl in early Tudor England, was harnessed to meet the ambitions and hopes of the Howard family at a young age. By 1531 it is likely that Katherine had been 'put out' by her father into the household of her step-grandmother Agnes, dowager Duchess of Norfolk, at Chesworth in Horsham, aged 7 or 8; as the Venetian visitor commented, young children – both male and female – were usually placed outside the home by this age.[35] In 1531, as noted, Edmund Howard was granted the controllership of Calais, which may have led to the dispersing of his household in England in order to reduce expenses. At the same time, a vacancy in the dowager duchess's household arose when her ward, Katherine Broughton, married the dowager duchess's son Lord William Howard.[36] Edmund undoubtedly would have viewed his daughter's entry into the dowager duchess's household as an honour. At an early age, aristocratic girls were instructed in the necessary skills of household management and in feminine pursuits, such as singing, dancing and learning musical instruments, which enhanced their attractiveness to potential suitors.[37] Usually, the girl's mother was deemed responsible for providing her daughter with this 'informal' education, although attendants and mistresses of the household also played a part.[38] As has been suggested, 'elite parents regularly placed their children in the homes of wealthier or better-connected friends and relatives to complete their educations and extend their personal contacts', with Agnes, dowager Duchess of Norfolk specifically performing this function for Katherine and three other grandchildren.[39] Because no mention in the interrogations during Katherine's downfall was made of a nurse or supervisor at Horsham, except for Katherine's step-grandmother, it is therefore possible that she was in her pre- or early teens, around 12 or 13, when she began receiving music lessons from Henry Manox in 1536, since she seemed to lack a governess.[40]

According to contemporary customs in the mid Tudor period and the expectations of her Howard relatives, which undoubtedly interacted closely with one another in a symbiotic relationship, it was reasonable, even ideal, for Katherine to live in her step-grandmother's household and obtain an education of sorts which focused on the aforementioned 'feminine' skills. The date of 1523 is thus more convincing as Katherine's birth date since, had she been aged 13 or older in the mid 1530s, it is likely that her uncle, the Duke of Norfolk, and perhaps her father would have sought an appointment at court for Katherine as a maiden in the household of her cousin, Queen Anne, who married Henry VIII in early 1533.[41] Proponents of a 1520–21 birthdate cannot explain why Katherine's ambitious relatives apparently failed to seek an appointment for her in the household of Anne Boleyn or Jane Seymour between 1533 and 1537 when, according to their theory, she would have been aged between 13 and 17. The most reasonable solution to that conundrum would be that she was not born as early as 1520–21. Dwelling in an environment with other young relatives who performed tasks for the dowager Duchess of Norfolk in return for lodging and sustenance, Katherine must have been aware of the importance of maintaining her family's honour through virtuous maidenly behaviour. The values which Katherine could expect to learn and emulate, intended specifically for young females, were as set out in *How the Good Wife Taught Her Daughter*: 'Reverence thy father and mother as Nature requires … Wipe thy mouth when thou shalt drink ale or wine on thy napkin only … Blow not your nose in the napkin where ye wipe your hand.'[42] In view of this context, alongside the fact that Katherine's father was constantly occupied in Calais, the suggestion that 'it was an evil hour for the little Katharine, when she left the paternal roof and the society of the innocent companions of her infant joys and cares, to become a neglected dependant in the splendid mansion of a proud and heartless relative' is demonstrably incorrect.[43] Her appointment to the household of the dowager Duchess of Norfolk was entirely conventional in the context of sixteenth-century aristocratic society, and it presented a range of opportunities to her that she would have been expected to understand and appreciate.

It is apparent that women within the Howard family were able to play important and sophisticated political roles as a means of consolidating and enhancing their family's prestige and furthering its influence both at court and outside of it, which is relevant in understanding Katherine's subsequent career both before and after she married Henry VIII in 1540. Perhaps the most obvious and inspiring example to Katherine would have been Anne of York, younger sister of Queen Elizabeth (wife to Henry VII) and wife of Thomas Howard, 3rd Duke of Norfolk, who as sister-in-law to Henry VII not only 'represented an important step' in the rehabilitation of the Howard family but brought this noble family closer to the Tudors, something which was to provoke the hostility and suspicion of the royal family who remained insecure about their dynastic future.[44] This couple's closeness to the Tudors was further enhanced in July 1510, when Henry VIII granted his aunt and Thomas Howard land in several counties as compensation for the land claimed in right of Anne's great-grandmother Anne Mortimer, wife of Richard, earl of Cambridge.[45] The fact that Anne was in constant attendance on her sister the queen also helped to ensure that Thomas's influence was represented in court affairs, his wife actively symbolising the Howard family's political and financial interests within the queen's privy chamber and strengthening the opportunity for the Howards to attain favour from the Tudors through their connection with the ruling family.

Yet Agnes Tilney, dowager Duchess of Norfolk and wife of the Earl of Surrey, arguably exacted even greater influence on behalf of the Howards by virtue not only of her prestigious status but her role at court. She served as godmother to Princess Mary, the only surviving child of Henry VIII and Katherine of Aragon, and acted as first lady of the queen's household after Henry VIII's sister Mary – higher even in rank than her stepdaughter-in-law Anne of York – and she was to play a public role at the coronation of Anne Boleyn, her relative.[46] By 1538 she was one of the highest-ranking women in the kingdom and was godmother to both daughters of Henry VIII. The dowager duchess divided her time between her residences at Horsham and Lambeth and her lodgings at court. Yet, as has been noted, 'clearly, Lady Norfolk did not govern her household well'.[47] By virtue of her prestigious social and political status and high-ranking role within the Howard family, the dowager duchess was expected to fulfil important ceremonial and political functions at court, especially with the ascent of her step-granddaughter Anne Boleyn to the position of queen in 1533, but this glittering arrangement was to have tragic repercussions in the long term for, in not exacting a firm rule over her household at all times, the dowager duchess exposed her granddaughter Katherine to sexual scandals which corrupted her name and undermined the Howard family, ultimately culminating in Katherine's execution and in the imprisonment of several members of the Howard family in the Tower of London.

The examples of Anne of York and Agnes Howard uphold Harris's claim that Tudor noblewomen 'participated with enthusiasm, persistence, and success in all the activities connected to forming, maintaining, and exploiting patronage networks' at court, which strengthened Howard family influence; in particular, the Howard women may have been extensively involved in the politics of marriage.[48] Even those Howard women such as Joyce Howard, mother of Katherine, who did not hold office at court, could still help to strengthen the family's fortunes and enhance its prestige by ensuring that, through marriage, Howard men acquired substantial influence in denoted geographical regions of the kingdom through their wives' rich landowning assets. These female relatives served as important, perhaps inspirational, examples for young Howard women such as Katherine Howard, who by virtue of her birth into a respected and influential noble English family could expect to acquire influence at court and contribute to her family's greatness through the politics of fertility and marriage and through a much-desired appointment to the household of the queen. She belonged to a noble family in which the women featured as 'important actors on a public, political stage'.[49] With the breakdown of Henry VIII's marriage to Katherine of Aragon in the late 1520s, the opportunities for the Howard family to become ever more socially and politically significant increased demonstrably, and these were opportunities in which women within the family would play essential roles.

2

A HOWARD QUEEN

IN ORDER TO FULLY appreciate the circumstances that facilitated both the queenship and tragic downfall of Katherine Howard in 1540–42, it is essential to understand the nature and development of fertility politics at the Henrician court within the period immediately before her marriage, for this political context directly or indirectly shaped the eventual fortunes and successes of Henry VIII's queens. The collapse of Henry VIII's marriage to Katherine of Aragon in the mid 1520s demonstrates how a queen's inability to bear her husband a male heir could cast both her womanhood and her status as queen in doubt, for by failing to bear a son she was viewed as not only subjecting her realm to danger and disarray, but failing in her biological duty as a woman and queen, the two of which were inextricably linked.

Religious and polemical literature produced either at the time or later in the century mostly chose to believe that it was not Katherine of Aragon's inability to bear a son that led to the collapse of her marriage, but Henry VIII's ultimately destructive passion for Anne Boleyn that was the direct catalyst for the annulment of his first marriage. During the reign of Katherine's daughter Mary I, the prevailing view in Venice ran thus:

> After the King her father [Mary's] had cohabited during 20 consecutive years with the Queen her mother in the most complete love and concord, he became enamoured of a damsel in the Queen's service, an English girl, by name Anne Boleyn, and wishing to enjoy her … as his wife, his flatterers, and principally the Cardinal of York, at that time the King's chief favourite, and who was unfriendly towards the Queen, had it represented to him by his Confessor that his marriage with Queen Katherine was invalid.[1]

Nicholas Sander, a Catholic recusant writing during the reign of Elizabeth I, agreed: 'Henry was giving the reigns to his evil desires, and living in sin'; while Wolsey, 'seeing that the king was becoming more and more estranged from Catherine, and that his own ambitious temper was extremely offensive to the latter ... resolved to bring about the divorce of the king and queen'.[2]

The reality was markedly different. On becoming King of England some weeks shy of his eighteenth birthday in 1509, the king had every reason to expect that, through siring several sons, the Tudor dynasty would be made invincible as the ruling family of England, firmly suppressing any lingering dangers of civil war which had plagued every king's reign with varying degrees since the early fifteenth century. Henry's personal family context – his elder brother Arthur, heir to Henry VII, had died unexpectedly in 1502 – would have fuelled the king's concerns and fears about the continuation of the Tudor dynasty. Katherine, aged 23, came from a fertile family and soon became pregnant, bearing a stillborn daughter in January 1510 before going on to deliver a son, Prince Henry, on New Year's Day 1511 who was, tragically, to die merely six weeks later. A succession of miscarriages and stillbirths followed, leading to increasing concern about the continuation of the Tudor dynasty, before the queen was delivered of a healthy daughter in 1516. The king informed the Venetian ambassador following this birth that, by virtue of the fact that both king and queen were still young, 'if it was a daughter this time, by the grace of God the sons will follow'.[3] Two years later, the birth of a stillborn daughter effectively signalled in the eyes of Henry VIII that the queen was unable to provide England and her husband with a male heir. It is worth noting that, in sixteenth-century England, women were routinely faulted for failures in pregnancy and childbirth as a result of the medical teachings and social customs of the time. While other kings without surviving sons, such as Henry I, had been content to find an alternative solution to the issues raised by the succession, Henry VIII was not one of them.

As early as 1514, when the king was aged only 23, rumours had circulated in Europe that he 'meant to repudiate his present wife ... because he is unable to have children by her'. The Duke of Buckingham, who was related to the Howards by marriage and was executed for treason in 1521, stated that 'God would not suffer the King's Grace's issue to prosper, as it appeareth by the death of his son, and that his daughters prosper not, and that the King's Grace has no issue male'.[4] Not only was Katherine unable to ensure the continuation of Henry VIII's dynasty through providing him with a surviving son, but matters of honour were at stake which negatively affected both king and queen, especially in the sense that 'it is women who confirm male honor and not the reverse'.[5] Henry VIII's belief that it was his queen who was to blame for failures in childbirth reflects not only his own confidence in his fertility and ability to sire a male heir, but also illustrates his adherence to contemporary medical and social learnings about the female role in pregnancy. The king's beliefs were shared by many male – and perhaps female – contemporaries who expressed fear and wonder at the workings of the female body. It is important to analyse the blame received by Katherine of Aragon for her supposed barrenness in the context of the fact that 'the body formed not only a vital part of female personal identity but was also a significant component of their public role', with expressions of shame directed towards the reproductive process during the early modern period because of discomfort associated with the fluids and processes of female physiology.[6] Menstruation was viewed with disgust since it was believed to demonstrate the 'power' of the female body, which had the ability to deceive and ensnare unsuspecting men.[7] From this perspective, the cruel comment made by the French king in 1519 about the English queen during Henry and Katherine's marital difficulties can be understood in the tragic context of her failures in pregnancy and how this subsequently impacted upon her husband, while also shedding light on contemporary perceptions of the female body: 'He has an old deformed wife, while he himself is young and handsome.'[8] At this time Katherine was 34 and Henry 28.

Despite – or perhaps in response to – the unsettling nature of the Tudor succession during his first marriage, the king promoted his only surviving daughter Mary as his heir and bestowed upon her an excellent education suitable for a European princess living in the wake of the Renaissance. She was educated in classical and modern languages, history, mathematics, theology, and was granted her own household as the effective Princess of Wales in 1527. However, Henry could not have been entirely hopeful about the future of the English succession when, aged 11, the princess met with her father and she was found to be 'so thin, spare and small'.[9] Katherine's failure to provide Henry VIII with a male heir effectively placed both her femininity and her status and honour as queen in jeopardy, while serving to undermine the political and dynastic honour of her anxious husband. 'No matter how successful the queen was politically, or how influential culturally, her primary duty was to produce a male heir.'[10] In the context of prevailing social and political beliefs about gender roles, especially within a monarchical context, this conclusion is unsurprising, since 'contemporaries usually blamed women for failures in childbirth and conception'.[11] Ultimately, as this situation was to prove, the success of a queen consort was overwhelmingly judged in terms of whether she was able to preserve the stability of the succession through bearing surviving sons. By failing to do so, despite the unquestioned suitability of her personal qualities and noble birth, Katherine had signified in the eyes of Henry that she was neither a successful nor a suitable wife.

The situation was compounded by, as Sander notes, Henry VIII's 'evil desires' and 'sin' with other women, remarking that the king was known to enjoy pleasures with more than one of Katherine's maidens at a time.[12] 'King Henry gave his mind to three notorious vices – lechery, covetousness, and cruelty, but the two latter issued and sprang out of the former.'[13] The king's lustiness was well known, although it was viewed as being less outrageous when compared with the behaviour of the French king, François I. The royal couple's marital situation was worsened in 1519 when Henry's mistress, Elizabeth Blount, bore the king a son, Henry Fitzroy. The birth of Fitzroy demonstrated to Henry VIII, if he had not known it already, that he could not be faulted for his lack of a sur-viving son with Katherine of Aragon. Six years after Fitzroy's birth, this bastard son was rewarded with the titles of the dukedoms of Richmond and Somerset and the earldom of Nottingham, the appointment of Lord High Admiral of England, Lieutenant North of the Trent, and Warden General of the Marches.[14] The queen was personally insulted, especially since the prevailing international situation, which had led to the king's disfavour with her family, the Habsburgs, further threatened her position as Queen of England.

In order to understand the political and dynastic context in which Henry VIII's first marriage collapsed, thus facilitating a further five remar-riages, it is necessary to perceive how the nature of fertility politics within Henry's court set in chain the events which eventually resulted in the annul-ment of the king's marriage to Katherine of Aragon. Although later Catholic writers such as Sander blamed both Cardinal Wolsey and Anne Boleyn for the breakdown of the royal marriage, the reality was that, had the queen borne the king a healthy male heir, both her marriage and her status as queen would never have been placed in doubt. These two actors were, ini-tially, external to the personal and political crisis that opened up between the king and queen as doubts set in as to whether the king's first marriage was lawful. Holinshed, writing later, disputed whether the cardinal had put doubt in Henry's mind about his marriage to Katherine, commenting that 'howe soeuer it came about, that ye king was thus troubled in conscience con-ceryng his mariage, this folowed, that like a wise prudent Prince, to haue the doubt clearly remoued, he called together the beste learned of the realme'.[15] Indeed, George Cavendish, who served in Wolsey's household, intriguingly stated that 'Wolsey on his knees sought to dissuade him but could not affect him', directly suggesting that it was the king who planned to look further into whether or not his marriage was contrary to the will of God, despite the cardinal's attempts to dissuade him from doing so.[16] Undoubtedly, as an absolute monarch preoccupied with the continuation of the royal dynasty, Henry VIII was determined to father a legitimate male heir and, unfortunately for Katherine, at 40 years of age it looked increasingly unlikely, if not impossible, that she would provide that male heir.

The marital crisis between the king and queen in 1526–27 was exacerbated by the king's love for Anne Boleyn, who had first arrived at the English court in 1522 following her return from the French court. Whether she actually resided in Katherine's household is uncertain, because the lists of Katherine's household attendants are no longer extant. Anne had been dismissed from court sometime in 1523 for her liaison with Henry Percy, later Earl of Northumberland, but she had returned to court by 1526 at the latest. How old she was when she captivated the king remains a matter of debate, but in view of Henry's obsession with fathering a legitimate male heir, it seems more likely that she was in her late teens or early twenties when he proposed marriage to her. Henry was captivated by this enchanting gentlewoman, whom Lancelot de Carles praised thus: 'For her behaviour, manners, attire and tongue she excelled them all, for she had been brought up in France. No one would ever have taken her to be English by her manners, but a native-born Frenchwoman.'[17] Other evidence presented by William Forrest during the reign of Mary I suggests that it was only after he had decided to annul his sonless marriage to Queen Katherine that Henry VIII fell in love with Anne and resolved to marry her, describing how 'in the Courte … theare dyd frequent a fresche younge damoysell, that cowld trippe and go, to synge and to daunce passinge excellent, no tatches shee lacked of loves allurement; she cowlde speake Frenche ornately and playne, famed in the Cowrte … Anne Bullayne'.[18] The king's intention to marry Anne was plain, for he promised her that 'I will take you for my only mistress, casting off all others besides you out of my thoughts and affections, and serve you only'.[19]

For the purposes of this study it is significant that Anne Boleyn was related to the Howard family, for her mother Elizabeth was the younger sister of Thomas Howard, Duke of Norfolk, and Edmund, father of Katherine; this made Anne and Katherine first cousins. Moreover, the association between the Howards and Boleyns became ever stronger during the period when Henry VIII began his courtship of Anne, for not only had her sister Mary been honoured – however briefly – as the king's mistress some years previously, but the Howard family's closeness with the Parker clan presented the opportunity for the only surviving Boleyn son, George, to wed Jane in around 1524, around the time of or shortly after their cousin Katherine Howard's birth.[20] The Howards' association with the Parkers had become closer some years previously when Alice Lovel, mother of Henry Parker and grandmother of Jane, married Sir Edward Howard, the Lord Admiral who died at Brest in 1513 and who was uncle to both Anne and Katherine.[21] Now, in the course of her increasingly intense relationship with Henry VIII, Anne confidently expected to be supported by her maternal relatives, the Howards, in a bid to attain the queenship. Her ambitious uncle, the Duke of Norfolk, could only have welcomed this opportunity for the Howard family to consolidate their prestige and their growing influence with the Tudor dynasty with a hitherto unlooked-for opportunity for a Howard woman to become Queen of England as the consort to Henry VIII.

It is apparent that Norfolk became closely involved in the matters pertaining to the king's efforts to obtain an annulment of his marriage to Katherine of Aragon. He had never been particularly favourable to Cardinal Wolsey; the cardinal's downfall in 1529 was believed to have been engineered by Norfolk acting together with the Duke of Suffolk, with Anne as the figurehead. While it is true that 'noblemen such as Norfolk and Suffolk had for years been irritated and frustrated by the proud way in which Wolsey had flaunted his possessions and power', contemporary documentation does not necessarily support the notion that the Howards, acting with Anne, and the Duke of Suffolk conspired to achieve the downfall of Cardinal Wolsey.[22] As late as the summer of 1528 Anne maintained friendly relations with the cardinal. Despite this, the Spanish ambassador's hostile comment that 'if the Lady Anne chooses the Cardinal will be dismissed, and his affair settled; for she happens to be the person in all this kingdom who hates him most and has spoken and acted the most openly against him', while almost certainly overstated, can be interpreted as providing evidence for the increasing hostility of Anne and her Howard relatives towards the cardinal, who they perceived to be obstructing the annulment of Henry's marriage.[23] Cardinal Wolsey was well aware of Anne's anger towards him, writing that 'if the displeasure of my Lady Anne be somewhat assuaged, as I pray God the same may be, then it should be devised that by some convenient mean she be further laboured … All possible means must be used for attaining of her favour'.[24]

The hostility of the Howard family towards the cardinal is seemingly further demonstrated in the dispatches of Eustace Chapuys, the Spanish ambassador at Henry VIII's court, although it is worth drawing attention to the limitations of this ambassador's dispatches since he vehemently opposed Anne and her relatives.[25] Nevertheless, the report in February 1530 that Norfolk 'began to swear very loudly that rather than suffer this he would eat him up alive'[26] in relation to the cardinal is plausible in consideration of the Howard family's belief that Wolsey was preventing not only the annulment of Henry VIII's marriage, but the elevation of their relative Anne to the politically and dynastically lucrative position of queen consort and the consequent extension of their own influence within the kingdom. As several scholars have noted, it is evident from

contemporary evidence that 'faction', in the modern sense of the word, did
not exist within the Henrician court. Rather, alliances and friendships were
centred on ties of kinship that were usually consolidated through betrothals
and marriages, which women played essential roles in both symbolically and
practically. As Starkey credibly suggests, Henrician faction cannot be seen as
'a universal, but rooted in certain institutions, and not as a constant, but flourishing or being repressed in accordance with the character and policies of
certain crucial figures – and the monarch above all'.[27] In view of this, there was
nothing especially strange or unusual about the influence exercised by Anne
Boleyn during this time, for as has been made apparent, women were actively
involved at the Tudor court in providing their family with power, prestige and
influence.[28] Approaching Tudor politics from a gendered perspective is fruitful
since 'looking at politics from women's point of view alters our understanding
of the development of the [Tudor] monarchy'.[29]

Nonetheless, this did not mean that women who played important political
roles within the operation of the Tudor court were universally accepted or
perceived to be political players on a par with their male counterparts; in some
circumstances, quite the opposite could prove true. This should be viewed in
the context of cultural and social mores that pervaded the sixteenth-century
court, for not only were women's bodies constructed in this period as the
absolute Other, but women's chastity and unchastity were continually proscribed, ridiculed and feared, which led to a preoccupation and obsession with
notions of honour and dishonour.[30] Dishonour focused overwhelmingly on
sexual sins, and eventually 'dismantled the trappings of higher status women's
rank'.[31] The female body itself was widely feared by men, for it 'was believed
to have magical effects, bewitching a lover, serving as an aphrodisiac, assisting
in conception'.[32] In view of this, the visible political influence wielded by
Anne within the Tudor court opened her up to ridicule that her male relatives, such as the Duke of Norfolk, did not face in the same respect by virtue
of both their biological sex and contemporary constructions of masculinity.
It is unsurprising that male commentators, such as the unknown chronicler
of *The Chronicle of Henry VIII of England*, blamed Anne for the annulment of
Katherine's marriage to Henry VIII, opining how 'he was ruined by Anne
Boleyn', while castigating Anne's 'wickedness' and 'the pleasure she took in
doing harm to the blessed Queen Katharine'.[33]

In order for women to exercise influence at Henry VIII's court, it was essential that they be seen to adhere to contemporary gender mores, rather than
undermine or challenge them by appearing to be 'manly' in the degree of
influence they exercised. Earlier queens consort, such as Margaret of Anjou,
became victims of contemporary gender expectations because they were

perceived to transgress the – often murky – boundaries between acceptable and unacceptable behaviour. Any influential woman who overstepped these boundaries rendered herself vulnerable to accusations of sexual transgressions, which usually proved the most effective means of dishonouring her and her family. This danger became a reality for Anne Boleyn in 1536, leading not only to her execution but also to the deaths of five men implicated with her.

Despite the censure she faced for her unique position in the annulment struggle, the kinship between Anne and her Howard relatives brought tangible benefits to her family, increasing the influence held by the Howard family at Henry VIII's court. The Venetian ambassador Lodovico Falieri was able to report by November 1530 that Henry 'makes use of him [Norfolk] in all negotiations more than any other person ... and every employment devolves to him'.[34] Similarly, Charles V in 1532 was informed that the Duke of Norfolk was 'a man who willingly takes trouble in this matter, but would suffer any-thing for the sake of ruling'.[35] In 1532 Norfolk's 13-year-old daughter, Mary, participated in the ceremony creating Anne Boleyn Marquess of Pembroke and was later to attend her during her first court appearance as queen. Rather more obvious and lucrative benefits were acquired in the period that witnessed the marriage and coronation of Anne Boleyn, when Norfolk was created Earl Marshal on 28 May 1533, four days before the public coronation of his niece at Westminster Abbey, who was then six months pregnant. Norfolk's role in the demotion of Katherine of Aragon, whose marriage had by now been formally annulled, was confirmed by Wriothesley:

> On Easter evening, Anne Boleyn, Marquess of Pembroke, was proclaimed Queen at Greenwich. The Wednesday before the good Queen Katherine was deposed at Ampthill, Bedfordshire by the dukes Norfolk and Suffolk; the mar-quis of Exeter; the earl of Oxford; the treasurer; and comptroller. On 29 May 1533 she was received as Queen of England by all the lords of England.[36]

Members of the Howard family played a prominent part in Anne's corona-tion proceedings, with her uncle Lord William Howard present acting as Earl Marshal and the dowager Duchess of Norfolk, step-grandmother of Anne and Katherine, present in the procession.[37] Other relatives, however, such as Elizabeth Stafford, the Duchess of Norfolk, aunt of the queen, personally opposed Anne's rise and openly expressed their sympathy for the old queen.

Although Anne's uncle was not personally present at the pinnacle of her triumph, the coronation in June 1533, since he was then on embassy in France, the summer of 1533 could well be interpreted as the golden age for the Howard family, when a member of the family won the heart of Henry VIII and was crowned as his queen consort, with an expectation that she would shortly give birth to the much-desired male heir. This close relationship between the Tudors and the Howards was further strengthened by the birth of Princess Elizabeth to the king and his new queen in September, although the ambitions of the Howard family and the dynastic expectations of the Tudors required that the queen present her husband with a son in order to secure her position beyond doubt. The reason for the rejection of Katherine of Aragon would always have been in the mind of Anne and her relatives. Traditionally, historians have interpreted Norfolk's relations with his niece the queen as being strained due to their differing religious beliefs – the Howards were renowned for their religious orthodoxy – and on account of Anne's abrasive character, but the duke and his niece maintained a mutually beneficial relationship during the initial years of Anne's marriage. Norfolk's mistress, Bess Holland, was appointed to the household of the new queen, and the Howards enjoyed additional glory in the winter of 1533 as a result of the marriage of Norfolk's 14-year-old daughter, Mary, to the king's bastard son Henry Fitzroy. Uberto de Gambara further proposed that the duke approach the king with the proposal of a marriage alliance between Mary Tudor, the bastardised daughter of Katherine of Aragon, and Henry Howard, Earl of Surrey, Norfolk's heir:

> Only the duke of Norfolk can persuade him to do this by his influence, and relationship to the new queen, pointing out that the peace of the Kingdom and the settlement of the king's son weighs more with him than the good of his own niece, and that if the king were to die before the son became a man, the next heirs might trouble the succession – the king of Scotland and the sons of the other sister and of the duke of Suffolk … I think I could point out to him that this course would so endear him to the emperor and the pope that they would enable him to have the princess for his son; whose right would not really be put aside, and they would afterwards help to maintain him by force.[38]

Whether this report can be credited is difficult to ascertain, for ambassadorial reports were usually influenced, directly or indirectly, consciously or unconsciously, by rumour, hearsay, and gossip that was currently in circulation at the English court. It was also the custom of English monarchs, moreover, to deliberately mislead foreign ambassadors at court. It is impossible to know whether or not the duke did suffer a long-term estrangement with Queen Anne, based on differing religious interests and Norfolk's increasing disillusionment with the assertiveness of his niece, for the Spanish ambassador reported that the queen personally scolded the duke as if he were a 'dog, so much so that Norfolk was obliged to quit the royal chamber', referring to his niece as a 'whore'.[39]

Historians have traditionally asserted that a personal crisis occurred in the relationship between Norfolk and the queen soon after the birth of Elizabeth, because Anne's assertiveness threatened his own religious and political interests, coupled with the fact that the turbulence of her relationship with Henry VIII placed the Howards in a potentially precarious political position. Although it is possible that Norfolk, like his male contemporaries, believed that women should not exercise excessive influence to the detriment of the male aristocracy at the court, the surviving evidence compiled by resident ambassadors must be considered sceptically since the queen had brought unprecedented prestige to the Howard family, firstly through her marriage to Henry VIII and secondly through her personal involvement in the marriage alliance between her cousin Mary, daughter of the duke, and Henry Fitzroy, son of the king.

It is unlikely that the duke would have forfeited his favour with his niece the queen on the basis of personal religious beliefs to the detriment of the overall fortunes of the Howard family, for Anne had been instrumental in ensuring that the Howards achieved greater influence and prominence at Henry VIII's court, which acted politically and ceremonially as a microcosm of the English state. Her female attendants included several Howards, with Mary Howard, Elizabeth Boleyn, Mary Shelton, Jane Parker, Lady Rochford and Mary Boleyn foremost among Anne's ladies-in-waiting.[40] Directly relevant to the life and circumstances of Anne's young cousin Katherine Howard was the fact that in 1535 the queen, acting together with Norfolk, successfully achieved for Edmund Howard some forfeited goods worth 200 marks.[41] The appointment of Howard women within the queen's household with the opportunity to exercise influence on behalf of the Howard family and enhance the family's influence at court forms a necessary context to a consideration of the age of Katherine Howard during her cousin's tenure as queen consort, for had Katherine been born in 1520–21, as historians traditionally believed, then surely her uncle or her step-grandmother the dowager Duchess of Norfolk would have sought a position for her within Anne's household as a maiden. That there is no evidence of them doing so surely indicates that Anne's cousin was still too young to serve at court.[42] Further rewards were granted to Norfolk by virtue of his association with the new queen, including a French pension and an invitation for his son Surrey to accompany the king's bastard son – and Norfolk's son-in-law – Henry Fitzroy, Earl of Richmond, to the French court.[43]

The suggestion here that the duke did not suffer a personal fall-out with his niece the queen has also been offered by other historians, who argue that 'when Norfolk suffered reduced power and influence after 1531, it was less the result of a strained relationship with his niece than his own lack of talent and commitment'; 'in terms of his leadership of the Howard clan and political faction at court, this senior member of the family [Norfolk] spent a lifetime chasing after the unattainable', 'he was no more successful as a politician at court'.[44] The dynastic and political goals of the Tudor dynasty, which consolidated and reaffirmed traditional perceptions of the queen's traditional role, meant that Anne's position as queen was not fully secure after she gave birth to Elizabeth in September 1533. A son was needed in order to publicly demonstrate her legitimacy as queen consort and to ensure the continuation of the Tudor dynasty. From the wider European Roman Catholic perspective, the new queen was no more than a mischievous harlot who had bewitched, or manipulated, a pliable king into annulling his marriage with a Spanish princess and marrying Anne instead, leading to the birth of a bastard daughter who was no more legitimate than Henry Fitzroy. In view of this political and dynastic context in 1533 it is possible that Norfolk counselled his niece on the necessity of bearing Henry VIII a male heir – if he even needed to – in order to make clear to her to avoid the fate of Katherine of Aragon and to ensure that the Howard family's glittering fortunes at court were consolidated and, if possible, elevated further. The arrival of a son would have been interpreted as a divine blessing, which by extension would have signalled God's approval of Henry VIII's decision to rusticate Katherine and marry Anne.

The succession troubles which affected the royal family directly involved the queen's relatives. Mary Tudor, aged 17 at the birth of her half-sister in 1533, refused to renounce her title as princess, leading to the king her father ordering Norfolk to visit her 'concerning the diminishing of her high estate of the name and dignity of Princess'. Visiting her at Beaulieu, the duke informed the king's eldest daughter that the king 'desired her to go to the Court and service of [Elizabeth], whom he named Princess', but Mary refused since the title of princess, in her eyes, rightfully belonged to her and not to her infant half-sister. The duke, however, informed her that 'he had not come to dispute but to accomplish the King's will', before Mary finally agreed to depart, 'with a very small suite'.[45]

Around the same time, the Duke of Suffolk was ordered to demand that Katherine of Aragon's servants refer to her as 'princess dowager' rather than queen, and he attempted to encourage the king's first wife to retire to Somersham. This mission proved to be spectacularly unsuccessful, with Katherine refusing to heed Suffolk's request and locking herself in her chambers in protest. The dynastic and political troubles associated with the English succession had brutal repercussions, with Bishop John Fisher of Rochester and Sir Thomas More, both of whom had formerly been close to Henry VIII, suffering execution for high treason in the summer of 1535 on account of their refusal to accept Henry VIII as Supreme Head of the English Church.[46] According to the Spanish ambassador, in a vocalisation of the contemporary belief that influential high-status women were usually to blame for their husbands' follies, after the executions of More and Fisher Queen Anne admonished the king 'that he does not act with prudence in suffering the Queen [Katherine] and Princess [Mary] to live, who deserved death more than all those who have been executed, and that they were the cause of all'.[47] Anne's evident fears and hostility towards the former queen and her daughter can be understood in the context of the prevailing concern about the Tudor succession within both the court and England as a whole. Well aware that Katherine had been rusticated for her inability to solve the succession crisis, Anne perceived that only by bearing Henry VIII a healthy son could her position as queen remain secure, for no blame would be attached to her husband were her pregnancies to end unsuccessfully. In view of this context in 1533–35, it is evident that 'by his divorce and remarriage Henry had created for himself a domestic tangle that was unusual for his day ... when his second consort presented him with a female child, confusion reigned in the minds of many about which daughter had the better claim to the throne'.[48]

Contemporaries generally adhered to the prevailing view that 'the queen's lying-in is the foundation of everything'.[49] Yet it is possible, even likely, that it was the king, rather than his queens, who was responsible for the lack of a son to succeed him to the throne.[50] This context will be discussed in greater detail during the queenship of Anne's cousin Katherine Howard, but it is worth emphasising here that Anne's failure to bear a son compounded her personal difficulties, for she was never a popular queen consort in the same way in which her predecessor Katherine of Aragon had been. The abbot of Whitby seems to have voiced the opinion of many when he declared that 'the king's grace was ruled by one common stewed whore, Anne Bullan, who made all the spirituality to be beggared and the temporalty also'.[51] Her association with Thomas Cromwell and reformist bishops such as the Archbishop of Canterbury, Thomas Cranmer, meant that Anne was viewed with even greater hostility among traditional Catholics within England, who resented the break from Rome and the rapid rate of religious changes occurring during the 1530s. The Succession Act, directed by Cromwell, which required every person in the country to swear an oath in support of Henry VIII's union with Anne, fuelled discontent with the king's new marriage. George Cavendish, who resented the queen and openly blamed her for Cardinal Wolsey's downfall, created an arrogant and vindictive Anne in his *Verses*, written during the reign of Mary I, in which he represented her as to blame for the unpopular religious and political changes: 'I was the author why laws were made for speaking against me … it was my full intent lineally to succeed in this Imperial crown.'[52] Cavendish's discontent seems to have been shared by many, for 'the people, horrified to see such unprecedented and brutal atrocities, muttered in whispers about these events and often blamed Queen Anne'.[53] On the other hand, it is possible that Anne's personal unpopularity has been overstated in modern historical accounts, but the overriding emphasis here is that her inability to deliver a son placed her in a vulnerable political and dynastic position, while also endangering the Howards.

Because, as has been noted, aristocratic women directly contributed to and affected the successes and failures of their families as daughters, wives, and widows, the Duke of Norfolk and his kin could only have been relieved to discover that the queen was apparently once more pregnant in the spring of 1534, especially against a backdrop of mounting discontent in England coupled with the (from the perspective of England) troubled state of international politics.[54] The king personally informed the Spanish ambassador in February 1534 that he would soon become a father again, while at court the queen's 'goodly' belly was remarked upon by those who observed her at royal events and ceremonies.[55] It is likely that both the ambassador and his master, Charles, feared the news of Anne's pregnancy, for were she to produce a son for the king this would undoubtedly mean that the Lady Mary, daughter of Katherine, could never succeed to the English throne. This was not to be, however, for some months later, on 23 September, Chapuys reported that the king believed that his wife was not truly pregnant, evidently signalling an end to the couple's hopes.[56] The failed pregnancy was shrouded in mystery and has remained a matter of contention among modern historians, for they have not been successful in discovering what the outcome of Anne's second pregnancy was, but the likelihood was that she had suffered a miscarriage in the late summer of 1534, probably weeks before her due date.[57]

The nature of the English succession was further undermined by developments in European politics, which were characterised mainly by a continuing refusal to accept Henry's second marriage as valid in view of the fact that not only was his first marriage lawful but his second wife had failed to provide her husband with the desired male heir, which would have strengthened her position immeasurably. Both Henry and Anne were desirous of maintaining their friendship with the French, inviting François's envoys, who resided in England during the spring of 1534, to convey their support of the marriage in meeting the new princess. Chapuys reported the interview: Elizabeth 'was brought out to them splendidly accoutred and dressed, and in princely state, with all the ceremonial her governess could think of, after which they saw her quite undressed'.[58] At the same time George, Lord Rochford, brother of the queen, departed for France to discuss plans with the French king for a marriage alliance between Elizabeth and Charles, Duke of Angoulême (third son of François I and Claude of France). Following the unsuccessful outcome of the queen's pregnancy that summer, however, relations between England and France swiftly deteriorated. Chapuys informed the emperor in January 1535 that, following a banquet at which the Sieur de Brion attended, Anne had burst out laughing, explaining that 'I could not help laughing at the King's proposition of introducing your secretary to me, for whilst he was looking out for him he happened to meet a lady, who was the cause of his forgetting everything'.[59] Palamedes Gontier, treasurer of Brittany, who met the queen that same month, was informed personally by her that:

> The Admiral must think of applying some remedy, and act towards the King so that she may not be ruined and lost, for she sees herself very near that, and in more grief and trouble than before her marriage. She charged him to beg the Admiral to consider her affairs, of which she could not speak as fully as she wished, on account of her fears, and the eyes which were looking at her, her husband's and the lords' present. She said she could not write, nor see him again, nor stay longer.[60]

It is evident that the queen found herself in a troubled personal and political situation by early 1535, for not only had she failed to provide Henry VIII with a male heir, which her marriage to him had apparently promised, but her daughter's legitimacy was placed in doubt when the negotiations for Elizabeth's marriage to Angoulême collapsed. Indeed, the king and queen were publicly humiliated when François instead offered his son's hand to Mary, daughter of Katherine of Aragon. Adding to her misery, hostile observers further recorded that Anne had suffered a breakdown in her relationship with the Duke of Norfolk, who complained that he had not received sufficient rewards from her who he had so vigorously supported.[61] Other evidence seems to indicate that other Howard relatives, aside from the duke, experienced mounting discontent with their kinswoman and the policies that they associated with her and Master Secretary Cromwell. During the royal couple's progress in the summer and autumn of 1535, Lady Rochford, sister-in-law to the queen, and Lady William Howard, the step-aunt of Anne, may have been among a number of wives of London citizens and some of the queen's ladies who demonstrated at Greenwich Palace in support of the Lady Mary. Chapuys later reported that:

The marchioness of Exeter sent to say that four or five days ago the king talking about the princess, said that he should provide that soon she would not want any company, and that she would be an example to show that no one ought to disobey the laws and he meant to fulfil what had been foretold of him ... he would be gentle as a lamb and at the end worse than a lion.[62]

Chapuys's report is telling in relation to who was the real author of Mary's ill treatment. In keeping with contemporary gender and political mores, however, like other male chroniclers the Spanish ambassador castigated the queen for her alleged cruelty and spite towards the king's firstborn daughter, either failing to recognise or choosing not to believe that it was actually Anne's husband who treated his daughter cruelly out of outrage towards her (from his perspective) disobedience and stubborn behaviour. Even if Anne had been content to ignore Mary's intransigence, Henry would not have been: at the least, he would have feared that his daughter's publicly uncooperative behaviour may have encouraged rebellion in the realm from those sympathetic to her cause.

The death of Katherine of Aragon in January 1536 and the welcome news of Queen Anne's third pregnancy around the same time enacted the beginning of a new phase in the fortunes of the Howard family, which was to have long-term consequences. As has been recognised by several historians, the death of the old queen should have ensured that Anne found herself in a stronger political and dynastic position than she had been since her marriage to the king, for Katherine's death might be thought to have encouraged both the King of France and the Holy Roman Emperor to come to terms, at least publicly, with Henry VIII and his union to Anne, even if privately they continued to view Henry VIII's second marriage as unlawful. Henry VIII's joy at Katherine's decease was made public at court:

The king was clad all over in yellow, from top to toe, except the white feather he had in his bonnet, and the Little Bastard [Elizabeth] was conducted to mass with trumpets and other great triumphs. After dinner the king entered the room in which the ladies danced, and there did several things like one transported with joy. At last he sent for his Little Bastard [Elizabeth], and carrying her in his arms he showed her to one and then another.[63]

Despite Katherine's death, and the discovery that Anne was pregnant for the third time, the queen would have feared that her enemies would not fail to move against her if she fell from the king's favour, for in the eyes of imperialist sympathisers the king was now a widower and could be encouraged to marry again and, perhaps, return to the Roman Church and resolve the English schism.

The queen's tragic miscarriage of a three-month-old male that month was directly ascribed to her, for sixteenth-century observers believed that women were to blame for failures in conception and pregnancy. Women's bodies were blamed for causing notorious vices, with women interpreted as being 'at the mercy of their wombs which could wander dangerously through the body causing hysteria and other maladies'.[64] The Spanish ambassador, writing less than two weeks after the queen's miscarriage on 29 January, recorded that:

> On the day of the internment [Katherine's funeral], the Concubine [Anne] had an abortion which seemed to be a male child which she had not borne 3½ months, at which the King has shown great distress. The said concubine wished to lay the blame on the duke of Norfolk, whom she hates, saying he frightened her by bringing the news of the fall the King had six days before.[65]

According to Chapuys, Anne's personal relationship with her uncle the duke had deteriorated to the extent that she personally held him responsible for her miscarriage, indicating that relations between the two had been hostile for some time, probably since at least the preceding year. The chronicler Edward Hall also made reference to the queen's miscarriage, commenting that 'and in February folowyng was quene Anne brought a bedde of a childe before her tyme, whiche was born dead'.[66] Wriothesley similarly documented that 'Queene Anne was brought a bedd and delivered of a man child, as it was said, afore her tyme, for she said that she had reckoned herself at that tyme but fiftene weekes gonne with child'.[67] Lancelot de Carles, who described the events of the queen's downfall in his verse, agreed with Chapuys in opining that the king's jousting accident caused his wife to miscarry 'un beau filz'.[68]

As with Queen Katherine during the 1510s, Anne was directly blamed for failing to bear a son. Rumours circulated at court that she was physically unable to bear sons, while claiming that both Elizabeth and her miscarried son were 'suppositious'.[69] Significantly, similar allegations of barrenness would arise during Katherine Howard's downfall five years later, albeit with no direct evidence that Katherine ever conceived a child by the king, let alone suffered a miscarriage or stillbirth. Anne's position as queen and the influence of the Howard family at court were both undermined by this miscarriage, and the resulting vulnerability of both queen and family was exacerbated by the king's increasing affection for Jane Seymour, an attendant to the queen who was fairly close in age to her royal mistress. Yet, somewhat unusually, despite her estrangement from the king and her perhaps increasingly strained relationship with her Howard uncle, the queen's situation was not as bleak as it might have initially appeared, for Emperor Charles had promised Cromwell, who had previously enjoyed an amicable relationship with Anne, that while 'the Princess Mary might be declared legitimate … He promised to use his good offices with the Pope, that, at the impending council, his good brother's present marriage should be declared valid, and the succession arranged as he desired'.[70] Paradoxically, despite her second miscarriage, Anne's position as queen during the early spring of 1536 was not undermined irretrievably by the increasing influence of the Seymours that arose from the king's flirtation with Jane, for Katherine's death and the changed international situation offered the opportunity for a reconciliation between England and the Holy Roman Empire that would be channelled through, while also facilitating, a diplomatic acceptance of the Boleyn marriage.

Although the king had not yet decided to end his marriage to Anne during the spring of 1536, it has been surmised that the Duke of Norfolk's hostility towards the queen led him to participate actively in the events leading to her downfall, largely because Anne had failed to bring sufficient rewards and prestige to the Howards and more importantly Norfolk himself.[71] It is difficult to place the Duke of Norfolk acting with Jane Seymour, her family, and so-called Imperialists in a 'faction' which aimed at the downfall of Queen Anne and her Boleyn relatives, for the evidence pointing to such a coalition against the queen and her supporters is scarce. It is unlikely that, following his niece's miscarriage, Norfolk conspired with the Seymours to effect Anne's disgrace in the confident belief that the king would accept their evidence and rid himself of his second wife, for the king, contrary to popular opinion, continued to outwardly support his consort, entreating the Spanish ambassador to publicly honour her on 18 April and writing abroad of 'the likelihood and appearance that God will send us heirs male by our most dear and most entirely beloved wife, the queen'.[72] For the time being, at least, Norfolk probably continued to support his niece by virtue of their kinship ties and his belief that she might yet deliver the much-desired male heir.

Although both Anne's personal relationship with the king and her friendship with Master Secretary Cromwell had been placed in difficulties by virtue of her miscarriages and her opposition to Cromwell's religious policies – although it is possible that this has been exaggerated by modern historians – Henry VIII's affection for Jane Seymour did not personally threaten Anne to a significant extent during the early months of 1536 as some historians have traditionally believed that it did. As has already been noted, the international situation was actually more favourable to the queen than it had been hitherto. Although her (possibly overstated) estrangement from Norfolk and the growing fear among the Howards that the success which they had attained on account of Anne's spectacular rise to the position of queen might be undermined by her uneasy relations with the king, the favour that Anne apparently enjoyed – for the time being – with her husband surely prevented Norfolk from actively colluding with the Seymours and other enemies of his niece as early as the spring of 1536 to bring about her disgrace, for the subsequent rise of the Seymours and their associates could not bode well for his family's fortunes. However, in late April, a series of events worked together to effect the downfall of Queen Anne and a number of residents at court, some of whom were closely associated with her through friendship or blood. Cromwell reported in mid May 'that the ladies of the queen's Privy Chamber had informed certain councillors of certain matters and there had followed interrogations of some of the Privy Chamber and a number of the queen's staff' pertaining to allegations of Anne's adultery committed with five members at court, one of whom was her brother George.[73] The queen's own indiscreet conversations with Henry Norris, a favoured courtier, her brother George, and the lowly musician Mark Smeaton meant that, as Starkey wryly notes, 'she [Anne] delivered herself'.[74]

There is a notorious lack of consensus among modern historians as to the nature of Queen Anne's unprecedented downfall in the early summer of 1536 and the degree of Henry VIII's involvement in it, with the majority of historians presently divided between the following theories:

> 1. That proposed by Eric Ives, that Anne was ruined by a factional conspiracy masterminded by Thomas Cromwell, who resented the queen's influence.
> 2. The theory that the birth of a deformed foetus in January convinced the king that his wife was a sorceress who had bewitched him into marrying her.
> 3. The suggestion that the queen was actually guilty of the charges brought against her.
> 4. The argument that it was the simple fact that her own indiscreet conversations with male courtiers planted suspicion in the mind of the king when rumours circulated of the queen's closeness with these individuals, gossip that perhaps originated in her household.[75]

The frustrating nature of the surviving evidence and the prejudiced and often misguided reports of ambassadors resident at court compound these problems with resolving the mystery behind Anne's downfall, but the fact remains that Anne had been in a relatively strong position as late as April 1536, calling into doubt the first three theories, none of which are satisfactory in explaining why the queen was charged, imprisoned, condemned and executed within a space of three weeks. The likelihood may be that the queen, unsettled by her second miscarriage that winter and fearful of the rising influence of Jane Seymour, failed to maintain a respectable distance from courtiers, participating in conversations with those whose company she enjoyed which could be sinisterly misinterpreted as evidence of treason and plotting the king's death. Most infamously, she berated Norris on 29 April, informing him that 'you look for dead man's shoes, for if aught came to the King but good you would look to have me', bringing his shocked reply that 'he would his head were off rather than think such thoughts'.[76]

Irrespective of Anne's own actions – and ultimately whether one accepts her actions as at least partly contributing to her downfall depends a great deal on one's interpretation of Anne's character – there is no doubt that her downfall and execution in 1536 took place with the express consent of Henry VIII. As an absolute monarch, the decision for Anne to become the first queen consort of England to suffer execution must be laid squarely at the door of her husband. No matter how influential Cromwell was at court, he could not have brought about the queen's ruin without the encouragement or involvement of Henry VIII, and the king's intimate involvement in the last weeks of his second wife's life would be mirrored in the downfall of Katherine Howard five years later.

Two days after Anne's conversation with Norris, on May Day, the king abruptly departed from the jousts, leaving the queen in some discomfort and bewilderment:

> On May day were a Solempne Justes kept at Grenewyche, and sodainly from the Justes the kyng departed hauying not above vi persons with him, and came in the evening from Grenewyche in his place at Westminster. Of this sodain departyng many men mused, but most chiefely the quene, who the next day was apprehended and brought from Grenewyche to the Tower of London.[77]

The following day, Anne was arrested on charges of adultery with three men (unnamed, with others to follow), incest and plotting her husband's death: 'About five of the clocke at night, the Queene Anne Bolleine was brought to the Towre of London by my Lord Chancellor, the duke of Norfolke, Mr. Secretarie, and Sir William Kingston, Constable of the Tower.'[78]

The lack of documented evidence relating to the Duke of Norfolk during the initial proceedings against the queen calls into question the suggestion that, in order to save both himself and his family, the duke allied himself with the Seymours and their friends in conspiring the downfall of Anne Boleyn. The first tangible mention of the duke in relation to the queen's downfall was in relation to his role in her arrest, for on the morning of 2 May the duke, alongside Sir William Fitzwilliam, treasurer of the household, Sir William Paulet, comptroller of the household, and other members of the Privy Council, accused the queen of adultery and incest before escorting her to the Tower that afternoon. Norfolk's fear for the future of his family was evident in the reports of the disapproval that he showed his niece, saying 'tut, tut, tut … in answer to her defence' during her journey to the Tower.[79] The duke's concern for the safety of his family is understandable, especially when another member of that family, the queen's brother George, Lord Rochford, was imprisoned in the Tower on a charge of incest committed with the queen. Yet any concern for the future of the Howard family led the duke, as one of the foremost peers in the realm, to serve as a member of the Oyer and Terminer Commission for Middlesex on 24 April, which sat at Westminster. This commission also included another Howard relative, the earl of Wiltshire, father to the queen. The duke later sat on the Oyer and Terminer Commission for Kent on 11 May at Deptford.[80]

As will be discussed in relation to the downfall of Katherine Howard five years after the disgrace of Anne Boleyn, contemporary gender mores lay at the heart of the downfall of Queen Anne, who was condemned in the indictments for her 'frail and carnal lust' entertained with male courtiers due to the 'malice' she held against the king.[81] Significantly, it was reported that 'the king … took such inward displeasure and heaviness, especially from his said queen's malice and adultery, that certain harms and perils have befallen his royal body'.[82] The implication, clearly, was that Anne had bewitched the king into marrying her and had rendered him impotent to the detriment of both the Tudor succession and the realm of England, which relied on political and dynastic stability to ensure its continuing harmony and wellbeing. The likelihood, or at least the impression that Henry VIII and his councillors wanted to provide, was that the king genuinely believed that his queen had employed sorcery to enact evil upon his body, for contemporaries believed that women were able to manipulate men's sexual organs and rob them of their manhood through sorcery and witchcraft. Henry VIII's insecurity about his manhood and his ability or otherwise to father a male heir reflected the concerns of many men living in the Tudor age, for manhood was commonly perceived to be a fragile achievement always open to threat from the malice of women.[83] This cultural context was graphically reflected in the charges brought against the queen and her co-accused, which included the humiliating accusation that she had discussed Henry's prowess in bed with her sister-in-law Jane Rochford.

Meanwhile the queen's Howard relatives readily participated in the proceedings against her irrespective of what their private feelings might have been, in order to preserve their honour and safeguard their lineage from being disgraced through association with her. Jane, Lady Rochford, sister-in-law to Queen Anne and the niece of the Duke of Norfolk through her marriage to

George Boleyn, was interrogated by the officers of the Crown and whatever she might have said was eventually used in the allegations made against the queen. Although the only extant reference to Jane during the downfall of the queen does not support the popular notion that she accused Anne of committing incest with her brother, she was to testify that the king's impotence had been discussed.[84] Despite the minimal evidence that she provided in the course of the proceedings, Lady Rochford has traditionally been perceived as a 'wretched woman [who] was actuated wholly by hatred of her own husband and the Queen, and it was upon her unsupported statements that the charges of incest were brought … She was largely instrumental in bringing Ann [sic] Boleyn to her death.'[85]

Bishop Burnet agreed with this condemnatory evaluation of the viscountess, believing that Lady Rochford 'provided the damaging evidence that there was a familiarity between the queen and her brother beyond what so near a relationship could justify'.[86] Significantly, however, hostile observers such as Chapuys and the author of *The Chronicle of Henry VIII* did not mention Lady Rochford in their discussions of her husband's downfall. It is more than likely that her uncle, the duke, encouraged her to co-operate with Cromwell and the king's councillors in the course of the interrogations in order to preserve the safety of the Howards, who were placed in considerable danger during April and May 1536. It is also possible, of course, that Lady Rochford was unaware of the fatal consequences of the testimony provided by the queen's attendants for her husband George Boleyn and her sister-in-law Queen Anne. No Queen of England had been executed before, and it is entirely plausible that the queen's household and the king's councillors might have predicted the annulment of the Boleyn marriage and the exile of Anne from court, but surely they could not have anticipated her execution. On 12 May, letters were directed to the Duke of Norfolk which appointed him High Steward of England for the trial of his niece and nephew, the queen and her brother, 'to give judgment according to the laws and customs of England and direct execution'.[87] That same day, four men accused of adultery with the queen, Henry Norris, Francis Weston, William Brereton and Mark Smeaton, were found guilty and sentenced to a traitor's death.

The minimal role of the Duke of Norfolk during the downfall of his niece, apart from in his role as High Steward of England during her trial on 15 May, appears to be confirmed by a letter written by William Paulet, comptroller of the Household, to Cromwell on 11 May:

My lord of Norfolk showed me that he had no knowledge that the indictment was found and asked me whether the parties should proceed to their

trial or not … he said he knew not how many were required nor whether they ought to be barons or not. Therefore he could not tell whom to name, and if he knew yet he would name none till he learned the king's pleasure so he willed me to advertise you.[88]

Although ambassadors at court during Anne's queenship, and modern historians since then, generally subscribed to the view that the duke became increasingly disaffected with his niece on account of her outspokenness and her conflicting religious views, the evidence supporting this argument is astonishingly slim. Rather than actively participating in the queen's downfall as a means of enacting revenge upon a niece he had come to loathe, or in the context of a faction battle in which the duke and Anne's enemies collectively united against her, the evidence indicates that Norfolk supported his monarch because of his unwavering belief in the necessity of doing his duty to the king, and in the belief that the future of the Howard dynasty was a more pressing concern than the survival of his niece as queen. He could surely not have happily anticipated the rise of Jane Seymour to the position of queen, for her family was hostile to his, meaning that his focus may have shifted from his niece the queen to his daughter Mary who, by virtue of her marriage to Henry Fitzroy, represented the opportunity for the Howards to increase their political influence at court. In the weeks immediately after Anne's execution, rumours circulated that Henry was seriously considering nominating his bastard son as his heir, and this would have been an alluring and entirely unexpected prospect for the ambitious Duke of Norfolk.

On 15 May, the queen and her brother were tried at the Great Hall within the Tower of London on charges of adultery, incest and plotting the death of the king. Wriothesley reports that:

There were made benches and seates for the lordes, my Lord of Northfolke sitting under the clothe of estate, representing there the Kinges person as Highe Steward of Englande and uncle to the Queene, he holding a longe white staffe in his hande, and the Earle of Surrey, his sonne and heire, sitting at his feete before him holdinge the golden staffe for the Earle Marshall of Englande.[89]

The queen maintained her composure when the charges were read out, 'whereunto she made so wise and discreet aunsweres to all thinges layd against her, excusinge herselfe with her wordes so clearlie, as thoughe she had never bene faultie to the same'.[90] Despite her firm answers and courageous demeanour, the twenty-six peers present unanimously found the queen guilty, leaving her uncle the duke to pass the sentence of death. Following her trial, her brother George was also found guilty on all charges and was sentenced to a traitor's death, although the king later permitted the more gracious method of decapitation, a privilege also granted to the other four men under sentence of death.

The Howard family, as one of the premier noble families in the kingdom with a long history of political service to the Crown, had been required to participate in the proceedings against Queen Anne and the five men accused of adultery and treason with her, although the duke grievously regretted the loss in his status as relative to the king and the dishonour enacted upon the Howard name. Following the execution of the queen's supposed lovers on 17 May, on 19 May Anne herself was beheaded within the walls of the Tower. Edward Hall, who served as chronicler at Henry VIII's court, reported her execution speech:

> Good Christen people, I am come hether to dye, for according to the lawe, and by the lawe I am judged to dye, and therefore I wyll speake nothynge agaynst it. I am come hether to accuse no man, nor to speae any thyng of that whereof I am accused and condemnped to dye, but I pray God saue the king and send him long to reigne oeur you, for a gentler nor a more mercyfull prince was there neuer: and to me he was euer a good, a gentle, & soueraigne lorde. And if any persone will medle of my cause, I require them to judge the best. And thus I take my leue of the worlde and of you all, and I heartely desyre you all to pray for me. O lorde haue mercy on me, to God I comende my soule.[91]

The brutal and unprecedented downfall of Anne Boleyn within a space of three weeks, bringing down five almost certainly guiltless men with her, is a clear demonstration of the dangerous nature of fertility politics at Henry VIII's court and the opportunities it presented for the hitherto unimagined disgrace and death of a queen consort. As with Katherine of Aragon during the 1520s, Anne's failure to bear a male heir, after suffering at least one and possibly two miscarriages, signified to her husband Henry VIII that he had made a grave error in marrying a woman who was, in his view, unable to produce a male heir with which to ensure the continuation of Tudor succession. It is not necessarily correct to interpret his relationship with Jane Seymour as one based on lust and desire, for by all accounts she lacked the charisma, beauty and wit of Anne Boleyn which had made that gentlewoman so irresistible to her monarch.[92] Instead issues of honour and masculinity were at stake, for the king speedily married Jane following his wife's execution – not necessarily because he was captivated by Jane and wildly impatient to marry her, but because Anne Boleyn's failure to produce a son had intensified the problems afflicting the English succession, while salacious rumours of her conversations with male courtiers and her sister-in-law placed the king's manhood and his fertility in considerable – and embarrassing – doubt. The charge that Anne had committed adultery with five men necessitated a brutal response from the king in order to preserve his honour. Historians, perhaps neglecting the social and cultural context of sixteenth-century manhood and beliefs about reproduction and fatherhood, have usually interpreted Henry VIII's marriage to Jane Seymour a mere eleven days after Anne's death as callous, proving that he had been so moved by hatred for his second wife that he could not wait to get rid of her.[93] The reality was that his honour and his manhood required that he speedily take another wife in order to sire a son, both for his own personal security and that of the kingdom, while ensuring that his honour was preserved in a climate of wild accusation and rumour.

The indictments produced at the queen's trial provide evidence of the king's belief that his wife had bewitched him into marrying her and had rendered him impotent. She would not be the last of his queens to be accused of inflicting impotence on her husband, the king. As Katherine Howard's disgrace five years later also illustrated, Henry VIII did not take kindly to accusations of marital disloyalty.

3

'HIS VICIOUS PURPOSE': MANOX AND DEREHAM, 1536–39

DURING ANNE BOLEYN'S UNPRECEDENTED rise at court and elevation to queenship, which brought unimaginable favour to the Howard family that was undermined only by the queen's tragic downfall, her young cousin Katherine Howard embarked upon her first steps into the adult world when she began receiving music lessons in 1536, the year of Anne's downfall, when she was aged about 12 or 13 years old, which would prepare her for an exciting future at court as an attendant to the Queen of England. It is reasonable to suppose that, had Queen Anne's son been born that summer, thus securing her position as queen consort beyond all doubt, negotiations might have been made for a place within Anne's household for her young cousin Katherine to serve as one of her maidens. Unfortunately, Anne's downfall put paid to any hopes the dowager Duchess of Norfolk might have had of placing additional Howard relatives within the queen's household. The brief tenure of Jane Seymour, moreover, similarly prevented the appointment of additional Howard women to the queen's household, which in any case was a highly competitive process.

At an unknown date after October 1536, the dowager duchess moved her household from Chesworth House in Horsham to the Howard residence at Lambeth.[1] The relocation coincided with her decision to appoint a local musician, Henry Manox, to instruct Katherine in music. The timing of his appointment may have coincided with Katherine's thirteenth birthday and perhaps signalled the dowager duchess's hope to have Katherine placed at court in the service of the queen.[2] Musical ability was a skill that was highly prized in young gentlewomen, with some going so far as to perceive it as 'not only an ornament but a necessity to the Courtier'.[3] Katherine's cousin, Anne Boleyn, had been especially celebrated for her musical talents, which attracted the notice of courtiers at the English court: 'She [Anne] knew well how to sing and dance … [and to] play lute and other instruments to drive away sorrowful thoughts.'[4] In late 1536 the dowager duchess arranged for Katherine to receive music lessons from a neighbour, Henry Manox, younger son of George Manox of Giffords, who had connections with the dowager duchess's household. Agnes Howard's decision to provide Katherine with music lessons were entirely conventional in the context of the theory and practice of education in the mid sixteenth century, for Honor, Viscountess Lisle, had similarly ensured that her daughter Anne became proficient in musical ability by sending her as a teenager to France in order to acquire fluency in French and for the purposes of developing her skills in 'her work, the lute and virginals'.[5] Anne's musical skills probably influenced the decision of Jane Seymour, queen consort of Henry VIII, to accept her as one of her maidens in 1537.

Before proceeding to a discussion of the nature of the relationship between Katherine Howard and Henry Manox, which occurred in the context of that music master's task of providing his young pupil with music lessons, it is useful to note that evidence of this relationship exists only in the indictments brought against the queen in 1541. Such documents are, by the very nature of their genre, inherently difficult to examine, for legal records often contained manufactured and manipulated evidence in relation to matters pertaining to marriage and sexuality.[6] Moreover, in causes of adultery, witnesses often transferred the blame from the defamers to the wives themselves.[7] These difficulties in relation to legal evidence have been recognised by historians in their discussions of the queen's adolescent experiences that led to Katherine's downfall in 1541, with one historian going so far to say that 'imagination largely supplemented memory … almost everyone concerned lied like a trooper'.[8] A critical reading of the surviving evidence about Katherine's relationships with both Manox and Francis Dereham in 1536–39, which takes into account the nature of the indictments of 1541 and more broadly the legal records of early Tudor England, will lead to the conclusion that Katherine's relations with both men were coerced; there is no impression that she loved either man or that she especially welcomed their advances.[9]

To reach a full understanding of the relationship between Katherine and these two young men, their interactions should be interpreted in the context of sixteenth-century beliefs about female sexuality, honour codes and the nature of the institution of marriage. Influential witchcraft treatises associated female sexuality with the most heinous of crimes, believing that females had the ability to render men impotent and destroy their souls, and it was warned that 'carnal lust … is in women insatiable'.[10] These treatises were undoubtedly influential in early modern Europe because they informed and encouraged the notorious witchcraft persecutions towards the end of that century and during the course of the seventeenth century, while shedding light on how early modern men could perceive their female counterparts. Helkiah Crooke, writing shortly after Queen Elizabeth's reign, argued that 'the imaginations of lustfull women are like the imaginations of brute beasts which have no repugnancy or contradiction of reason to restrain them'.[11] Heterosexual relations during this period can be regarded as 'the most fundamental site of repression' and 'the key to … patriarchal power'.[12] Attitudes that we might deem today as misogynistic were widely held in early modern England; women were perceived as mysterious or threatening creatures who had the power to unman their male contemporaries, bewitch them into loving them, and cause them diabolical harm if angered or betrayed. These early modern gender mores should be borne in mind when analysing the indictments for evidence of the relationship between Katherine and the men dwelling in the household of the dowager Duchess of Norfolk during Katherine's teenage years. This task is complicated when it is remembered that 'carried out under the threat of torture … the language men and women use in criminal trials is clearly forced discourse', meaning that the evidence provided by both the queen and her acquaintances in her step-grandmother's household cannot necessarily be taken at face value as a true reflection of the reality of those pre-marital experiences.[13] The witnesses were providing details about events that had taken place between three and five years prior to the interrogations. Their responses to the interrogators' questions would have been shaped, consciously or unconsciously, by early modern perceptions of gender relations, sexuality and notions of honour. Katherine's relations with both men were striking in the sense that both were socially inferior to her; as a niece of the Duke of Norfolk, she would reasonably have expected to wed a young nobleman or member of the gentry of an equivalent status to her own. Her responses to both Manox and Dereham should be interpreted in this social and political context: it would have been unthinkable for Katherine to have considered marrying either of them.

Placing their relations with one another in the context of early modern beliefs about female sexuality is useful because it offers illuminating insights into the relationship between Katherine and Henry Manox which occurred while he was expected to offer her lessons on the virginal and lute, perhaps in readiness for an appointment to the household of the queen. The chaplain of Thomas Cranmer, Archbishop of Canterbury, opined that 14-year-old maidens were 'desirous to be married … to the end that they may be fruitful'.[14]

Believing that this was the case, the belief was propagated that, because they were oversexed, women desired to be raped, a notion which had prevailed since the medieval period, with a specific saying demonstrating this idea: '*Un coq suffit a dix poules, mais dix hommes ne suffisent pas a une femme*' (A rooster is enough for ten chickens, but ten men are not enough for a woman).[15] Yet, despite prevailing ideas that equated female sexuality with sin, honourable women were expected to be chaste and modest, retaining their honour through avoiding sexual sin and consequently upholding their family honour.[16]

Although it is impossible to know for certain, there is no evidence to indicate that Manox instructed other young gentlewomen who resided in the dowager duchess's household in music, although some of Katherine's female relatives surely dwelled there, including perhaps her younger sister. This suggests that the dowager duchess might have specifically chosen her young step-granddaughter to receive music lessons as a way of enhancing her future prospects, thus making her more attractive to prospective suitors who favoured such attributes in well-born maidens. It has been suggested in light of this that Katherine's noble lineage and kinship to the duke and dowager duchess meant that other individuals within the household who were aware of the nature of her relationship with Manox decided not to inform the duchess against Katherine.[17]

Manox's cousin Edward Waldgrave served as a gentleman-in-waiting to the dowager duchess, which might have led her to favour Manox as tutor to Katherine. According to the indictments drawn up at the time of the queen's disgrace, interpreted here in the context of sixteenth-century notions of female sexuality and culpability, Manox reported that he had asked Katherine, who was then aged around 13, to let him 'perceive by some token that you love me'. Apparently Katherine, fearful of the consequences both to herself and to the honour of the Howard family, responded uneasily: 'What token should I show you? I will never be taught with you, and able to marry me you be not.' Far from demonstrating arrogance or even callousness, as some writers have alleged, Katherine can be viewed as earnestly seeking to remind the lowborn Manox that, because of her kinship with one of the premier noble families in the kingdom that was connected by blood and marriage to the ruling family of England, he would compromise both her own personal honour and that of her family through his attempts to seduce her. Considering how young maidens were warned to preserve their chastity, surely the dowager duchess had emphasised to both Katherine and her relatives that the honour of the Howard family could not be undermined at any cost, especially in the wake of Anne Boleyn's disgrace. Manox, however, was not satisfied with the answer with which Katherine provided him, perhaps because he subscribed to prevailing notions of interior consent to sexual acts even when the other party apparently refused.[18] He continued to harass Katherine, desiring that she allow him to fondle her body, and eventually compelled her to agree to his requests. Later, when the two met in the dowager duchess's chapel chamber 'in the dark evening' – where others were not present to act as witnesses to what occurred there – the music master 'felt more than was convenient'.[19] Manox later swore that he 'never knew her [Katherine] carnally'.[20] At some point, the dowager duchess appears to have discovered the two alone together and probably dismissed Manox from her household for threatening the honour of the Howard family, for he later held a post in the household of Lord Bayment. Interestingly, Manox may have later married Margaret Munday, widow of Katherine's father Edmund. His wife, Katherine's stepmother, had a negative or 'unnatural' opinion of him, perhaps because she blamed him for his relentless seduction of her disgraced stepdaughter.[21]

Katherine's responses to the manipulative Manox were informed by the contemporary belief that women were expected to contribute to the successes of their families and strengthen their families' honour, while also preserving their own.[22] The dowager duchess's decision to relocate her household to Lambeth from Horsham had the effect of intensifying Katherine's desperation to be rid of Manox, for his desire to achieve sexual satisfaction with her was becoming stronger. There, one of Katherine's acquaintances, a chamberer named Mary Lascelles, heard from a fellow servant, Alice Restwold, a rumour circulating within the dowager duchess's household which alleged that Katherine and Manox were betrothed. Mary, aware of the reputation of the Howard family and the displeasure of the dowager duchess were she to discover such a tale, reprimanded Manox, in which she upbraided him for his seduction of Katherine: 'Man, what mean thou to play the fool of this fashion'; 'know not thou that if my lady of Norfolk knew of the love betwixt thee and Mistress Howard, she will undo thee', warning Manox of Katherine's position within 'a noble house' and, were he to 'marry her some of her blood would kill thee'.[23]

Manox's reply to Mary Lascelles, documented in the indictments drawn against Katherine in 1541, demonstrated scornfully his intimacy with Katherine and his attitude towards her: 'I know her well enough', informing Mary that 'she [Katherine] hath said to me that I shall have her maidenhead though it be painful to her, not doubting but I will be good to her hereafter'.[24] Thus in the indictments the blame for their relationship was transferred neatly from the lowly musician to the noble step-granddaughter of the dowager Duchess of Norfolk. It also appeared to confirm the early modern perception of women as unswervingly desirous of sexual fulfilment. Whether Katherine promised Manox anything of the kind is unlikely, considering her earlier behaviour towards him. Undoubtedly aware of the necessity of preserving her virginity and her family's honour in order to achieve a respectable marriage, she appears to have attempted to offer him a compromise by permitting him caresses but stopping short of sexual intercourse, for in that way she could preserve her maidenhead and, by association, the purity of her family name. Manox later attempted to conceal his pursuit of his young student by excusing his actions, believing himself to be 'so far in love' with Katherine that he was unable to control himself. He certainly managed to retain control over Katherine, despite the attempted intervention of Mary Lascelles, for Katherine later accompanied him on a walk in the orchard of her step-grandmother, 'they two alone'.[25] Possibly, Manox sought to seduce her further in an attempt to acquire means of influence within the Howard family. Whether he actually ever considered marrying her is impossible to know.

The dowager duchess's regular duties at court and her age restricted her abilities to manage her household successfully, for had she been fully aware of the manipulation of her step-granddaughter, she almost certainly would have done something to aid her relative in order to preserve her honour and that of the Howard family. The 'flattering and fair persuasions' of Manox placed Katherine in a position of some danger, for in an age which identified young females with licentiousness and the ability to sexually entrap men, she surely recognised that she might earn little sympathy or pity were her relatives to become aware of her experiences. Indeed, when Lord William Howard discovered Mary Lascelles's reports of his niece Katherine's plight, he took no moves to intercede on her behalf, lamenting only: 'What mad wenches! Can you not be merry amongst yourselves but you must thus fall out?'[26] Although it is anachronistic to interpret Katherine's experiences as constituting child sex abuse, as they were not interpreted as such in the mid sixteenth century, it is intriguing that, as Martin Ingram noted in his analysis of the abuse of English females within early modern society who were aged between 8 and 15, 'children are as individuals and as a group among the most vulnerable elements in any society'.[27]

Why Manox decided to abuse his position as music master and seduce the young Katherine cannot be known from the indictments, although most modern historians, perhaps sharing Mary Lascelles's beliefs, suggest that he may have hoped to marry Katherine and align himself with the noble Howard family. To be sure, that could account for his persistent attempts to seduce Katherine in the belief that she consented to his advances, for the 'age of consent to marriage was … tied to an understanding of the age at which young people were deemed capable of having sex and so of conceiving children'.[28]

However, the timing of this affair in the context of the Howard family's political and dynastic position at that time could suggest Manox's desire to sexually manipulate the young step-granddaughter of the dowager duchess in a period when the Howards were perhaps perceived to be more vulnerable. Anne Boleyn's downfall that year had placed the Howards in a more ambivalent position and had raised the danger of both her uncle and the family in general becoming tainted with her disgrace, although Norfolk had willingly served his monarch in acting as High Steward at Anne's trial and personally sentencing her to death. Perhaps believing that the Howards were in a weaker position than they had been hitherto, Manox presumed to take control of Katherine's future by taking advantage of his position and seducing her, despite the attempts of both Katherine and Mary Lascelles to discourage him from this pursuit. Later, subscribing to notions of aggressive female sexuality and believing that Katherine had willingly consented to his sexual advances, Manox blamed her for the affair and insisted that he had only acted because she had entrapped him into loving her. Yet an understanding of this relationship can only be achieved by having 'the sensitivity to hear the female voices embedded in documents', for there is no evidence that Katherine enjoyed the affair, or that she ever encouraged Manox in his seduction of her.[29]

When these events took place, Katherine was 13 or 14 years old. Her step-grandmother may have hoped to secure for her a position in the household of Queen Jane, which meant that Katherine's honour – which was primarily defined and understood in a sexual sense – needed to be protected. The dowager duchess's decision to relocate to Lambeth, however, might have afforded Katherine some hope that she could escape Manox's pursuit of her, for it is possible that he had sworn to marry her despite her efforts to dissuade him.

At Lambeth, Katherine became acquainted with Francis Dereham, who was distantly connected to the Howard family and served as one of the Duke of Norfolk's gentleman-pensioners. Dereham was born between 1506 and 1509, which made him fourteen to seventeen years Katherine's senior.[30] Initially, Dereham had been involved in a liaison with Joan Bulmer, one of Katherine's acquaintances who served the dowager duchess and who permitted Dereham to visit the 'maidens' chamber' at Lambeth. It was not long, however, before Dereham's attentions were transferred from Joan, who was then aged around 19 (having been born in 1519), to her younger companion Katherine. It is possible, as Warnicke suggested, that Dereham initially became acquainted with the step-granddaughter of the dowager duchess in the guise of her protector, when he discovered that she was being coerced by the persistent Manox.

If Katherine hoped to escape Manox's attention, however, she soon discovered that Dereham was also attracted to her.

From a careful reading of the evidence produced in the indictments against a backdrop of early modern perceptions of female sexuality, it will be suggested here that Dereham may have coerced Katherine, psychologically if not physically, leading her to later accuse him of rape, which most historians have perhaps been too unwilling to address in their analyses of her life.[31] This view questions the traditional assumption that Katherine's relationship with Dereham constituted a love affair, as proposed by Baldwin Smith in 1961 and subsequently accepted by the majority of historians as fact. It is worth noting that, since the initial publication of my own biography in 2014, other historians have suggested that Katherine was molested by Dereham, including Josephine Wilkinson and Lucy Worsley.[32]

The chamber in which Katherine dwelled with other maidens was frequently visited by young gentlemen who resided within the household of the dowager duchess, as Katherine was later to recall, in which she remembered how the door of the chamber was unlocked 'as well at the request of me, as of others'.[33] Edward Waldgrave, cousin of Manox and esquire, was one such frequent visitor, as was Francis Dereham. Having seduced Joan Bulmer, Dereham attempted to flatter Katherine, having heard that her involvement with Manox had shortly concluded beforehand. Charles de Marillac, who served at the court of Henry VIII as the French ambassador, later reported that Dereham had violated the young Katherine from her thirteenth year, five years before her downfall, placing their liaison in around 1537.[34] Although Marillac was incorrect about the duration of this affair, he seems to have been truthful in documenting the true nature of the relationship between Katherine and Dereham, for there is little evidence to suggest, as with Manox, that Katherine consented to Dereham's advances, either sexual and material.

An examination of Katherine's confession pertaining to her liaison with Dereham will be discussed later in the context of the investigation into her pre-marital life, but it is worth noting here that, according to the indictments drawn up in 1541, gifts were exchanged between the two during Katherine's residency in the household of the dowager Duchess of Norfolk. Dereham provided Katherine with 'a French fennel, some velvet and satin for a billyment and sarcenet for a quilted cap'. An embroidered friar's knot was also presented to Katherine, apparently as a symbol of the love between the two. Katherine also recalled that she had given him a band and sleeves for a shirt and, during the 1541 progress, £10 as payment for his earlier gifts. Following Katherine's appointment to court in 1539, Dereham left an indenture and obligation of

£100 at Lambeth following his move to Ireland which, he promised, would be hers if he never returned.[35]

Many seductions during this period began with games, joking or direct sexual touchings, as a means of implying the woman's consent to sexual activity.[36] One observer within the maidens' chamber later reported how Katherine 'was so far in love' that the couple kissed 'after a wonderful manner, for they would kiss and hang by their bellies together as they were two sparrows'.[37] However, as Roper compellingly notes, 'the language men and women use in criminal trials is clearly forced discourse. In other contexts, men and women would have spoken differently about sexuality.'[38] Like Manox, Dereham believed that Katherine consented to his advances, failing to appreciate that her desire to protect the honour of her family and her own chastity – the quality most valued in early modern gentlewomen – might have prevented her from doing so.

When Manox discovered that Dereham had made sexual advances towards Katherine, he angrily wrote an anonymous letter to the dowager duchess informing her of the night-time escapades occurring in the maidens' chamber:

> Your Grace, it shall be meet you take good heed to your gentlewomen for if it shall like you half an hour after you shall a-bed to rise suddenly and visit their Chamber you shall see that which shall displease you. But if you make anybody of counsel you shall be deceived. Make then fewer your secretary.[39]

Manox's comment, 'you shall see that which shall displease you', may have been a veiled reference to the exact nature of the sexual acts taking place under the dowager duchess's roof, for contemporaries strongly prohibited sexual practices which deviated from those advocated by the Church as a means of procreation. Canon lawyers of the age held that if a woman engaged in sexual positions other than the approved one (beneath her partner) it was utterly sinful, being worse than incestuous relations with a male relative.[40] In view of contemporary notions about female sexuality, it has been suggested that 'the female offender's deviation from her ascribed role, therefore, was not only an offence against an individual, but a serious threat to the entire system of order'.[41] It is ironic that Manox sought the assistance of the dowager duchess, for had she been aware that he had been systematically abusing her step-granddaughter from the age of 13, she would likely have expelled him from her household immediately for placing the honour of the Howard family in jeopardy. Manox may also have resented his loss of control over Katherine, for sexual jealousy and cuckoldry anxiety among men in early modern England was widespread. This, of course, explains why the regulation of female sexual-ity was favoured by men in an attempt both to safeguard their own honour and ensure their successful performance of masculinity, which might account for Manox's interference.[42]

When she learned of Dereham's attraction, Katherine was understandably desirous of protecting her personal honour, and to avoid placing her family name in disrepute she 'stole the letter out of my Lady's gilt coffer and showed it to Dereham who coped it and thereupon it was laid in the coffer again'.[43] Probably, she revealed the letter to Dereham as a means of warning him of the danger in which his seduction of her placed both herself and her family, and may have signalled to him that he should leave her alone as a result. The dowager duchess, when she discovered the goings-on in the maidens' chamber, reacted with understandable fury, for this placed the honour of the Howard name and their reputation in danger and cast doubts on the suitability of herself as guardian for the young people within her household.

Scattered pieces of evidence from the indictments suggest that not only did Katherine fail to consent to Dereham's sexual advances, but also that he may have coerced her emotionally if not physically. According to the queen's confession in 1541:

> Fraunceʒ Derame by many persuasions procured me to his vicious purpose and obteyned first to lye uppon my bedde with his doblett and hose and after within the bedde and wodin he lay with me nakyd and used me in suche sorte as a man doith his wyff many and sondry tymeʒ but howe often I knowe not.[44]

Suggesting that she did not consent to the advances of Manox or Dereham, Katherine was to plead the king to take into account her 'youthe, my ignorans [and] my fraylnez'.[45] Following her confession, Katherine reported to Archbishop Cranmer that Dereham's actions constituted 'importune forcement, and in a manner, violence, rather than of her own free consent and will'.[46] The reference to Dereham's 'vicious purpose' and 'many persuasions' establish direct similarities with Manox's relentless seduction of Katherine, suggesting that, like Manox, Dereham saw an opportunity to be exploited in Katherine's noble lineage and familial connections. This might explain his apparent desire to marry her as a means of social and political advancement.

A further comment made by Katherine, which has almost certainly been misinterpreted by early historians, indicates that Dereham may have coerced her in order to fulfil his own sexual desires. Margaret Benet, a fellow maiden at Lambeth, later reported that she had heard Dereham say 'that although he used the company of a woman a C [hundred] times yet he would get no child except he listed and that the queen [Katherine] made answers thereto and likewise that a woman might meddle with a man and yet conceive no child unless she would for herself'.[47] Baldwin Smith took this to mean that Katherine was referring to the use of contraception, as have other modern historians.[48] It is possible, however, in light of prevailing sixteenth-century beliefs about reproduction and sexuality, that Katherine meant something else, for contemporaries continued to adhere to the widespread medieval notion that 'conception was believed to take place only if the woman omitted a seed, which she would do only if the experience of sex was pleasurable'.[49] Since Dereham seems to have viewed Katherine as his wife, it seems unlikely that he would have permitted the use of contraception, for were she to fall pregnant, it might force her family to marry them in a hasty attempt to conceal the true nature of the affair. It is likely that, knowing that contemporaries believed that women were expected to enjoy sexual intercourse in order to conceive a child, Katherine's reference to not conceiving a child indicates that she had not enjoyed her sexual encounters with Dereham. Thus 'if she did not wish to have sexual relations with him, then she would have considered herself forced to please him and would have found the experience unpleasant. She could believe, therefore, that her emotions controlled whether she became pregnant.'[50]

The behaviour of Katherine and the nature of her relationships with both Manox and Dereham have been unsatisfactorily explained by the majority of modern historians, who have concluded that Katherine was light in living conditions, flighty, and the instigator of both affairs. The approach taken in this biography, supplementing the findings of historians such as Warnicke and Wilkinson, has indicated that Katherine was coerced by both men in the household of her step-grandmother, despite her persistent attempts to preserve the honour of the Howard family by attempting to deflect their attentions, for she was well aware that she would be ruined if news of these escapades reached her uncle the duke.

The dowager duchess's inability to control her household and protect her charges compounded the unenviable position in which Katherine found herself, for the dowager duchess's duties at court simply meant that she could not, on a regular basis, manage the daily life of her household as closely as she might have liked. In the indictments drawn up against her Katherine was blamed for both affairs, which makes sense when beliefs regarding female sexuality prevalent in the mid sixteenth century are considered. Moreover, in early modern Europe rape and seduction became more closely aligned and were linked more closely with normative male heterosexual behaviour, meaning that perhaps Dereham's persistent seduction of Katherine did not shock observers who continued to adhere to the accepted belief that women desired to be raped, by virtue of their overflowing carnal desires.[51] However, rape and sexual assault were prohibited by law and condemned as sexually deviant by both lawyers and clerics, who regarded these offences as unlawful and offensive to God. How Katherine later presented her experiences at the hands of both Dereham and Manox probably depended a great deal on the gender of her accusers, for, aware that these male prosecutors viewed her by virtue of her sex in a negative and suspicious light, it was necessary to emphasise the degree of force she had suffered; in contrast, her fellow females within the duchess's household may have been able to work out for themselves more clearly Katherine's reaction to her ordeals.[52]

Perhaps Dereham believed that Katherine was his lawful wife. Katherine later admitted that 'there was Communication in the House that we Two should Marry together … wherefore he desired to give me Leave to call me Wife, and that I should call him Husband … And so after that, commonly he called me Wife, and many times I called him Husband'.[53] When one observer opined that it seemed as if 'Mr Dereham shall have Mrs Katherine Howard', Dereham responded 'By St John you may guess twice and guess worse'.[54] Seeking to legalise his affair with Katherine, Dereham persistently bothered her with 'the question of marriage'.[55] Possibly, Dereham's giving of gifts to Katherine publicly demonstrated his desire to marry her, for gifts were understood as an important and accepted aspect of courtship in early modern England, and coins, rings, and gloves were especially popular among lovers.[56]

Despite the political and dynastic policies and concerns of the Howard family, which would have centred on noble marital alliances for the sons and daughters of the house, Dereham may have adhered to the accepted belief that 'merely … uttering the appropriate words' was sufficient to contract a marriage, without the presence of witnesses, priest or church, or the goodwill of Katherine's Howard relatives.[57] It may be noteworthy in light of Katherine's experiences that some women only agreed to marry following a sexual attack. In the fifteenth century, Agnes Grantham of York agreed to marry her attacker using words of present consent, fearing further instances of rape.[58] Probably because she never consented to Dereham's sexual advances, Katherine later vehemently denied ever being his wife, and her belief that her lack of consent meant that she was not Dereham's spouse was shared by canon lawyers who required that marriage vows be freely given and not coerced by others.[59] Significantly, Katherine defined her experiences in terms of 'force' brought about by Dereham's 'vicious purpose'; as has been intriguingly suggested, 'in most narratives rape was defined in terms of male violence, not sex'.[60] Whether Dereham ever actually raped Katherine is unknown; the majority of modern historians have dismissed Katherine's allegation in 1541 because they believe that she was lying in a desperate bid to save herself from being ruined. Even if there was no physical aspect, a strong argument can be made that the attentions of both Manox and Dereham in 1536–39 constituted psychological coercion.

Dereham's pursuit of Katherine was to have fatal consequences for both of them. However, Katherine's youth and status during the period in which the Manox and Dereham liaisons took place rendered her unable to end her abuse. Not only was her step-grandmother often at court to carry out her duties and thus unable to provide her with assistance, but sixteenth-century English law regarding unconsented sexual liaisons worked against the young Katherine. Only women who belonged to a father, husband or master could make public accusations against those who assaulted them – and although Katherine's father may still have been alive, his duties and his absence from his daughter's life rendered him unavailable to assist her. In early modern England the rape of virgins was an offence punishable by death, and even in eighteenth-century England the sexual assault of children was perceived to be far worse to the rape of adult women. Although it is likely that Katherine had begun puberty by the time of her relations with Dereham in 1538–39, interestingly the death penalty was merited for the sexual molestation of a girl who had not yet reached puberty.[61] If Henry VIII believed that Dereham had violated a pre-pubescent Katherine, this could account for the especially savage execution granted to him in 1541, in which he was hanged, drawn and quartered while Culpeper was only beheaded. Dereham's irresponsible and coercive behaviour shattered Katherine's reputation and rendered her, in the eyes of her contemporaries, dishonest and deceitful, for 'girls who had already lost their virginity were regarded as more culpable for their sexual relationships'.[62] Moreover, in cases of rape women struggled to prove any allegations they made 'because the very law suspects her of having invited the assault … the law puts women on the defensive'.[63] If Dereham somehow injured Katherine sexually during their relationship, this might account for her failure to conceive a child after she became queen. It has been recognised that the long-term physical impacts of sexual abuse can encompass damage to the urethra and vagina, sexual and reproductive health problems, and other problems associated with sex.[64] The evidence is insufficient to suggest that Dereham either raped or sexually assaulted Katherine, but the contemporary details of their relationship do not support the popular notion that theirs was a romantic love affair and do seem to suggest that Katherine was susceptible to emotional coercion as she had been with Manox previously. Moreover, Dereham's aggressive behaviour during Katherine's queenship testified to his predatory attitude towards her.

It should be considered why Katherine's fellow relatives and acquaintances who shared the maidens' chamber with her did not inform the dowager duchess of the sexual relationship between her step-granddaughter and Dereham within her household. By contrast, Mary Lascelles had been pivotal in attempting to put an end to the affair with Manox. Possibly, if other individuals within the establishment believed that Katherine and Dereham were actually married, then it could explain why they did not intervene to protect Katherine's honour and discourage Dereham in the same way in which Manox had been confronted. Dereham's behaviour supports this interpretation, from his reply to an acquaittance discussed earlier.[65] Although she was to chastise her step-granddaughter for her behaviour with Dereham, it is probable that 'the Dowager may have been unaware of the full extent of the relationship' between Katherine and Dereham.[66] Katherine's fellow residents within the dowager duchess's household were only to provide details about the full nature of the Dereham affair during the queen's downfall, when they were forcibly required to. Possibly they mistakenly believed that Katherine consented to Dereham's advances, while excusing his aggressiveness. Significantly, the contemporary language utilised for describing male sexual misbehaviour was the same as that of ordinary male heterosexual activity: 'lustfull Desires' and 'pleasures'. John Wolfe, when accused of violently raping a maiden, declared that he had 'pulled up her clothes and asked her whether she was willing as I'. Katherine's acquaintances reported that Dereham, like Wolfe, had plucked Katherine's 'clothes above her navel so that he might well discern her body'.[67] Yet, as has been recognised, 'men often claimed that sex, not rape, had occurred. They dramatised female consent verbally (by a woman's assent or invitation), physically (by her acquiescence or little resistance), and association (by claiming that she was of "lewd" disposition)'.[68]

It is worth addressing one recent misconception about the interpretation offered here of Katherine's relationships with Manox and Dereham, which occurred from 1536 to 1539. In her 2005 biography, Joanna Denny speculated that Manox's attentions, in particular, constituted 'child abuse', which is an unfortunate characterisation of Katherine's relations with him (and likewise with Dereham) because of the modern connotations associated with the term. In her study of early modern child victims of rape and sexual assault, Sarah Toulalan noted that early modern England lacked an age of consent that 'align[ed] neatly with contemporary ideas about the boundaries of childhood'.[69] Martin Ingram discovered that most modern historians concluded 'that behaviour that we would interpret as the abuse of children was certainly not a central feature of early modern English society'.[70] In his research, however, Ingram learned that the majority of abusers 'were servants, apprentices or other employees of the children's parents, step-parents or guardians', and he concluded that 'child sexual abuse ... both existed and was recognized to exist in Tudor and Stuart England'.[71] Despite Ingram's important findings, several historians have disputed whether the concept of child abuse actually existed in early modern England. In his biography, Gareth Russell doubted that Katherine 'was a survivor of childhood abuse'.[72]

To be sure, aside from Denny, no other modern historian has actually referred either explicitly or implicitly to Katherine as a victim of child abuse, mainly due to her age: she was 13 when Manox first became attracted to her and 15 when Dereham pursued her. Legally, girls could marry at 12 years of age in sixteenth-century England. The concept of childhood, moreover, was less clear-cut than it is today; in a society in which noblewomen could marry in their early teens, it is doubtful whether a teenager was regarded as a child or even as an adolescent. On the other hand, leaving aside the issue of childhood, one does not need to interpret Katherine as a victim of child abuse to suggest that she was coerced by both men. Coercion need not be physical – the affair with Manox, in particular, strongly argues for the presence of psychological coercion, as has been argued here. Katherine's lukewarm responses to Dereham both during and after her affair, including when she was appointed to court, hardly support the traditional interpretation that she loved him or even cared for him, and his reckless and aggressive behaviour during Katherine's tenure as queen placed both himself and Katherine in danger.

Responding to Gareth Russell's interpretation of Katherine's relations with the two men between 1536 and 1539, Carolyn Harris has emphasised that 'Catherine seems to have been in a vulnerable position in spite of her rank because her mother was dead and her father was fleeing his creditors in Calais. Her situation, in the household of an inattentive guardian, attracted the attention of the arrogant, aggressive men whom she encountered in her adolescence.'[73] Harris's interpretation is rare in modern accounts of Katherine's life prior to her marriage to Henry VIII, although the recognition that Katherine was 'in a vulnerable position' is slowly becoming more widespread in modern scholarship. The dowager Duchess of Norfolk certainly could not have predicted that Manox and Dereham would actively seek sexual relations with Katherine, for whom she was probably hoping to arrange an advantageous marriage, but her inattention was to prove fatal to her step-granddaughter. When the extant evidence concerning Katherine's liaisons with both Manox and Dereham in 1536–39 is read in the light of early modern gender relations and perceptions of female sexuality, it indicates that Katherine was vulnerable to emotional coercion at the hands of both men within the household of her step-grandmother. As she was the niece of the Duke of Norfolk, both men probably saw a golden opportunity in Katherine to increase their political and social influence.

Because of the importance attached to female honour and the influence of the Howard family, a ducal family in the kingdom in which women could and did play a prominent part as family members, it is reasonable to suppose that Katherine's uncle, the Duke of Norfolk, was not aware of his niece's sexual experiences when he sought a place for her at court in the autumn of 1539, especially since he had participated at the trial of his niece Anne Boleyn and was thus surely well aware of the suspicion and hostility that could be aroused by female sexuality. Instead, probably through hearing reports of his niece's beauty and charm, Norfolk sought a place for her at court that year to serve Henry VIII's new queen, Anne of Cleves, as part of a process in which he also sought appointments for Katherine Carey and Mary Norris to the queen's household. Although she had not necessarily consented to, or welcomed, the sexual experiences she had undergone between the ages of 13 and 15, Katherine's pre-marital liaisons would eventually return to haunt her.

4

'STRANGE, RESTLESS ... YEARS': THE HOWARDS AT COURT, 1537–40

THE DOWNFALL OF ANNE Boleyn, and the subsequent rise of the Seymour family, in 1536 inaugurated a period of ambivalence for the Howards, who had forfeited the major source of their influence with the king as a result of the queen's disgrace. The Seymours, who initially shared the religious conservatism of the Howards, were to become the Howards' greatest rivals within the kingdom, ushering in a period of hostility and suspicion between the two families which was to endure throughout the later years of Henry VIII's reign.

Following Anne's execution, 'the weke before Whitsontyde the kyng maryed Jane doughter to the right worshipfull sir John Seymour knight, whiche at Whitsontyde was openlye shewed as Quene'.[1] The unknown author of *The Chronicle of Henry VIII of England* approvingly described Jane as 'this good lady', who was 'much beloved by all' for the kindness she showed to Henry's daughter Mary.[2] On the following Tuesday, Jane's elder brother Edward, who had played a prominent role in encouraging and facilitating his sister's relationship with the king during Anne's queenship, was created Viscount Beauchamp, while Sir Walter Hungerford was made a lord.[3] The king agreed, 'at the humble entreaty of his nobility ... to accept that condition [of marriage] and has taken to himself a wife, who in age [Jane was between 25 and 28] and form is deemed to be meet and apt for the procreation of children'.[4] Often interpreted as indicative of his callousness and hatred for his former wife, the king's speedy marriage to Jane Seymour actually demonstrates the precarious nature of the Tudor succession and his urgent desire, more than ever, to sire a male heir to ensure a peaceful succession. The rise of the

Seymour family led to a considerable loss of influence for their opponents, namely the Howards. On 10 July Cromwell was made Lord Cromwell and Baron Cromwell of Wimbledon, replacing Thomas Boleyn, father of the late queen, as the Lord Privy Seal on 29 July. Later, Cromwell's son Gregory was married to Elizabeth, younger sister of the new queen, strengthening the alliance between the Master Secretary and the queen's family.

During the parliament that assembled in June, however, Lord Thomas Howard, half-brother of the duke, 'without the kynges assent affied the lady Margaret Douglas daughter to the quene of Scottes and nece to the kyng: for whiche … acte he was attainted of treason … and so he dyed in the Tower, and she was long there as prisoner'.[5] The love affair between Thomas Howard and Henry VIII's niece, Margaret Douglas, daughter of the Scottish queen Margaret, dishonoured the Howard family, for it was alleged by their enemies that Thomas Howard had conspired to seize the throne through his marriage with the king's relative. The Act of Attainder brought against him recorded that 'he aspired to the throne by reason of so high a marriage … that he had a firm hope and trust that the subjects of this realm would incline and bear affection to the said lady Margaret being born in the realm and not to the King of Scots her brother'.[6] It was later recorded by Wriothesley that 'this yeare [1537], on All Hallowe Even, the Lord Thomas Howarde, brother to the Duke of Northfolke, died in prison in the Tower of London, and his bodie was caried to Thetforde, and there buried'. At the same time, Margaret Douglas returned to court, having been pardoned by her uncle the king, although 'she tooke his [Thomas's] death very heavilie'.[7] The duke must have reacted to the news of his half-brother's liaison with Margaret Douglas with fury, for the honour and security of the Howard family had been threatened as a result of such rash behaviour. The downfall of Anne Boleyn, coupled with Thomas Howard's misalliance with Margaret, weakened the position of the Howards, which was exacerbated by the rapid rise of the Seymours and their increasing favour with the king.

Notwithstanding these setbacks, the Howards continued to play important political and ceremonial roles within the kingdom, which indicated that their influence remained significant. Cromwell, in a letter written to Sir Brian Tuke on 12 June, mentioned that the king of arms had been sent to 'the lorde William Howarde' then serving in Scotland as 'ambassade'.[8] The Duke of Norfolk continued to bear 'the golden staffe as Marshall of Englande' during celebrations for the new queen.[9] During the process of reconciliation between the Lady Mary and her father, the king, in early June, Norfolk headed a delegation of the council at Hunsdon, entreating Mary to acknowledge her father as her sovereign lord and to accept all the laws and statutes of the realm, while accepting him as Supreme Head of the English Church and repudiating the jurisdiction of the pope, and agreeing that her parents' marriage had been invalid. When she refused, Norfolk brutally informed her, in the company of the other councillors, that he 'would knock her head so violently against the wall that they would make it as soft as baked apples'.[10] Later the duke, alongside the Lord Chancellor of England, escorted the new wife of the heir of the Earl of Oxford, who was daughter to the Earl of Westmorland, to her new home.[11]

However, the fortunes of the Howards suffered a blow with the death of the king's bastard son Henry Fitzroy, Duke of Richmond and husband of the duke's daughter Lady Mary Howard, on 23 July at St James Palace. He was aged only 17; his cause of death was then unknown but was attributed by some to the use of poison by the late queen and her brother. He and Mary Howard had failed to consummate their marriage, meaning that 'she [Mary] is maide, wife, and now a widowe'. Fitzroy was buried at Thetford in Norfolk, the traditional burial place of the Howards.[12] The widowed duchess struggled to obtain payment of the dowry settled upon her, before receiving in March 1539 or 1540 the manor of Swaffham in Norfolk and other Crown properties.[13]

The death of Fitzroy in the summer of 1536 could be viewed as severing the blood relationship of the Howards to the Tudor dynasty, a process which had been initiated with the downfall of Queen Anne scarcely two months previously. In a matter of weeks the influence of the Howard family had decreased rapidly and their rivals had overtaken them within the king's court. Unsurprisingly, it has been suggested that 'those ... years, between 1536 and 1540, are strange, restless, memorable years in the annals of the house of Howard – years replete with bitter hates and passionate loves that ended in bitterness ... During that brief period, the story of the Howards was the story of the English Court.'[14] The increasing suspicion in which the king may have regarded the Howards during this period was exacerbated by the rapid rate of religious changes within England, which not only offended the religious conservatism of the Howards but encouraged and facilitated the rise of individuals who sympathised with the evangelical cause, such as Thomas Cromwell and Thomas Cranmer, Archbishop of Canterbury, to the detriment of religious conservatives such as the duke. Following the disgrace of Thomas Howard in July 1536, what came to be known as the Ten Articles was passed, 'the which the bishopps of this realme should cause to be declared in their dioces[es]'. Cromwell was appointed Vicegerent in September and, while proceeding with the dissolution of the smaller monasteries, quickly sent out his first set of injunctions to the prelates and clergy, desiring 'the vertuous living of the said cleargie'.[15] At the same time the Lady Mary, daughter of the king by his first marriage to Katherine of Aragon, was reconciled with her father.[16]

However, the religious changes which Cromwell and Cranmer now began to inaugurate with increasing intensity in England in the summer and autumn of 1536 were to provide an unexpected opening for the Duke of Norfolk, especially during what came to be known as the Pilgrimage of Grace. According to Hall:

> The inhabitauntes of the North ... altogether noseled in supersticion and popery, and also by the means of certayne Abbottes and ignorant priestes not a little stirred and prouoked for the suppression of certain Monasteries ... & thus the fayth of holy churche shall vtterly be suppressed and abholished: and therefore sodainly they spred abrode and raysed great and shamefull slanders only to moue the people to sedicion and rebellion, and to kyndle in the people hateful and malicious myndes against the kynges Maiestie and the Magestrates of the realme.[17]

Other chroniclers likewise recorded that certain individuals had incited rebellion among the commoners, in which they publicly opposed the religious changes that threatened traditional practices and beliefs. Wriothesley recorded that 'in the beginning of October ... the people made an insurrection, and made of them tow captaines, the one being a monke and the other a shoomaker, and so increased to the number of twentie tow thousand persons or more' in Lincolnshire, while 'their was an insurrection in Yorkeshire, and they made of them a captaine called Robart Aske ... they were so oppressed with taxes and putting downe of religious howses'.[18] Royal favourites such as the Duke of Suffolk were sent to suppress the riots, while Norfolk, as lieutenant of the north, alongside the Earl of Shrewsbury, negotiated with Aske and his followers on the king's behalf. Norfolk encouraged the rebels to ask the king for pardon, before riding back to the king to inform him of the suppression of the rebellion.[19] On 26–27 October, the king thanked Norfolk for his 'politique devise', urging him 'never to give stroke ... unless you shall, with due advisement, thinke yourself to have greate and notable advauntage for the same'.[20]

In response to the king's orders, the duke set upon a campaign of brutal vengeance in Yorkshire, punishing the rebels for daring to rise against their monarch. In early 1537, the king instructed the duke to 'cause such dreadful execution upon a good number of the inhabitants, hanging them on trees, quartering them and setting their heads and quarters in every town, as shall be a fearful warning'.[21] In February, following a further insurrection in Westmorland involving around 8,000 rebels, Norfolk took the captains as prisoners, hanging them on the walls of Carlisle.[22]

In Yorkshire, during Francis Bigod's rebellion, Norfolk rode as the king's lieutenant 'to appease the sayde rebells and kepe the countrye in peace'.[23] Later, in the summer of 1537, prominent rebels such as Aske, Lord Darcy, Sir Thomas Percy, John Hussey and Sir Robert Constable were publicly executed in London as traitors.[24] The duke's ruthlessness and military capabilities somewhat restored his influence with the king, but his weariness soon began to show, leading him in June 1537 to complain to Cromwell:

> I aske your Lordeship to take in good parte that I do not followe your advise in offring my poure person to remayne lenger in thies parties ... for, and I shold tary here when the cold tyme of the yere should comme, I knowe surely my deathe shold shortely insewe witheowte remedy ... My Lord this contrey is more cold than those that hath not experimented the same, wold believe, wherefore, if ye woll have my liff to contynewe any tyme, help that His Majesties promise, made to me in his last letters, may be observed.[25]

Only in November 1537, however, following the death of the queen, was Norfolk able to lay down his office.[26]

Although the king's confidence in Norfolk had been restored as a result of his brutal efficiency directed towards the insurgents implicated in the northern rebellions, others at court resented the return of the Howards to favour, fearing the subsequent loss of their own influence with the king. The Seymours speedily accused the Earl of Surrey, son of the duke and cousin to Katherine Howard, of connivance with the northern rebels during the insurrections. Insulted, Surrey reacted violently, striking his accuser. Surrey was arrested and summoned before the council, leading Norfolk to write to Cromwell from the north: 'What chawnces of informations hath ben of my son falsely ymagined, no man knoweth better than ye. And nowe to amende the same in my hert, by chaunce of lightlihode to be maymed of his right arme.'[27] Fortunately Surrey did not lose his arm, but he was imprisoned in Windsor Castle.[28]

Following the brutal retribution exacted in the aftermath of the Pilgrimage of Grace, somewhat happier news reached the king that his third wife, Jane, was pregnant. On 27 May 1537, Trinity Sunday, 'there was Te Deum sounge in Powles for joye of the Queenes quickninge of childe ... the same night was diverse greate fyers made in London, and a hogeshed of wine at everye fyer for poore people to drinke as longe as yt woulde last'.[29]

A persistent legend – and one that is perhaps false – is that Henry VIII loved Jane Seymour more sincerely than he had his other queens, for the reason that she bore him a surviving male heir. Whether this is true or not is doubtful, for his behaviour towards her during her short period as queen does not support the view that he loved and cherished her during her own lifetime. Barely a week after his marriage to Jane, Henry had become acquainted with two beautiful young women, leading the king to state that he was 'sorry that he had not seen them before he was married'.[30] During the lifetime of Queen Anne, Jane had sought to intercede for the Lady Mary, begging Henry to restore her as princess. The king condemned her as a fool, warning her that she 'ought to solicit the advancement of the children they would have between them, and not any others'.[31]

Whatever the true nature of his private life with the queen, the king reacted with understandable joy when he discovered that she was pregnant. However, Queen Jane was well aware that it was essential for her to bear the king a son; were she to deliver a daughter, her position and future as queen – not to mention that of her family – would remain uncertain. The public rejoicing and demonstrations of joy at the news of the queen's pregnancy call into serious doubt one writer's belief that the reason Katherine Howard was removed from power by reformers in 1541 was because of rumours that she was pregnant for, if this was the case, one might question why no moves were made to remove either Anne Boleyn or Jane Seymour while they were pregnant with the king's heir.[32]

Shortly after Cromwell achieved even greater influence after being made a Knight of the Garter, the queen delivered a son, Edward, at Hampton Court Palace on 12 October 1537, the eve of St Edward. Indicating that his influence and favour with the king had been speedily restored, Norfolk served alongside the Archbishop of Canterbury as godfather to the new prince at his christening, while Lady Mary served as the prince's godmother.[33]

While both she and her newborn son lived, Queen Jane had emerged triumphant in the potentially deadly game of fertility politics which pervaded the court of Henry VIII. Where both her predecessors had failed, the king's third wife had demonstrated that her union with the king was divinely blessed through the deliverance of a healthy prince, while also signalling that the king was not responsible for his previous wives' inability to produce a living male heir. As has been noted, contemporaries generally blamed women for unsuccessful pregnancies or infertility, so the birth of a healthy son in 1537 very publicly demonstrated divine approval of Henry's decision to marry Jane. Celebrations took place in London the whole day, with banquets, hogsheads of wine, thanksgivings and the ringing of bells in parish churches until ten o'clock at night demonstrating the people's joy at the birth of a son to the king and queen.[34] Supporters of the queen received further rewards. William Fitzwilliam, Lord Admiral and vice treasurer, became Earl of Southampton; Beauchamp, brother to the queen, became Earl of Hertford; Sir John Russell, controller of the king's household; Heneage, Long and Knevett of the king's privy chamber, knights; and Thomas Seymour, another brother of Jane, also became a knight.[35]

The mood of celebration in the court and kingdom at the birth of a son, however, soon turned to one of grief and mourning with the death of the queen probably from childbed fever on 24 October, less than two weeks after her dynastic triumph. Norfolk summoned Cromwell from London, asking him on the evening of the 24th 'to be here tomorrow early to comfort our good master, for as for our mistress there is no likelihood of her life, the more pity, and I fear she shall not be in life at the time ye shall read this'.[36] According to Hall, who was present in his capacity as the court chronicler, 'of none in the Realme was it more heavelier taken then of the kynges Majestie himself, whose death caused the kyng imediatly to remove into Westminster wher he mourned and kept him selfe close and secret a great while'.[37] On 13 November, the queen was buried at Windsor 'withe greate solempnitie', with the Lady Mary acting as the chief mourner for her dead stepmother. The king remained in mourning apparel until Candlemas 1538.[38]

Queen Jane's achievement ushered in a new phase of English politics, for the Seymours had now triumphantly displaced the Howards as the English family connected most closely with the Tudor dynasty. By virtue of the birth of Prince Edward, their blood relationship with the Tudor dynasty was firmly established. Notwithstanding this, the Howards could feel confident once more for two major reasons. Firstly, the duke's success in quashing the rebellions known collectively as the Pilgrimage of Grace restored the confidence and trust of the king, following the suspicion with which the king may have briefly viewed him during the downfall of his niece. Secondly, the death of the queen meant that the king would require a new wife who could bear him a second son, for the Tudor succession, in spite of the birth of Jane's son, was still not completely secure. The example of the death of Prince Arthur, and the circumstances of Henry VIII's own succession, demonstrated that a 'spare' heir was needed, should the first die at an early age. Although it is unnecessary to believe, as some historians have done, that the Howards set about grooming their female relatives as a means of seducing the king and ensuring that a Howard became the Queen of England, it is likely that the Howards hoped that the king would marry someone, perhaps a foreign princess, who was favourable to their conservative religion and political interests.

The king's own unpredictable health emphasised the need for him to marry again and father a second son. Louis de Perreau, Sieur de Castillon, was to write to Anne de Montmorency on 14 May of how 'the King has had stopped one of the fistulas of his legs and for ten or twelve days the humours which had no outlet were like to have stifled him, so that he was sometimes without speaking, black in the face, and in great danger'.[39] While the king's health remained uncertain the rate of religious changes in England continued to accelerate, something which surely alarmed conservatives within both the court and the kingdom. Cranmer was instrumental in early 1538 in ensuring that 'the people might leave their idolatrie that had bene there used' in relation to the use of holy images in churches.[40] At around the same time, it was ordered that the Bible should be published in English for the common people to read.[41] Later in September, Cromwell issued his second injunctions as Lord Privy Seal and Vicegerent, which ordered that every parish church in the realm should have a Bible in English for the parishioners to read, while instructing that holy images and roods should be removed. He also ordered curates should keep a book or register which recorded every wedding, christening and burial which took place within the parish. While this occurred, abbeys and monasteries continued to be dissolved and the profits obtained by the king.[42]

Meanwhile the hostility between the Howards and Seymours worsened, which was primarily aggravated by the actions of the duke's son, the Earl of Surrey. It is intriguing, therefore, that an alliance between the Seymours and the Howards by virtue of a Seymour marriage to the widowed Duchess of Richmond, daughter of the Duke of Norfolk, was briefly mooted, although it eventually came to nothing.[43] During the summer and autumn of 1538, the duke sold some of his manors to the king and others favourable to him:

> Sold to the King, the manors of Claxton and Fyndon, 70*l;* the manor of Hunsdon, with the parks, 50*l.* To Sir John Dudley, the manor of Acton Burnell, 98*l.* To James Lauson, the manor of Wollerhampton, £27. To George Throgmorton, the manor of Sullyhill, £34. To Gostwicke, the manor of Willyngton, 46*l.* To my lord of Suffolk (when I went to Ireland), the manor of Cossey, 110*l.* Also divers other manors to the value of 133*l* 6*s.* 8*d.* Total 568*l* 6*s* 8*d.* Bought the manors of Wynthering, Snape, Alborough, Romborowe, and some other lands. Annual receipts: – The Treasurership, fee of 378*l.* An annuity of my lord of Suffolk, 413*l.* 6*s.* 8*d.* The Stewardship of the Augmentation, 100*l.* The stewardship of Winchester, 100*l.* Of suppressed lands given by the King, 200*l.* Of Sipton, 200*l.* Whereof, to the quondam and other monks, 72*l.* To my wife and son, 400*l.* And so remaineth to me, clear, 2638*l.*[44]

In April 1538, Lady Elizabeth Howard, mother of Anne Boleyn and sister to the duke, died and was buried at Lambeth, where her brother Edmund, father of Katherine, acted as chief mourner at her funeral.[45] Edmund continued to suffer personal financial difficulties, leading him to seek Cromwell's assistance, for his staff consisted of seven clerks and he was obliged to keep four horses and a groom. Despite Edmund's personal difficulties and his inability to live in the political and financial state expected of a Howard nobleman, his brother Lord William, who had earlier chastised his niece Katherine for her behaviour within the household of the dowager duchess, 'was steadily climbing the ladder of political success' as 'a diplomat of rare merit', namely as the English ambassador at the court of James V of Scotland and later in Scotland. It is ironic that he was employed, along with other diplomats, with the task of selecting an appropriate royal consort in Europe as a fourth bride for his king, merely months before his niece Katherine became the fifth queen of Henry VIII.[46] Edmund did not long survive the death of his sister, dying in the spring of 1539 nine months or so before his daughter Katherine departed for court in order to serve the new queen as a maiden. As with Jane Seymour's father, Edmund Howard did not share in the success of his daughter's family when she was unexpectedly elevated to royalty, although unlike John Seymour, Edmund did not actually witness the extraordinary feat of his daughter marrying the English king.

The inauguration of the reformed religion in England correspondingly led to an attack on conservatives who were known to favour papal authority. The treachery of Cardinal Reginald Pole, who had wholeheartedly supported the cause of Katherine of Aragon and who had printed and distributed in late 1538 his book which personally vilified the English monarch and his decision to annul his first marriage, fuelled the king's displeasure with the Pole family and led Cromwell to seek evidence of treason committed by members of that family. On 5 November, Henry Courtenay, Marquess of Exeter, Edward Neville, the Earl of Devon, and Henry, Lord Montague were arrested for treason and imprisoned in the Tower of London. The Lady Marquess of Exeter was shortly afterwards imprisoned there too.[47] Montague and Exeter were tried for treason in December and, on 9 January, were beheaded alongside Edward Neville on Tower Hill. Montague's brother, Geoffrey Pole, was pardoned on account of the evidence he had provided against his relatives.[48] In March 1539, Sir Nicholas Carew was also executed. The execution of these prominent noblemen did not occur solely on account of their religious interests and kinship with the traitorous Reginald Pole, but at least partly because of their royal blood: they were known as the 'White Rose' on account of their dynastic connection with the house of York. Fearing the still uncertain nature of the English succession, the king appears to have become increasingly suspicious of noble families, such as the Poles, who could lay claim to the throne of England on account of their royal lineage. This demonstrated further the need for the king to take a fourth wife who could bear him a second son and ensure that the succession was safeguarded against all possible dynastic threats.

While Cromwell rooted out evidence of treason among disaffected nobles, the king's advisers pressed ahead with plans for a fourth marriage. In the autumn of 1538, the king was rumoured to favour the 17-year-old Christina, Duchess of Milan, as a possible consort, but she was not ecstatic about a marriage alliance with the ageing king (he was 47 at this time).[49] During negotiations with the Schmalkaldic League that year, Cromwell was believed to be 'most favourably inclined to the German nation', intending 'very dearly, that the King should wed himself with the German Princes'.[50] The Duke of Cleves, as early as September 1538, sought a marriage alliance between Henry VIII and his sister Anne as a means of countering the Emperor's influence in Europe.[51] This occurred in the context of England's increasing isolation on the European continent, for the inauguration of the reformed religion had alarmed and angered the Catholic powers of France and the Holy Roman Empire, who opposed what they came to perceive as heresy, and they condemned both Cromwell and Cranmer as heretics and schismatics. In January 1539, the bishop of Tarbes, Caros and Granvelle signed a letter which was sent to both Charles V and François I promising 'that no new alliances, agreements or accords with the King of England whether for marriages of himself, the Princess, his daughter [Mary] or the Prince his son, or any treaties whatsoever without mutual consent, were to be made'.[52] In view of this, it is more likely that Henry VIII sought an alliance with Cleves through a marriage to Anne because of England's diplomatic isolation caused by the 1538 alliance between Charles, François and the pope, rather than being an international alliance masterminded solely by Thomas Cromwell to achieve his religious goals.[53]

The king, fearing the consequences of England's diplomatic isolation and perhaps increasingly resentful of the rapid rate of religious changes masterminded by Cromwell and Cranmer, called a meeting of parliament in April 1539 in which a new religious settlement, centred around the conservative Act of Six Articles, was inaugurated. In May, Norfolk was personally authorised to put forward the Six Articles to parliament for discussion.[54] It is possible that Henry VIII personally selected Norfolk because he was aware of the extent to which the Howards favoured traditional religion and their opposition towards the reformed settlement. Norfolk's disagreement with Anne Boleyn during her queenship had perhaps occurred mainly because of conflicting religious interests, for she was known to favour the reformed cause, something which may have been unacceptable to her conservative relatives.[55] This parliament passed the Act of Precedence which confirmed, among others, Norfolk's power and influence as Lord Treasurer of England and Earl Marshal, second only to the positions of Lord Chancellor Audley. Suffolk, Cromwell, Oxford and Southampton were also confirmed within the act.

By then, the king had agreed to marry Anne of Cleves in an alliance that would bolster England's security against the hostility of the European powers of France and the Holy Roman Empire. The English ambassador Christopher Mont visited the court of Cleves and personally reported on the appearance of Anne, promising to Cromwell that 'everyman praiseth the beauty of the said Lady [Anne], as well for the face, as for the whole body, above all other ladies excellent … She excelleth as far the Duchess [of Milan], as the golden sun excelleth the silvern moon'.[56] In August, John Wotton, writing from Cleves, reported that both Anne and her sister Amelia had been brought up in the household of their mother, the Duchess of Cleves, 'a wise lady and one that very straitly looketh to her children'. Believing Anne to be 'of very lowly and gentle conditions', Wotton wrote that Anne was accomplished in needlework but did not speak French or Latin, nor was she musically gifted, 'for they take it here in Germany for a rebuke and an occasion of lightness that great ladies should be learned or have any knowledge of music'.[57] Warnicke has recently demonstrated that the Cleves court was not unsophisticated, as some historians have supposed, and the reasons for Henry VIII's early rejection of Anne have a psychological dimension that has perhaps not been adequately considered in previous studies of their marriage.[58] In the autumn of 1539, negotiations were made for her journey to England in order to marry Henry VIII.

Although, alongside other conservatives such as Bishop Gardiner, the Duke of Norfolk may not have personally favoured the king's alliance with Cleves and his prospective marriage to Anne, the king's impending fourth marriage did offer the opportunity for the duke to seek appointments within the new queen's household for his relatives. Aristocratic women were well placed to advance their family's fortunes and exercise influence within the queen's household through serving her in the capacity of maidens and ladies-in-waiting, and families were expected to mobilise all their connections and contacts at court in order to secure appointments to the queen's household for their daughters, who 'functioned as members of dense kin networks'.[59] The difficulty in attaining a place within the household of the queen, however, was demonstrated in the case of Katherine Basset, whose sister Anne had served Jane Seymour and later Anne of Cleves. Lady Lisle, mother of both girls, sought the assistance of her cousin the Countess of Rutland in the matter, the countess replying that the king himself had limited the number of maidens allowed at court, but if Lady Lisle would 'make some means unto mother Lowe', who was 'mother of the Dutch maids' brought from Cleves, she might accomplish her purpose of achieving a place for Katherine.[60] Anne Basset reported that she had approached the king regarding her sister's appointment, but he replied that he had not decided upon the final number or selection of the queen's maidens, but that they would have to 'be fair and as he thought meet for the room'. Anne encouraged her mother to 'send to some of your friends that are about his grace to speak for her'.[61] The case of the Bassets demonstrates the critical role that women played in achieving, or at least influencing, the appointments of female relatives to positions in the queen's household. When Anne had sought a place in the household of Queen Jane in 1537, her mother's niece Mary, Countess of Sussex, and her stepfather's cousin the Countess of Rutland, wife of the queen's lord chamberlain, had provided invaluable assistance.[62]

In the autumn of 1539 the duke, probably assisted by his stepmother the dowager Duchess of Norfolk, achieved appointments at court within the queen's household for his niece Katherine Howard and his great-nieces Katherine Carey and Mary Norris. They were to serve the queen as her maidens, alongside other young women such as Anne Basset and Dorothy Braye, while other Howard relatives, such as the widowed Duchess of Richmond and Lady Jane Rochford, were selected to serve the queen as her ladies-in-waiting.[63] Katherine's half-sister Isabel Leigh was the wife of Sir Edward Baynton, who served the king's later queens as vice-chamberlain, while her sister Margaret was married to Sir Thomas Arundell, Anne of Cleves's receiver and later the chancellor to Katherine.[64] That Katherine Howard was chosen to serve Anne of Cleves as her maiden, alongside her young cousins Katherine Carey and Mary Norris, provides a further clue to her age. Katherine Carey was born most likely in the spring of 1524, and Mary Norris, daughter of the disgraced Henry Norris (who had been executed alongside Anne Boleyn for treason), had been born around 1526 in Berkshire, suggesting that Katherine Howard was fairly close in age.[65]

Since the duke had probably had little contact with his niece Katherine due to his various political and diplomatic duties both in the north and at court, it seems plausible that he would have relied on reports provided by his stepmother which advised him as to the suitability of Katherine as a maiden to the new queen. It is likely, however, that he would have met with his young niece perhaps in the autumn of 1539 prior to her appointment at court. That the dowager duchess was at least partly, if not fully, aware of Katherine's pre-marital liaisons is evident from the examinations of 1541, but it seems unlikely that the duke was aware of the full extent, or nature of, his niece Katherine's sexual experiences prior to her appointment at court, for the Howards surely would not have risked the threat to their family honour were rumours of their relative's past to surface at court and expose them to scandal. It is likely that the duke had heard pleasing reports of his young niece which convinced him that she would be an asset to the Howards by serving Anne of Cleves. He might have been further convinced to seek her appointment at court once he had met with her at the dowager duchess's residence. Aged 15 or 16 in the second half of 1539, she appears to have blossomed into a young lady of noteworthy beauty, with reddish-gold, or auburn, hair, blue-grey eyes, pale skin and a dainty figure, while being 'of very diminutive stature', according to Richard Hilles.[66] One writer later complimented her as the most beautiful lady at court, if not in the kingdom.[67] The speed with which she captivated Henry VIII further illustrates her physical charms. The dowager duchess's activities as a fosterer to her Howard relatives, including Katherine, assisted in the selection of Katherine as a maiden to Anne of Cleves in late 1539, and the dowager duchess later instructed Katherine on how to please Henry VIII.[68] As Warnicke argued, 'Katherine's most important female supporter' in promoting her as an attendant to the new queen 'was her step-grandmother',[69] and 'women might deserve some credit' for her appointment at court.[70]

The announcement that Katherine had been chosen to serve the new queen instigated the conclusion of her affair with Francis Dereham. Dereham's later confession conveys his possessiveness of Katherine and desire to retain control of her, for he promised that 'he should never live to say thou hast swerved'. Katherine, exasperated with his behaviour, replied that he 'might do as he list'.[71] Clearly, she was eager to leave him and the perhaps undesired nature of his attentions behind, for she later admitted that 'for all that knew me, and kept my company, knew how glad and desirous I was to come to the court'. Later at court, having returned from Ireland, Dereham confronted Katherine with the rumour that she had promised to wed Thomas Culpeper, a distant relative and a favoured servant of the king. She replied: 'Why should you trouble me therewith, for you know I will not have you; and if you heard such reports, you heard more than I do know.'[72] Dereham's manipulative and controlling behaviour illustrates his sexual jealousy and fear of cuckoldry, in an environment which perceived female sexuality to be potentially excessive and harmful to the honour of men, which could give rise to an atmosphere of jealousy, anxiety, and violence. Indeed, 'the force with which women's unchastity was imagined, ridiculed and proscribed made for a culture in which the possibilities of dishonour seem almost to erase those of honour'.[73]

Meanwhile, in October Anne of Cleves was given a safe-conduct to travel to England, which the king had agreed to.[74] The future queen left Dusseldorf in November and arrived at the English keep of Calais on 11 December. Admiral Fitzwilliam, who provided hospitality for Anne during her sojourn in Calais, informed the king that 'she played as pleasantly and with as good a grace and countenance as ever in all my life I saw any noblewoman'.[75] Eventually, Anne arrived in England amid stormy weather on 27 December. The Duke of Suffolk reported that she was 'desirous to make haste to the King's Highness'. At Canterbury, Archbishop Cranmer welcomed her with a speech, while the mayor and citizens received her with torches and a peal of guns. Fifty ladies in velvet bonnets visited her in her chamber. Suffolk reported that this 'she took very joyously … that she forgot all the foul weather and was very merry at supper'.[76] On New Year's Eve, Anne travelled to Rochester where she was personally met by Norfolk and Lord Dacre. Alongside Lord Mountjoy, the knights and esquires of Norfolk and Suffolk and the barons of the exchequer, 'all in coates of velvet with chaynes of gold', escorted Anne to Rochester.[77]

The king himself decided to visit his new queen at Rochester, a matter of days before their marriage. The nature of the meeting has become a subject of controversy, even myth, with the king's decision to visit Anne at Rochester often attributed to impatience or curiosity on the king's behalf. Yet it is likely that the actual nature of this meeting formed 'part of the elaborate courtship ritual based on chivalrous antecedents', with Henry's greeting constituting 'a sophisticated adaptation of fertility ritual and chivalric ceremonies concerned with the rites of passage, because the begetting of male children was the ultimate goal of the marital union', while demonstrating the king's excellent hospitality and social position within his kingdom.[78] Hall reported that Anne 'was sumwhat astonied' at meeting with the king in such a manner, but he 'spoke & welcomed her, she w most gracious & louyng coutenance & behauiour him receiued & welcomed on her knees, whom he gently toke vp & kyssed'.[79] Sir Anthony Browne, however, who served as gentleman of the privy chamber and master of the horse, believed that the king spoke barely twenty words to the woman who was about to become his wife and parted from her company without giving her the New Year's gift of bejewelled sables which he had brought with him.[80]

The king's disappointment with his new wife will be addressed in the next chapter, but to fully understand their relationship one needs to view the king's opinion of his queen, and his desire to marry again, in the context of early modern concerns about fertility, reproduction and the English succession. Although the king had sired a healthy prince in 1537, his own childhood reminded him of the urgent necessity of fathering multiple sons, for, if the eldest son were to die young and there was no brother to replace him, the succession could be cast into doubt, potentially leading to dynastic conflict or civil war as had happened in the fifteenth century. Thus the emphasis on fertility within the ritual used to welcome Anne of Cleves reminded her that she had been selected as queen consort because of the need for her to bear her king a second son, to fully secure the Tudor succession beyond all possible doubt. The king had utilised ritual before to remind his queens of the ultimate reason why he had chosen to marry them. The pageants in Anne Boleyn's coronation were centred on the themes of fertility, with verses hoping 'may

Heaven bless these nuptials, and make her a fruitful mother of men-children'.[81]
Further verses opined:

> Fruitful Saint Anne bare three Maries; the off-spring of her body, by a strange
> conception, bare the first founders of our holy Faith. Of that daughter was
> born Christ our Redeemer, foster-father of a vast family. Not without
> thought therefore, Queen Anne, do the citizens form this pageant in your
> honour. By her example, may you give us a race to maintain the Faith and
> the Throne.[82]

During Jane Seymour's period as queen, the celebrations at Corpus Christi
indicated hope for the royal couple's 'long life together' and future children
born to them.[83] Moreover, as will become clear, contemporaries at court were
obsessed with the possibility of Katherine Howard producing a son.

Only in the context of prevailing sixteenth-century social and cultural
beliefs about fertility, reproduction and sexuality can Henry VIII's decision to
marry not only Anne of Cleves, but also his other queens, be fully understood.
Because the queen was traditionally selected by her spouse first and foremost
on account of her perceived aptitude for bearing sons, the king did not select
Anne merely as a means of protecting England from the hostility of other
European powers, who were then diametrically opposed to him in their religious policies and activities. He must have been convinced that, by virtue of
her reported fertility and 'convenient' age, she would provide an answer to the
pressing issues which continued to plague the English succession. Her inability
to do so provides an essential context for understanding the subsequent rise
of Katherine Howard and her spectacular attainment of the queenship only a
matter of months after the Cleves marriage took place.

5

THE FOURTH QUEEN

THE CIRCUMSTANCES THAT LED to the elevation of Katherine Howard to the position of Henry VIII's fifth queen in the summer of 1540 have traditionally been explained as the culmination of factional intrigues masterminded by the conservative Duke of Norfolk and Stephen Gardiner, Bishop of Winchester, in an attempt to dislodge both Anne of Cleves and the reformist Thomas Cromwell, who had organised the king's marriage to Anne, from power. Apparently, 'it was plain to the Catholic chiefs, that if a suitable lady of their own faith could be found, she might win Henry back to what they considered the true fold', leading Norfolk and Gardiner to select Katherine, 'whose good looks and supposed Spartan upbringing seemed to fit her peculiarly for the perilous rank of Queen-consort'.[1] Baldwin Smith agrees: 'Catherine was selected by the conservative party for such a role' as Norfolk and Gardiner 'planned their strategy accordingly' through influencing their king 'by means of feminine guile'.[2] One writer goes further, alleging that 'Norfolk was quite ready to use Katherine to further his own political agenda' and Katherine was 'the victim' of 'a reformist conspiracy' instigated by her uncle and Gardiner.[3] It will be argued in this chapter, through a close and critical reading of surviving evidence in the light of political and cultural customs, that these views are largely misguided and do not accurately reflect the state of affairs which resulted in the annulment of Anne of Cleves's marriage, Cromwell's execution and Katherine's marriage to the king.

Norfolk's decision to appoint three of his female relatives to the household of the new queen, Anne of Cleves, illustrates his desire to consolidate and extend the influence of the Howards within the intimacy of the queen's chambers, but it does not signal that he intended for one of them to attract the attention of the king and emulate Anne Boleyn in becoming a Howard

Queen of England. Indeed, a rather more realistic aim of the duke was for his kinswomen to achieve respectable marriages, a political and social goal which would increase the influence and prestige of the Howard family within the setting of the court and in the regions outside of it, depending on the land-owning assets brought to the marriage. As has been noted, like other noble families the Howards appreciated that women within the family could play important roles, especially in marriage alliances, in contributing to the glory of the family. Since rumours were to circulate shortly after Katherine's arrival at court that she was about to marry Thomas Culpeper, gentleman of the king's privy chamber, it is possible that the duke, aware of the family connection with the Culpepers, considered marrying his niece to an individual who enjoyed enviable influence and proximity to the king. Katherine, however, was ignorant of such rumours, informing Francis Dereham when he accused her: 'What should you trouble me therewith, for you know I will not have you, and if you heard such reports, you heard more than I do know.'[4]

Female relatives at court played an essential role both in maintaining their family's honour and in actively contributing to the glory of the dynasty through the creation of marriage alliances. The renowned court poet Thomas Wyatt cynically opined: 'In this also see you be not idle: thy niece, thy cousin, thy sister or thy daughter, if she be fair, if handsome by her middle, if thy better hath her love besought her, if thy better hath her love besought her, advance his cause, and he shall help thy need.'[5] Aware of the dangers of the court, it is certain that both the duke and the dowager duchess instructed Katherine and her cousins on the necessity of maintaining their modesty and chastity, for any scandal that threatened the Howard name would be injurious, both to themselves and to the family. Chastity and modesty were highly prized qualities in the queen's maidens. In 1537, when Anne Basset was appointed to serve Jane Seymour, it was emphasised that she should 'be sober, sad, wise and discreet and lowly … and to be obedient' to the queen and 'to serve God and to be virtuous'. If she did not do so, it would have grave consequences for the honour of her family, to their own 'discomfort and discontentation'. The dangers of the court were well known, being 'full of pride, envy, indignation and mocking, scorning and derision'.[6]

Katherine would have been well aware of the prestigious nature of her appointment, for competition to become a maiden to the queen was intense. These attendants were expected to dress fashionably, maintain a modest and sober demeanour in court functions, possess musical capability, accompany the queen in court functions and processions, and sing and dance well as ornaments to their royal mistress. The repeated emphasis on maintaining their honesty and chastity can be understood in the light of prevailing cultural and social beliefs which associated the female body with evil, licentiousness and whoredom. One popular rhyme ran thus: 'Nine times a night is too much for a man / I can't do it myself, but my sister Nan can.' Nicholas de Venette was to warn that women 'are much more amorous than men, and as sparrows, do not live long, because they are too hot and too susceptible of love', associating a woman's caresses with sin and 'a capital crime'.[7] Robert Cawdry, writing in the reign of Elizabeth I, warned that for 'a maid, the honesty and chastity is instead of all ... the which thing only if a woman remember, it will cause her to take great heed who, and be more a wary and careful keeper of her honesty, which alone being lost ... there is nothing left'.[8] In view of this, it is inconceivable that the duke and his stepmother the dowager duchess would have sought an appointment for Katherine within the household of Anne of Cleves had they been fully aware of her adolescent affairs with Manox and Dereham. Deeply concerned with maintaining the family's honour, they would almost certainly have sought a place for an alternative female relative whom they knew was unquestionably chaste and virginal; potentially, Katherine's younger sister. The court actively upheld contemporary gender standards and any woman with a dubious sexual reputation would not expect to be honoured with an appointment.

In December 1539, Katherine received a maiden's stipend, probably having already travelled to Greenwich Palace in anticipation of Anne of Cleves's imminent arrival.[9] On 3 January Anne became acquainted with the Dukes of Norfolk and Suffolk and the Archbishop of Canterbury, and was welcomed by nobly born ladies including Margaret Douglas, niece of the king and daughter of the queen of Scotland; another royal niece, Frances Grey, Marchioness of Dorset; the king's erstwhile daughter-in-law Mary Howard, Duchess of Richmond; and the Countesses of Rutland and Hertford. Following these greetings, the gentlemen of the king's privy chamber, 'some apparelled in coates of velvet embrodered', the barons, the bishops, the earls, foreign ambassadors, and finally Cromwell among other officers rode forth to meet their new queen. The king himself shortly followed:

> Apparelled in a coate of purple velvet, somewhat made lyke a frocke, all ouer embrodered with flatte golde of Dammaske with small lace mixed betwene of the same gold, and other laces of the same so goyng trauerse wyse ... the sleues and brest were cut lyned with cloth of golde, and tyed together with great buttons of Diamondes, Rubyes, and Orient Perle ... his bonnet was so ryche of Iuels that fewe men coulde value them.[10]

Hearing of the king's arrival, Anne came forth to greet him:

Bbeyng apparelled in a ryche goune of cloth of golde reised, made rounde without any trayne after the Dutche fassyon, and on her head a kall, & ouer that a rounde bonet or cappe set full of Orient Perle of a very propre fassyon, & before that she had a cornet of blacke velvet, & about her necke she had a partelet set full of riche stone which glystered all the felde.

Riding forth to the king, Anne was personally welcomed and 'embrased ... to the great reioysyng of the beholders', replying with 'sweete woordes and great thankes'.[11] It is likely that Katherine was present at this glittering occasion, for Hall records the presence of 'Ladies, Gentlewomen & Maydens in a gret nombre'.[12] The new queen's household comprised great ladies, including Mary Arundell, Countess of Sussex; Frances Grey; Lady Margaret Douglas; Elizabeth Grey, Lady Audley; Mary Howard; the Countess of Rutland; gentlewomen including Lady Wriothesley and Lady Elizabeth Cromwell; and maidens including Katherine Howard, Katherine Carey and Anne Basset, who had previously served Queen Jane.[13]

Unfortunately for the new queen, her marriage got off to the worse possible start when the king failed to consummate it on their wedding night or in the weeks immediately after the wedding. Evidence suggests that the king was not personally delighted with his prospective wife, lamenting: 'I see nothing in this woman as men report of her', speaking 'very sadly and pensively.' He continued: 'And I marvel that wise men would make such report as they have done.'[14] Cromwell, who had been closely involved in the marriage negotiations, asked the king how he liked his new wife. Replying that he found her 'nothing so well as she was spoken of', the king insisted that Cromwell find a 'remedy'. Yet Cromwell was forced to admit that he knew 'none', adding that 'he was very sorry therefore'.[15] The king, however, was required to put aside his personal feelings for the needs of the kingdom and married Anne on 6 January at Greenwich:

> On Twelfe daie, which was Twesdaie, the Kinges Majestie was maried to the said Queene Anne, solemply, in her closett at Greenwych, and his Grace and shee went a procession openlie that daie, she being in her haire, with a rytch cronett of stones and pearle sett with rosemarie on her Graces heade, and a gowne of rich cloath of silver, and richlie behanged with stonne and pearle, with all her ladies and gentlewomen following her Grace, which was a goodlie sight to behold.[16]

The new queen, dressed in a gown of rich cloth of gold set with large flowers and orient pearl, with her 'fayre, yelowe and long' hair loose, chose the motto for her wedding ring: 'GOD SEND ME WILL TO KEEP.'[17]

The next day, Cromwell visited the king in his privy chamber to ask 'how [he] liked the Queen', presuming that the newlywed royal couple had consummated their marriage. The king bluntly responded:

> Surely, as ye know, I liked her before not well, but now I like her much worse. For I have felt her belly and her breasts and thereby, as I can judge, she should be no maid. [The] which struck me so to the heart when I felt them that I had neither will nor courage to proceed any further in other matters.

He then admitted, 'I have left her as good a maid as I found her.'[18] When read in light of cultural customs and contemporary beliefs about the female body, the king's comments take on new meaning. Contemporaries believed that maidens should have small breasts and flat stomachs, while demonstrating modest behaviour and a 'sober' appearance.[19] Believing that his new wife was not a virgin, Henry may have feared that she would steal his manhood or bewitch him into loving her.[20] He seems to have believed that she was actually the lawful wife of Francis, Duke of Lorraine, to whom Anne had earlier been betrothed. As Warnicke argued, this knowledge might have prevented Henry from consummating the marriage in the winter and spring of 1540.[21] The king's concerns with his wife, specifically with her body, occurred at a crucial time, for governments during this era interpreted women's fertility as a political and dynastic concern.[22] Henry's response to Anne and his subsequent behaviour after the wedding should be interpreted in this political and cultural context, and the king reported that 'he found her [Anne's] body in such sort disordered and indisposed to excite and provoke any lust in him', and 'could not in any wise overcome that loathsomeness, nor in her company be provoked or stirred to that act'. Yet he 'thought himself able to do the act with other, but not with her'.[23] As will be demonstrated in relation to Katherine Howard's marriage, Henry VIII was deeply concerned about the continuation of his dynasty, and it was this concern, rather than Anne's supposed ugliness, which led him to seek the annulment of his marriage to Anne.

Evidently, the modern notion that it was Anne of Cleves's physical ugliness which offended her husband is incorrect, for the king's comments demonstrate that, once more, fertility concerns threatened the future of his marriage. Indeed, court observers unanimously praised the new queen's beauty, with Cromwell informed that 'everyman praiseth the beauty of the said Lady [Anne], as well for the face, as for the whole body, above all other ladies excellent'.[24] The king's disgust with his wife's breasts and belly signifies his fear that she had surrendered her maidenhead to another man.[25] Anne herself may have been well aware of her predicament, for she allegedly informed her ladies-in-waiting that her husband had failed to consummate the marriage: 'She knew well she was not with child.' The Countess of Rutland, an experienced courtier who was aware of the king's fixation on the English succession, warned her mistress: 'Madam, there must be more than this, or it will be long ere we have a Duke of York.'[26] It has been argued that these reported conversations did not actually take place, but were invented as part of the evidence required to dissolve the marriage on the grounds of non-consummation.[27] Cromwell, fearful in light of his close and well-known involvement in the making of the Cleves marriage, instructed the Earl of Rutland, lord chamberlain of the queen, to inform the queen that she should behave more pleasingly towards the king her husband, in an attempt to encourage the consummation of the marriage and, more broadly, ensure the continuation of the Tudor dynasty through the deliverance of a son.

Anne's marital problems were compounded by the fact that the king had fallen in love with her maiden Katherine Howard either before or shortly after Anne's wedding. Most historians have interpreted the king's affection for the young Katherine as an unforeseen consequence of his marital difficulties, occurring only in the late spring or early summer of 1540 when the king had set in process the events which would culminate in the annulment of his fourth marriage.[28] It is possible, however, that when Henry VIII had first become acquainted with Katherine in the closing months of 1539, before the arrival of Anne, he had developed a strong affection and love for her which consequently impaired his relations with his fourth wife. Katherine's step-grandmother was later informed that the 'King's Highness did cast a fantasy to Catherine Howard the first time that ever his Grace saw her'.[29] If Henry had personally presided over the selection of maidens for his wife's household, as has been conjectured, then he may have fallen in love with Katherine before his wife had even arrived in the kingdom.[30] It is interesting that ambassadors who resided at court only learned of the king's new love in the summer of 1540, when his disaffection with Queen Anne had become obvious. It is likely that Henry maintained discretion and secrecy in his relations with his wife's maiden, especially if as seems likely he was concerned about maintaining Katherine's reputation, for the French ambassador reported only in July that the king planned to marry 'a lady of great beauty' who was a niece of the Duke of Norfolk.[31]

The king's desire for Katherine probably occurred mainly due to her renowned beauty, for several of her contemporaries agreed that she was highly attractive. Nikander Nucius, who appears to have served the imperial ambassador at Henry VIII's court, remembered her as 'the most beautiful woman of her time'.[32] George Cavendish emphasised Katherine's 'beawtie freshe and pure', while Marillac commented on Katherine's gracefulness.[33] The glaring contrast between Katherine and Anne only made the king more determined to annul his marriage and remarry, for he publicly admitted that he was unable to consummate his fourth marriage. Henry's subjects, however, were perhaps not as understanding of the king's concerns, for they viewed the king's frequent visits to the dowager duchess's residence at Lambeth or to Gardiner's Winchester Palace as evidence of adultery: 'The bishop of Winchester also very often provided feastings and entertainments for them in his palace; but the citizens regarded all this not as a sign of divorcing the queen, but of adultery.'[34]

Had Henry been convinced that his union with Anne of Cleves would result in the arrival of offspring and that it would provide a favourable solution to the pressing issues that continued to plague the Tudor succession, it is reasonable to assume that Katherine would have become merely his mistress, as both Elizabeth Blount and Mary Boleyn had been previously. The fact that Dereham became aware of rumours in the spring of 1540 which suggested that Katherine was betrothed to Thomas Culpeper, a gentleman of the king's privy chamber, may provide evidence of the initial secrecy surrounding the relationship between Henry VIII and Katherine, for it is possible that the king had been in love with Katherine as early as December 1539. Almost certainly Culpeper would not have dared to pursue a flirtation with Katherine if he was aware of his master's feelings towards her. However, the king's intention to annul his marriage to the queen and marry Katherine as his fifth wife seemed to be confirmed when she was granted the forfeited goods and chattels of two murderers on 24 April. In May, Katherine was granted twenty-three quilts of quilted sarcenet.[35] Similarly to the Dereham affair, the king provided Katherine with elaborate gifts as a means of courting her and signalling to the court his intent to marry her, for, as has been noted, gifts formed an essential part of courtship during this period.[36] The Howards, appreciative of Katherine's efforts to elevate their family to royalty, commended and praised her 'for her pure and honest condition'.[37]

Henry's conviction that marriage to Katherine, whom he believed to be both fertile and virginal, would provide a welcome remedy to the pressing issues of the English succession cast Cromwell into further political and personal difficulties, for he had been known to favour the now unwanted alliance with Cleves. Notwithstanding this, the king chose to reward him in the spring and early summer of 1540, culminating in Cromwell's acquirement of the earldom of Essex and the position of Lord Great Chamberlain in April.[38] However, with the benefit of hindsight observers later believed that 'this was all an artifice' in which Henry was presented in the best possible light and Cromwell's treachery was made to look worse.[39] But, as Richard Hilles stressed in his letter abroad to Henry Bullinger, the king's fourth marriage was questioned openly by the nobility only when 'they had perceived that the king's affections were alienated from the lady Anne to that young girl Catharine, the cousin [sic] of the duke of Norfolk, whom he married immediately upon Anne's divorce'.[40] Intriguingly in light of later events, on 12 June Thomas Culpeper, a distant cousin to Katherine and a favourite of the king, was granted reversion of properties in Crown leases in Yorkshire 'grant in fee, in consideration of his true and faithful service', some of which had previously been held by the Yorkshire gentlemen Sir Ralph Ellerker and Sir William Fairfax.[41]

Culpeper's rewards must be set in the context of the political and social nature of the Henrician court. The court emerged as the centre of national politics during Henry's reign, leading to a distinct form of court politics which modern historians have tended to interpret as factional but which had medieval antecedents, as recorded by Chaucer in *The Knight's Tale*: 'And therefore, at the Kynges court, my brother, Ech man for himself, ther is noon other.'[42] David Starkey's seminal research demonstrated the fundamental divisions within the royal household, with the 'below-stairs' comprising rooms such as the hall and kitchens run by the lord steward, while the 'above-stairs' encompassed private apartments headed by the lord chamberlain. The private apartments gradually became increasingly complex, which granted the king greater privacy. The privy chamber itself had its own staff, headed by the groom of the stool, and included half a dozen other grooms and pages of modest gentry background who served the king intimately.[43]

Culpeper, as demonstrated by his intimate position within the royal household, was visibly one of the king's favourites. He had possibly began his career as a page who lit fires and warmed his sovereign's clothes, before progressing to the office of groom and then becoming a gentleman of the privy chamber in around 1537.[44] His influence was well known, for in 1537 Lady Lisle and John Hussey had disputed as to whether Sussex or Culpeper was in a stronger position to be helpful at court and who should be granted a hawk as a gift. They both agreed that 'there is no remedy; Culpeper must have a hawk'.[45] Lady Lisle also granted him two bracelets, promising 'they are the first that ever I sent to any man'.[46] On 5 May 1540, at the annual May Day celebrations, Culpeper participated in the jousts as a defendant and was overthrown by Sir Richard Cromwell, challenger.[47] Culpeper was distantly related to Katherine, for he was the second son of Sir Alexander Culpeper of Bedgebury and Constance Harper. His father probably died sometime in 1540–41, for his will was made on 20 May of that year.[48] The eldest son of that union was also, somewhat confusingly, named Thomas, and he had served Thomas Cromwell. Later, in May 1542, five months after Culpeper's execution, Richard Hilles described the younger Thomas thus:

Two years before, or less, [he] had violated the wife of a certain park-keeper in a woody thicket, while, horrid to relate! Three or four of his most profligate attendants were holding her at his bidding. For this act of wickedness he was, notwithstanding, pardoned by the king, after he had been delivered into custody by the villagers on account of this crime.[49]

Predictably, this alleged rape and possibly the later murder of a villager has coloured historians' assessments of Thomas Culpeper and his later relationship with Katherine; these historians have argued that, as a violent and cruel individual, Culpeper manipulated 'Lady Rochford to assist him in obtaining political control of Katherine'.[50] This negative perception of Culpeper has also appeared in the medium of television, with Torrance Coombs's Culpeper in *The Tudors* committing rape and murder before his relationship with Katherine. It is possible, however, that Hilles confused Thomas with his elder brother, who shared the same name, because surviving evidence indicates that this eldest son was physically violent and aggressive; in a dispute over land with a reverend:

The said Thomas Culpeper broke the bow of the said William; clerk, with the shaft of a knife so that the blade ran down his face in the presence of this deponent … then the said Culpeper gave the said William, clerk, a blow or two with a staff for he was not able to sing mass for a fortnight after, and thereupon the said clerk plucked the said Culpeper down by the beard in the sight of the wife of the said Culpeper who with one or two of her servants came running to help to beat the said William clerk, so that he was forced to cry to the said William Playce and Robert Fulcher for aid … and by report the said Culpeper drew his dagger at another time to strike the said William, clerk, and more he cannot depose.[51]

Because of Culpeper's intimacy with the monarch and the fact that positions within the privy chamber were highly competitive, it is surely inconceivable that Henry VIII would have kept within his household an individual who committed the crimes of rape and murder with no apparent qualms, for that cast doubt upon both Culpeper's honour and the honour of the king, for it suggested that he was unable to properly govern his household and those who served within it, while also indicating that he condoned acts of crime. Rape in particular was perceived to be a sexual deviance and was to become prohibited by law, with a bill passed in 1548 protecting young males from sodomy and another in 1576 protecting girls under the age of ten from forcible rape.[52]

It is more likely, in view of the evidence relating to the elder Thomas's aggressive conflict with Reverend Williams, that Hilles unknowingly confused the younger Thomas with his elder brother, who was clearly violent. In the absence of any definitive evidence which illustrates the younger Thomas's personal characteristics, the trust which the king had in him and his favourable relations with contacts such as Lady Lisle would seem to indicate that he was a respectable young gentleman, as opposed to being a murderer and rapist. On the other hand, it is impossible to entirely dismiss Hilles's story and the interpretation offered later in this book of the younger Thomas's relationship with Katherine in 1541–42 might seem to support Hilles's identification of the younger Thomas as the brother involved in the unpleasant incident with the park-keeper's wife.

While both Culpeper and, especially, Katherine enjoyed enviable favour and rewards from the king during the early summer of 1540, Norfolk was apparently plotting with Stephen Gardiner, Bishop of Winchester, the downfall of Cromwell and with it the annulment of the Cleves marriage and Katherine's elevation to the queenship. Herbert did later record that 'he [Cromwell] was odious by reason of his low birth to all the Nobility, and hated particularly by Stephen Gardiner and all the Roman Catholiques, for having operated so much in the dissolution of Abbies', and mentioned specifically that Norfolk was chosen by the king to arrest Cromwell at a council meeting on 11 June.[53] He did not, however, associate Gardiner with the duke in a plot against Cromwell, recounting only that the bishop's hatred of Cromwell was shared by fellow Catholics at court. Hall made no mention of Gardiner and Norfolk plotting to remove Cromwell from power, merely recounting, like Herbert, that Cromwell was detested by conservative clergy who 'rejoysed' and 'triumphed together that night'.[54]

Although contemporaries were aware that Gardiner provided banquets and entertainments at his residence, which provided a convenient social setting for the king to court Katherine, there is no convincing evidence that demonstrates that the duke and bishop, contrary to popular belief, joined forces as a Catholic party in order to bring down Cromwell and marry Katherine to the king. Glyn Redworth noted that the two men belonged to different generations and were not connected through family alliances or patronage networks.[55] Both men were, however, undoubtedly hostile to Cromwell and resented his religious and political policies. Cromwell's closeness with German Lutherans, and his backing of the alliance with Cleves, was believed by the French ambassador to be the principal reason for his downfall.[56] Norfolk corresponded intimately with the French king regarding his desire to effect Cromwell's downfall, with François reporting to Marillac on 15 June: 'Norfolk will be able to remember what I said of it to him when he was last in France.'[57] Katherine's personal desire, in fact, to reconcile the mutual hostility between her relatives and the reformers represented by Archbishop Cranmer was demonstrated in late June when she personally promised Cranmer: 'You should not care for your businesses, for you should be in better case than ever you were.'[58] In effect, she seems to have promised that, were he to loyally support her and serve her well as queen, she would gladly support his advancement and vouchsafe his security.

While evidence was provided which allegedly proved Cromwell to be guilty of both treason and heresy, the king's desire to marry Katherine only increased. Marillac reported to King François on 1 June that, on 22 May, Queen Mary, wife of James V and niece by marriage of Henry VIII, had given birth to a son, whom the King of Scots hoped to make lord of Ireland or to establish in France.[59] Although Henry was believed to be joyous at the news of the birth of his grandnephew, the prince's birth must surely have heightened his fear and unease about the English succession; for although Queen Jane had provided him with an heir, the fact that Edward had no brothers with whom to completely safeguard the succession did not necessarily bode well for the future, especially when the circumstances of Henry VIII's own succession to the throne are considered. Henry only became king in 1509 after his father's death because his older brother Arthur had unexpectedly died in 1502.

With this context in mind, why the king decided to select Katherine as his queen consort needs to be considered. Although she was reportedly beautiful, youthful, charming, sweet-natured and gentle, the king was probably moved more by the promising signs of her fertility, for her mother had given birth to at least three sons during her second marriage and several by her first husband. Katherine's physical appearance probably also suggested to the king that she was likely to be fertile, whereas the bodily features of Anne of Cleves had indicated to Henry that she was not a virgin. As with Katherine of Aragon, Henry believed that Anne of Cleves had never been his wife, apparently signalled by her unacceptable bodily appearance which suggested that she had surrendered her maidenhead before she married the English king. The Howards, who knew little or nothing of Katherine's sexual experiences, emphasised her purity and, more importantly, her fertility, convincing their monarch of the suitability of the young Katherine as queen consort.

Although the king may have been involved with Katherine as early as late 1539, his relationship with her only became public in the early summer of 1540, when his desire to annul his marriage to Anne was obvious. On 20 June the queen herself complained to the Cleves ambassador Carl Harst of the king's affair with her maiden, although he comforted her by dismissing the affair as merely a 'light romance'.[60] Two days later, she was in better spirits because of Henry's kindness towards her, but she cannot have been unaware of the rumours circulating at court about both her future and Katherine's relationship with her husband, the king. On 24 June the queen was ordered to leave court and remove herself to Richmond Palace, allegedly because it enjoyed a better climate at a time when plague was feared, but in reality in order to begin the proceedings which would culminate in the annulment of her marriage.[61] Several ladies within the queen's household, Lady Rutland, Lady Rochford and Lady Edgecombe, 'gave such communications as was between the Queen's Grace and themselves, the Tuesday or Wednesday before midsummer day last at Westminster to the effect that the Queen had confessed to them the non-consummation of the marriage'.[62]

It is possible, as has been suggested, that these conversations did not actually take place and these ladies deliberately provided false evidence in order to ensure the annulment of the queen's marriage.[63] Certainly, in annulment cases, evidence was manufactured or embroidered whatever the cost in order to void a marriage.[64] Lady Rochford may have willingly participated in the proceedings against Queen Anne on account of her own conservative religious beliefs and her kinship ties to the Howard family, which required that she support their candidate, Katherine Howard, in her rise to the queenship, but it cannot be known for certain and she probably had little choice in the matter.

As has been noted, 'sexual attraction was quite obviously important for the King to achieve the male heirs necessary to continue the Tudor dynasty'.[65] It is interesting in view of this that contemporary observers believed that the king had consummated his relationship with Katherine several months before she became queen.[66] It is probably unlikely that Henry enjoyed a sexual relationship with his wife's maiden before their marriage, for social customs and contemporary gender mores dictated that a maiden should guard her chastity and virginity and only yield it to her husband once married. That Henry was determined to ensure that Katherine's reputation remained intact can be seen by his decision to court her in the presence of her relatives, as he had done with both Anne Boleyn and Jane Seymour previously. Repulsed by his current wife's body, the king seems to have been strongly attracted to the 16-year-old Katherine because her bodily attributes signalled, in his eyes, that she was a virginal maiden who had yet to be initiated in sexual experiences. Since both the potency of men and the fertility of women were profound political concerns in early modern governments,[67] it is likely that Henry was convinced that Katherine, by virtue both of her age and her fertility, would provide a second male heir to safely establish the Tudor succession once and for all, where his fourth queen had failed. Reassured by her Howard relatives, Henry was convinced that Katherine was honourable by virtue of her modesty and chastity, namely because she was apparently unexperienced in sexual relations.[68] By contrast, Queen Anne was accused of preventing her husband from consummating the marriage, inciting his suspicion that she had never been his lawful wife. As had similarly occurred in the moves that led to the dissolution of the Aragon and Boleyn marriages, the king's fourth consort was entirely blamed for the non-consummation of the marriage, for contemporaries adhered to the accepted view that women were usually to blame for failures in conception and pregnancy.

Following her departure to Richmond, the queen was met by certain lords on 6 July who informed her that her marriage to Henry VIII 'was not lawfull', meaning that, in effect, the king was now once more a free man.[69] There was some confusion as to whether or not Anne actually agreed with the king that their marriage should be judged by Convocation, with the councillors later reporting that she had given her consent and was 'content always with your Majesty's [desires]', but the Cleves ambassador believed that she had never consented to such a request.[70] He reported that the queen suffered an emotional collapse when her consent to the proceedings of the annulment was required, allegedly protesting: 'She knew nothing other than that she had been granted the King as her husband, and thus she took him to be her true lord and husband', making 'such tears and bitter cries, it would break a heart of stone'.

Anne's reaction was entirely understandable, for the annulment of her marriage and the loss of her status as queen placed her in an ambiguous position. Denounced by her husband as physically repellent and believed to be the lawful wife of another man, it is extremely unlikely that Anne rejoiced at her new status, as some historians have suspected. Rather, both her position and reputation had been fatally undermined by Henry's rejection of her and the rumours of her pre-contract to the Duke of Lorraine effectively prevented her from remarrying, if she had been inclined to do so, by placing her sexual reputation in doubt. However, by 11 July Anne had sufficiently recovered to accept the settlement her former husband was prepared to grant her. Referring to Anne as his 'sister' in a letter written to her on 12 July, the king granted her an income of £4,000 per annum, which included the residences of Richmond, Bletchingley and Hever, and she was welcomed to visit court.[71] Scarcely more than two weeks later, Cromwell was executed on Tower Hill, stating in his execution speech that he died 'in the Catholicke faithe' and describing himself as 'a very wretche and miser' who deserved death, before submitting himself to death by the axe, wielded by 'a ragged and Boocherly miser'.[72]

Cromwell's execution was not the culmination of factional intrigues masterminded by the so-called Catholic faction, led by the Duke of Norfolk and Stephen Gardiner, bishop of Winchester, who allegedly manipulated the king into favouring their 'candidate' Katherine Howard and, consequently, influenced his decision to execute his chief minister for treason and heresy. Instead, Cromwell was most likely beheaded for two separate reasons. Firstly, his radical religious beliefs, which were demonstrated in his close correspondence with the German Lutheran princes, proved unacceptable to England's conservative king, who was consistently ruthless in stamping out heresy in his desire to maintain a form of Catholicism which was essentially traditional despite the break from Rome. Secondly, Cromwell served as a scapegoat for the embarrassing failure of the king's fourth marriage, since it is likely that Henry held his chief minister personally responsible for his failure to consummate the marriage, believing that he had been bewitched into marrying a woman who had been promised to another. As with his first two queens, Henry believed that other individuals were always to blame for his marital failures. Anne, whom he openly proclaimed to be physically repugnant and capable of rendering him impotent, experienced arguably a more positive fate by virtue of the annulment of her marriage, but the king's chief minister was not as lucky. Indeed, on the day Cromwell died, his king was to marry for the fifth time, believing that his new queen would, finally, resolve the disturbing problems that plagued the English succession once and for all.

6

QUEEN KATHERINE

ON 28 JULY 1540, the day of Cromwell's execution, the king married Katherine Howard as his fifth queen consort at the pleasant 'hunting-box' palace of Oatlands in Surrey, with Edmund Bonner, Bishop of London, officiating. In the course of making her vows, Katherine promised to 'take thee, Henry, to my wedded husband, to have and to hold from this day forward, for better for worse, for richer for poorer, in sickness and in health, to be bonair and buxom in bed and at board, till death us depart'.[1] Although the chroniclers Edward Hall and Charles Wriothesley both gave the wedding date as 8 August at Hampton Court, this was in fact the date on which Katherine's marriage was openly celebrated at court, with Katherine appearing as queen for the first time, thus signifying a marriage celebration, not the actual wedding day.[2] Hall stated that it was on 8 August that 'the Lady Katheryn Haward, nece to the duke of Norfolk, and daughter to the lord Edmond Haward, shewed openly as Quene at Hampton Court'.[3]

This confusion surely arose due to the secrecy with which the king had married for the fifth time. Only his foreign-born consorts – Katherine of Aragon and Anne of Cleves – were honoured with public weddings as a means of glorifying both the English commonwealth and the Tudor dynasty. The private, even secret, circumstances in which Henry VIII married Katherine were further reflected in the fact that some observers were of the opinion that the new queen was pregnant when she married the king. Marillac had opined on 21 July that Katherine was 'already *enceinte*', while John III of Portugal was informed several days later that the king had married 'an English lady, niece of the duke of Norfolk, daughter of his brother … she is already with child'.[4] Marillac believed that the king's new queen was not universally popular among the English people, who had greatly favoured Anne of

Cleves as 'the sweetest, most gracious queen they ever had or would desire'.[5] According to one later chronicler, the king's marriage to Katherine was celebrated with 'grand rejoicings' at court.[6] Certainly, a week after Katherine was publicly 'showed' as queen at Hampton Court, prayers were made in church for herself, the king and Prince Edward.[7] It has been erroneously asserted that a gold medallion was struck to commemorate the king's new marriage, in which Katherine was symbolised by a crowned rose and the initials KR (*Katerina Regina*).[8] Consequently, she has since been popularly immortalised as 'the rose without a thorn'. However, the gold medallion has no association with Katherine and has been dated to 1509–26. David Starkey proposed that the medallion's legend 'RVTILANS ROSA SIE SPIA' refers to Henry VIII as opposed to Katherine Howard or, indeed, any of his other wives.[9]

Since the eleventh century, it had been customary for the king's wife to be honoured with a coronation, either alongside her husband or more often alone. J.L. Laynesmith argued that 'the coronation was primarily concerned with the queen's role as an integral part of the king's public body'.[10] Some historians have indicated that, after neither Katherine of Aragon nor Anne Boleyn presented him with a surviving son, Henry VIII was reluctant to honour any of his subsequent wives with a coronation until they demonstrated that they had been divinely favoured by producing a male heir. However, the coronation was not merely 'a glorified fertility rite', for it publicly demonstrated the queen's unique role and offered the opportunity to express 'the widest variety of ideologies of queenship', while 'affirming the political structures of the realm, for affirming kingship'.[11]

It would be too simplistic, therefore, to argue that Henry refrained from crowning his last four wives solely on the basis of their successes in childbirth, but it is entirely possible that this overriding political and dynastic goal of the king did influence his decision as to whether or not to crown his consort. One might assume that Jane Seymour would have been honoured with a coronation had she survived the birth of Prince Edward in the autumn of 1537, but her unexpected death means that it remains uncertain whether a coronation for her would have taken place. Intriguingly, the French ambassador Marillac reported on 10 April 1541 that 'this Queen [Katherine] is thought to be with child, which would be a very great joy to this King, who, it seems, believes it, and intends, if it be found true, to have her crowned at Whitsuntide'.[12] Marillac could only have been repeating court rumours, none of which were necessarily truthful or even plausible. No other extant evidence indicates that Katherine's contemporaries suspected her to be pregnant in the months after her marriage to the king, but the ambassador's report is fascinating in indicating that, had she produced a son, Katherine would have been crowned by her grateful husband, perhaps in a drive to affirm both 'the political structures of the realm' and 'kingship', as Laynesmith wrote in her study of the fifteenth-century coronations of English consorts.

When she consented to Henry's proposal of marriage in the late spring or early summer of 1540, Katherine would have been aware that, as queen, she would spend varying periods of time in a range of castles, palaces and manors belonging to the Crown. Her marriage took place at Oatlands Palace in Surrey, a perhaps surprising choice in view of the fact that none of Henry VIII's other five weddings took place at that residence. The palaces most regularly visited by the king's court included Hampton Court, where Katherine was officially proclaimed queen for the first time in early August; Whitehall Palace; Greenwich Palace; and Windsor Castle. When the court departed on the northern progress in June 1541, Katherine also experienced the opportunity to visit a number of residences with which her predecessors had not been acquainted. These included Grimsthorpe Castle, the bishop's palace in Lincoln, Pontefract Castle and Chenies Manor House. Katherine also briefly visited Fotheringhay Castle in October 1541; the birthplace of Richard III in 1452, the castle would later become known as the execution site of Mary, Queen of Scots in 1587. As a niece of the Duke of Norfolk and attendant to Anne of Cleves, Katherine would have been acquainted with the grandeur and luxury of Tudor aristocratic residences, but her experiences of them changed immeasurably when she married the king in 1540 and became the first lady of the kingdom. The most lavish apartments were now hers, while custom and protocol dictated that her every wish was to be granted. The speed with which she was promoted from maiden to the rejected Anne of Cleves to Queen of England in Anne's place was nothing short of extraordinary.

Katherine's marriage represented a period of triumph for the Howard family, enabling them to attain positions of power not previously enjoyed since Anne Boleyn's heyday several years previously, although it would be incorrect to suggest that the Howards were ever wholly politically marginalised at court in the years prior to 1546, when the Duke of Norfolk and his son, the Earl of Surrey, provoked the wrath of Henry VIII. As with her cousin Anne Boleyn and her relatives Anne of York and Agnes, dowager Duchess of Norfolk, Katherine's experiences proved that Howard women were capable of playing, and were expected to play, essential roles within court politics as a means of bolstering and furthering the power and influence of the Howard family.[13]

Katherine's elder brother George became a gentleman of the king's privy chamber, in the same capacity as her distant cousin Thomas Culpeper, and by October 1540 he had been granted a pension of 100 marks in tail male, before receiving the manors of Berwick, Hulcott, North Newnton, Wiltshire and Wylye; later, in June 1541, he and his brother Charles were granted a licence to import 1,000 tons of Gascon wine and Toulouse woad.[14] George was described by the unknown Spanish chronicler as 'a gentleman-in-waiting', who earned a 'good' income, suggesting that his success was well known beyond the immediate confines of the court.[15] Charles Howard was appointed to the position of the king's spear, and was granted £100 while his half-sister Lady Baynton and her children were granted 100 marks.[16] Katherine's brother-in-law, Sir Edward Baynton, was also granted possession of the manor of Semleigh, while her female relatives occupied important positions within the queen's household.

The queen's household was headed by the Earl of Rutland as lord great chamberlain, Sir Thomas Dennys as chancellor, and Sir John Dudley as master of the horse. Katherine's great ladies included her cousin Mary Howard, Duchess of Richmond, who was also the former daughter-in-law of Henry VIII; her half-sister Isabel Baynton became a lady of the privy chamber alongside her cousin Lady Jane Rochford; while Howard relatives such as Margaret Arundell and Lady Dennys, the queen's cousin, served as gentlewomen attendants. Other highborn ladies such as the king's niece Lady Margaret Douglas, the Duchess of Suffolk, and the Countess of Rutland served the queen. The king's niece Frances Grey née Brandon did not reside in Katherine's household, but she may have visited court from time to time. On 25 August 1540, Frances delivered a second daughter, Katherine, at Bradgate Park. It seems probable that the baby was named after Henry's fifth queen, although it is unlikely that the queen acted as godmother to her namesake.[17] Katherine decided to promote several ladies whom she had known from her childhood, with Katherine Tylney and Margaret Morton among her chamberers.[18]

Why Katherine decided to appoint women who were aware of her pre-marital sexual liaisons to important and favoured positions within her household should be considered. The indictments later brought against her suspected that it was because they, as her friends and confidants, were needed by Katherine to help facilitate the queen's sexual encounters with gentlemen at court, including her past lovers. It is rather more likely that Katherine feared the consequences were she to refuse favour to those who knew the truth about her experiences in the years 1536–39. Probably, she believed that she could more successfully control and manage these women were she able to keep an eye on them at court. Her behaviour was not idiotic or dangerous, as some historians have traditionally assumed, for queen consorts were customarily expected to promote those within their households who had been close to them, either through kinship or friendship. Some two weeks before Katherine's marriage to the king, her old acquaintance Joan Bulmer, then residing in York, wrote to Katherine, promising 'her love for her' and declaring her misery because of her unhappy marriage and begging Katherine to provide assistance. Praising Katherine's 'perfect honesty' and promising 'unfeigned love that my hearth hath always borne towards you', she concluded hopefully that 'the quyne of Bretane wyll not forget her secretary'.[19]

It appears, however, that Katherine refused her former acquaintance's request. Most historians have assumed that Katherine agreed to Joan's desire for a position within her household, and granted her the office of chamberer. However, the lists for the queen's household name only four chamberers, none of whom were Joan Bulmer: Tylney, Morton, Friswith, Lufkyn.[20] Joan Bulmer, therefore, never served Katherine Howard, either as chamberer or in any other position. The lists for the queen's household make no mention of her, and she does not appear as a prominent witness in the later interrogations. In fact, in her letter to Katherine it is possible that Joan had not asked for a position within the queen's household but instead sought 'some room, the nearer her the better'. It appears that Joan was eager to escape her unhappy marriage and desired to depart for London where she could meet and converse with the new queen, perhaps to confide in the severe difficulties she was experiencing. Why Katherine may not have responded to Joan's letter is unknown. Possibly it was because of her own so-called illiteracy, which will later be discussed, but more probably it was because she felt that, days before she married the King of England, she should restrict the number of attendants appointed to serve her who had previously resided in the household of the dowager Duchess of Norfolk. On the other hand, perhaps Joan's husband refused her permission to meet with Katherine.

It cannot be doubted, as has been noted, that 'we still do not know enough about the position of the queen consort in England', which reflects 'the essential maleness of history'.[21] This is especially relevant in relation to Henry VIII's queens, for while those who made a notable impact both religiously and politically, namely the king's first two queens and to an extent his sixth consort, have left considerable evidence of their activities, patronage, and interests. However, the activities of Henry's later wives, who were married to the king for much shorter periods, are less well known. In contrast with the Renaissance humanism espoused by Katherine of Aragon based on her education, and the evangelical French humanism of Anne Boleyn, Katherine Howard is commonly thought to have been illiterate and entirely conventional in her religious beliefs.[22] Katherine of Aragon had been educated as a foreign princess; Anne Boleyn's father, as an influential courtier and diplomat, had successfully mobilised his talents and utilised his connections with the courts of Burgundy and France to ensure that his daughter received an education quite unique at that time for an English gentlewoman. By contrast, Katherine Howard's education – befitting her position – was more typical of her day, for it had never been envisaged at her birth that she might one day become a queen. Despite this, the king's fifth queen is often popularly assumed to have been frivolous, uneducated, and even stupid; in the words of one writer, she had 'little more than puppy fat for brains'.[23]

However, there is actually no evidence to support this claim – it is Katherine's alleged adulteries during her period as queen which lead most to assume that she lacked common sense or wisdom. As with Jane Seymour and Anne of Cleves, who were both married to Henry VIII for similarly short periods of time, there is very little extant documentation that sheds light on the true personality of the king's fifth queen. As will be discussed with regard to her later activities, it is more likely to have been Katherine's youth and inexperience at the Tudor court, rather than her alleged stupidity, which influenced her actions as queen. Without compelling evidence from the early period of her queenship to demonstrate her personal characteristics, it is surely both unfair and unwise for historians to characterise Katherine in a negative light. Thus the suggestion that her personality comprised 'wild hysteria and agonizing self-appraisals with haughty disdain and senseless cheerfulness' is not necessarily at all accurate, for surviving source material makes no mention of these supposed traits during the months of her marriage.[24]

It is difficult to form a rounded picture of Henry's new love from the extant sources. Tradition has suggested that she was spoiled, for as the unknown Spanish chronicler later commented, 'the King had no wife who made him spend so much money in dresses and jewels as she did, who every day had some fresh caprice'.[25] None of her contemporaries at court accused Katherine of pestering her husband to buy her jewellery, and it is questionable whether a 17-year-old newly married queen would have presumed to interfere in the expenditure of her much older and more financially experienced husband, or that she had any real control over it. Nonetheless, presumably on the basis of the chronicler's version of events, Weir believed that Katherine was 'a frivolous, empty-headed young girl who cared for little else but dancing and pretty clothes'.[26] Crawford similarly characterised her as 'a spoilt child' who cared for nothing but 'enjoying herself'.[27]

Unlike Anne Boleyn, who had resided at the courts of Burgundy and France and almost certainly served Queen Katherine prior to Henry VIII's courtship of her, and Jane Seymour who had similarly been in royal service for around seven years prior to Henry's flirtation, Katherine was inexperienced at the Tudor court, for it seems apparent that Henry had decided to marry her within months of their first meeting. Having served Anne of Cleves from the winter of 1539–40, at the time of her marriage in July 1540 the new queen had been at court for just seven or eight months. Furthermore, when she married the king she may not yet have been 17 years of age. Indeed, she was the youngest woman to become Queen of England since Margaret of Anjou almost a century earlier, in 1445.[28] Surrounded by knowledgeable and educated women within her household, most of whom were several years older than her, it is perhaps not going too far to suggest that Katherine may have been somewhat out of her depth when she became Queen of England. This reality is essential to bear in mind when considering her later activities as queen. This political context has too often been ignored in modern judgements of her character, in characterising her as stupid, greedy and reckless.

Like her predecessors, the new queen's image was almost certainly immortalised in portraits painted by the prominent court artists, although it is possible that there are now no extant portraits of Katherine. The French ambassador described Henry's new wife in the summer of 1540 as a lady of 'great beauty', but upon meeting her in September 1540 found her to be 'of moderate beauty, but of very attractive deportment, little and strong, of modest demeanour and mild countenance'.[29] He also added that she favoured French fashions and encouraged her ladies to follow her tastes in fashion, which is interesting in potentially shedding light on Katherine's portraiture in terms of the clothing that she would have worn when sitting for her portrait.[30] Certainly during her period as queen, it seems likely that Katherine would have been painted by the masterful Hans Holbein, who had created images of previous Tudor queens such as Jane Seymour and Anne of Cleves. However, whether any portraits of Katherine painted by Holbein survive today has been the subject of considerable controversy. In the nineteenth century, a portrait of a young woman around her twenty-first year was identified as Queen Katherine. As has been pointed out, at this time Holbein was in much favour with Henry VIII, making it likely that the king would have commissioned Holbein to paint his young queen.[31]

There are three extant versions of the portrait, housed today at the Toledo Museum of Art in Ohio, the National Portrait Gallery in London and at Hever Castle. In the portrait the sitter, probably under 21, wears a rich gown of black silk. There is some controversy as to whether this signifies that the sitter is a widow, and thus dressed in mourning apparel, or whether or not the black apparel actually portrays her high status and excellent lineage, for black was an extremely expensive dye during this period and, as such, only the wealthiest were entitled to wear it.[32] It is instructive that in most of her portraits (none of which were painted during her lifetime) Queen Anne Boleyn is attired in gowns of black.

On the basis that the sitter's attire signifies that she is a widow, and because of a supposed resemblance to Queen Jane, some historians have cautiously suggested that the image portrays Elizabeth Seymour, younger sister of Queen Jane, who was a widow in 1534 following the death of her first husband Sir Anthony Oughtred. However, there are some difficulties in accepting this identification; firstly, that Elizabeth's birth date is actually unknown and so it cannot be known for certain whether she was aged 20 or 21 in the mid 1530s, when she was widowed. Moreover, as Weir has suggested, it might have been considered extraordinary for a younger daughter of a mere knight (Sir John Seymour) to wear such extravagant costume, when she herself was relatively unknown in the mid 1530s before her elder sister rose to prominence, and it may seem unlikely that, given the proliferation of the image – three versions exist – the sitter was merely a maiden to Anne Boleyn. It is also doubtful whether or not the sitter really does resemble Jane Seymour, for her colouring, in particular, seems somewhat darker than that of Henry VIII's third queen.

That said, however, a strong case has been made for the portrait's re-identification as an image of Elizabeth Seymour, especially in view of her marriage to Thomas Cromwell's son in 1537. Elizabeth subsequently became a baroness when her husband was elevated to the peerage in December 1540. Thomas Cromwell himself may have commissioned the portrait between January and June 1540, prior to his arrest for treason. Indeed, it is entirely possible that the portrait was painted not after the death of Oughtred but actually shortly after his widow's remarriage to Gregory Cromwell in August 1537. Teri Fitzgerald and Diarmaid MacCulloch have recently drawn attention to the possibility that this group of portraits depicts Elizabeth Cromwell, wife of Gregory.[33]

Certainly it would seem problematic to identify the sitter as Queen Katherine Howard. A further issue is the sitter's age, for, as has been suggested in this study, the queen was aged 16 or 17 in 1540, and almost certainly never reached her twenty-first birthday. Because there are no extant descriptions of Katherine's physical appearance, aside from the French ambassador's brief report, it is impossible to determine whether Holbein's sitter shares the same physical features as the queen. The sitter wears a serious, thoughtful expression, suggesting a matronly propriety. Her hair appears to be reddish-brown, or auburn, with dark eyes, pale skin, a prominent nose and firm chin. The sitter sits with her hands clasped and the fingers interlaced, displaying lavish jewellery. She wears a French hood edged with white, embroidered in gold, with a black veil; a popular headdress which had become fashionable in England during the 1520s and later became erroneously associated with Anne Boleyn. By the late 1530s and early 1540s, the headdress began to be worn further and further back on the head until it required a strap worn beneath the chin to keep it in place, as evidenced in this particular portrait. The sleeves are adorned with gold embroidery, with rich cambric ruffles at the wrists. The sitter's jewellery is also noteworthy, for she wears a narrow necklace, clearly expensive, set with pearls and diamonds, with a large pendant jewel attached. She wears a brooch on her gown from which hangs a circular jewel, edged in gold, with a diamond prominent in the centre. This has intriguingly been suggested as a depiction of the story of Lot's wife and the flight of Lot from Sodom.[34] Yet 'it is strange that Catherine Howard should have selected so ominous a subject, so suggestive of the frailty and irresolution of the female mind'.[35] As noted previously, other versions of the portrait exist, with a copy housed in the National Portrait Gallery which dates from after 1612 and was purchased in 1898. Another version sits at Hever Castle, and was recently identified by David Starkey as a portrait of Katherine Howard on the basis of the sitter's jewellery and expensive costume.

Certainly Katherine was well known for the jewellery that she enjoyed as queen. Indeed, the author of *The Chronicle of Henry VIII of England* subsequently remembered her as the 'wife who made him [the King] spend so much in dresses and jewels … who every day had some fresh caprice'.[36] At New Year 1540–41, the queen was presented with a 'square containing 27 table diamonds and 26 clusters of pearls', a brooch constructed of 33 diamonds and 60 rubies with an edge of pearl, and a 'muffler of black velvet furred with sables containing 38 rubies and 572 pearls'.[37] At the time of her downfall Katherine's jewellery was delivered to Anne Herbert, sister of the queen's successor Katherine Parr. During her period as queen Katherine owned, doubtless among other luxurious items, an 'upper habiliment of goldsmith's work enamelled and garnished with vij. Fair diamonds, vij. Fair rubies and vij. Fair pearls'; 'an upper habiliment containing eight diamonds and seven rubies'; a 'carcane for the neck, of goldsmith's work, wherein is set in gold vj. very fair table diamonds, and v. very fair rubies, and betwixt every of the same stones is two fair pearls containing in the whole xxiiij'; a 'collar' of sixteen diamonds; two 'laces' of 'xxvij fair table diamonds and clviij fair pearls'; 'a rope of fair large pearl containing cc pearls'; 'one fair brooch of gold enamelled with white having a border of antique boys about the same, with a very fair square diamond holden by a man whose coat and boots are enamelled with blue, and a king, crowned, with a sceptre in his hand at th'one end thereof'; 'a gold brooch with 35 small diamonds and 18 rubies with three persons and two horses in the same being the story of Noye'; 'a Jesus of gold containing xxxij diamonds having three pearls hanging at the same'; seventeen girdles of gold; twenty-three pairs of beads; eight chains of gold; tablets of gold – the sheer amount of expensive jewellery that Katherine enjoyed is incredible. She also made presents of jewellery to her ladies, including to both of the king's daughters and his niece Lady Margaret Douglas.[38]

In view of Katherine's inventory, it has subsequently been theorised that the sitter in Holbein's portrait must be the queen. However there are noteworthy issues with this identification, namely the sitter's age and her appearance. According to the French ambassador, who met Katherine in the autumn of 1540, the new queen was 'small and slender', even 'very diminutive', whereas Holbein's sitter does not necessarily appear to have been either small or slender. Katherine's beauty was also consistently remarked upon by her contemporaries, with the court observer William Thomas for example describing her as 'a very beautiful gentlewoman'.[39] George Cavendish also repeated Katherine's 'beawtie' in his *Metrical Visions*.[40] It might be questioned whether Holbein's sitter in this portrait can be called 'beautiful', which might further call into question whether the sitter actually is Katherine, although of course it is nonetheless true that early modern standards of beauty differed significantly from those prevalent in the modern West. Holbein's sitter wears a matronly, serious expression, and may appear worn and tired. Although the lavish costume and expensive jewellery certainly indicate that the sitter was well-born, possibly royal, it may not necessarily represent Queen Katherine. If the portrait dates from the late 1530s rather than the early 1540s, it is possible that it depicts a different royal woman, for during this period there were four other royal women at Henry VIII's court, all of whom could have been the sitter in this portrait. These women were Mary Tudor, daughter of Henry VIII and aged 20 in 1536–37; Lady Margaret Douglas, niece of Henry VIII and aged 20 in 1535–36; Frances Brandon, niece of Henry VIII and aged 20 in 1537–38; and her younger sister Eleanor, aged 20 in 1539–40. It is perhaps noteworthy that Holbein's portrait was originally identified as a portrait of Eleanor Brandon, Countess of Cumberland, and later as Mary Tudor.[41]

It is also interesting that the portrait was found in the collection of the Cromwell family.[42] Although Katherine herself may not personally have played a prominent role in Thomas Cromwell's downfall, it would have been extraordinary for the Cromwell family to have owned a portrait of the woman associated most closely with his downfall and execution, especially in terms of her Catholic beliefs which would have been unacceptable to the reformist Cromwell family. If one takes this further, not only may the sitter have had some connection with the Cromwells, but her religious beliefs were perhaps reformed or evangelical in nature, for Thomas Cromwell was associated with the suppression of medieval Catholicism within England and thus it may seem highly unlikely that his family would have retained a portrait of a Catholic sitter in an era of conflict between traditionalists and evangelicals. If this thinking is correct, then Katherine Howard must logically be ruled out as the sitter in view of several points: her age; her religious beliefs; her appearance; and the dating of the portrait.

It is likely that this portrait, which survives also in later copies, was painted between 1535 and 1540. At that particular point the fortunes of the Lady Mary were uneven, for while she had been in disgrace during Anne Boleyn's period as queen, she had later been restored to her father's favour during his marriage to Jane Seymour and later to Anne of Cleves. Because she spent much greater time at court in 1536–37, it is possible that Mary is indeed the sitter in Holbein's portrait. However, the sitter's features do not square with what is known of Mary's appearance, whose portraits evidence much paler skin, grey eyes, compressed lips, a high forehead, golden hair and a delicate frame.[43] Her Catholic faith and her uneasy relationship with Thomas Cromwell also call into doubt her likelihood as the sitter. More pertinently, there is also no record that a portrait by Holbein was commissioned for Mary during these years.

It is likelier that the sitter could be Margaret Douglas, niece of Henry VIII and later Countess of Lennox. Reported in 1534 to be 'beautiful and highly esteemed', the king's niece is believed to have had 'heavy-lidded, deep-set eyes, a long nose, broad jaw, and fairly thin lips', features evident in Holbein's portrait.[44] Aged 20 in 1535–36, she enjoyed good relations with Queen Anne and became engaged to Thomas Howard, uncle of the queen, in the spring of 1536. However, the king was furious when he learned of his niece's engagement, and imprisoned both Howard and Margaret in the Tower of London. Margaret was only released on 29 October 1537. It is intriguing, in light of this discussion, that Margaret reputedly offered Howard a miniature portrait of herself during their courtship. She also appears to have enjoyed a courteous relationship with Cromwell, for she referred to herself as 'her that has her trust in you' in a letter written to him in June 1537 in which she abandoned Howard. She promised to 'pray our Lord to preserve you both soul and body'.[45] However, the issue of her faith might call into question whether the Cromwells would have owned a portrait of a Catholic member of the royal family; although it is possible, since she was the grandmother of the Protestant king James I of England, that she was associated with the Protestant and Stuart dynastic cause. Alternatively, the portrait may represent one of the Brandon sisters, who were prominent at court in the late 1530s; in Frances's case, her status as mother of the Protestant queen Lady Jane Grey might have made an image of her an attractive gift for the Cromwell family.

It is therefore extremely unlikely that Holbein's portrait of this young woman aged in her twenty-first year depicts Katherine, for although the splendid jewellery could support her candidacy as the sitter, it should be taken into account that other royal women, including the king's daughters and nieces, were entitled to wear expensive items of jewellery, making it arguably more likely that the sitter is one of Henry VIII's three nieces at court in the 1530s: Margaret Douglas, Frances Brandon or Eleanor Brandon. Gareth Russell has recently suggested that the portrait may depict Frances Brandon or Mary Tudor, eldest daughter of Henry VIII.[46] There was, after all, no queen consort in the period from October 1537 to January 1540. Alternatively, interesting arguments have been offered for the sitter's identification as Elizabeth Cromwell, and the portrait may have been commissioned in 1537 shortly after she married Gregory.

More conventionally, a miniature by Holbein in the Royal Collection at Windsor has usually been identified as a portrait of Queen Katherine, perhaps painted during her first winter as queen. A second version exists in the collection of the Duke of Buccleuch. Most of the queen's biographers have accepted it as a likeness of her. Starkey confidently asserted that, on the basis of the sitter's jewellery and costume, 'the picture is of her [Katherine]. It can even be dated as a wedding portrait.'[47] By the mid nineteenth century, the sitter had been identified as Henry's fifth queen but may not have been viewed as such before the eighteenth century. Painted watercolour on vellum, the portrait measures 6.3cm in height. The earliest reference to the portrait miniature in the Royal Collection dates from the Restoration of 1660–61, when it may have been identified as 'a small peice Inclineing of a woman after ye Dresse of Henry ye Eightes wife by Peter Oliver'. The version owned by Buccleuch can be traced back to Thomas Howard, Earl of Arundel, in whose collection it was engraved by Wenceslaus Hollar as unnamed. Yet in neither case was Katherine Howard identified as the portrait's sitter. The fact that the portrait in the Buccleuch Collection was owned by Thomas Howard, a descendant of Queen Katherine, could lend support to the fact that the sitter was a Howard and, perhaps, the queen herself.

However, as with Holbein's portrait of a woman in her twenty-first year formerly identified as Katherine Howard, there is no conclusive evidence that Katherine is indeed the sitter, despite Starkey's interpretation. Although the sitter's jewellery indicates a royal status by virtue of the fact that the large ruby, emerald and pearl jewel which she wears appears to be the same as that worn by Jane Seymour in her portrait painted by Holbein, this does not necessarily prove that the sitter is Jane's successor as queen. Queen Jane is known to have made gifts of jewellery to her ladies-in-waiting, including Mary, Lady Monteagle (*c.*1510–40/44), whom some have suggested is a possible candidate for the miniature under discussion because of the sitter's alleged resemblance with authenticated portraits of Mary.

More possibly the sitter could be Lady Margaret Douglas, niece of Henry VIII and daughter of Margaret Tudor, queen consort of Scotland. Viewed 'as an important prize on the international marriage market', Lady Margaret was involved in the autumn of 1538 in a series of prospective marriage alliances proposed by her uncle the king to Emperor Charles V, in an attempt to secure the emperor's friendship against François of France. Reported to be 'beautiful and esteemed', the features of the sitter in the miniature are strikingly similar to those of a portrait of Margaret as Countess of Lennox (*c.* 1572), including a prominent nose, thin lips and heavy-lidded eyes.[48] The sitter's costume indicates that the portrait may have been painted in the autumn or winter; Margaret may have sat for this miniature in October 1538 during negotiations for a European marriage alliance. Moreover Queen Jane herself had made gifts of jewellery to Margaret, which would account for why that lady may have worn the queen's own jewels in a portrait miniature. In Greek, 'margarite' or Margaret can be translated as 'pearl'.[49]

While the portrait was originally owned by the Howards as the Earls of Arundel, it is uncertain whether the Howard family retained portraits of the ill-fated Katherine for in the wake of her execution, as with Anne Boleyn, they hastily dissociated themselves from Katherine and logically would have destroyed or hidden any images of the queen which they had once proudly owned. The Duke of Norfolk was to remember his niece as 'ungrateful' and declared that Katherine should be burnt at the stake, and if his attitude was representative of the feelings of his relatives it would seem unlikely that they would have desired to continue housing portraits of Katherine, especially since several Howards had been imprisoned and harshly punished on her account. By contrast, a portrait of Margaret may have been a more desirable gift to own. There is extant evidence to indicate her good relations and intimacy with the Howard family, namely in her love affairs with Thomas and Charles Howard. Margaret's closeness to the English throne, her royal connections and her beauty and charm would have made a portrait of her a worthy possession of any noble English family. More importantly, Margaret was of course the grandmother of the first Stuart King of England, James I. In terms of physical appearance, the features of the sitter in the portrait miniature may not be easily reconciled with what is known of Katherine's appearance or figure, who was reported to be 'slender' rather than plump. The queen's hair may also have been golden in colour, rather than auburn, if the figure of the Queen of Sheba in the window of King's College Chapel at Cambridge can be viewed as a possible likeness of Katherine, as some historians have argued.[50] It is impossible to conclude whether the Holbein miniature depicts Queen Katherine, Lady Margaret Douglas or another lady entirely, but in the absence of definitive evidence to support the Margaret Douglas identification, it can be speculated that the portrait does depict Katherine and may have been painted in 1540–41.

Housed in the Metropolitan Museum of Art in New York is a portrait also painted by Hans Holbein that may well depict Queen Katherine. Dating from *c.* 1540–45, the portrait was painted oil on wood, measuring 28.3 by 23.2cm, and was acquired from the Jules Bache Collection in 1949, having been housed originally by Prince Joseph Poniatowski and held in Vienna until at least the mid 1920s. It is noteworthy that this young woman is aged ANNO ETATIS SVAE XVII, 'in her seventeenth year', which was almost certainly Katherine's age in 1540–41 during her period as queen. The sitter wears a rich gown of black lined with pearls and gold along the breast, with slashed red sleeves, gold embroidered cuffs, and a brooch of gold hanging from the breast set with what appears to be a mythological or classical image. She wears a gold necklace set with diamonds and three pearls; her French hood is embroidered with gold, trimmed in red and set with precious gold stones. The costume and headdress are probably French, which is interesting in view of the fact that Katherine was reported to favour French costume during her period as queen.[51] The sitter's complexion is rosy, with sensuous red lips, a prominent nose, red-gold hair and blue eyes.

The portrait was first suggested by G.F. Waagen in his *Die vornehmsten Kunstdenkmäler in Wien* (Vienna, 1866, pp. 336–37) as a representation of an English lady, later confirmed by Paul Ganz in *Hans Holbein d. J.: Des Meisters Gemälde* (Stuttgart, 1912, p. 245) as a portrait of an English lady dating from 1540. *Duveen Pictures in Public Collections of America* (New York, 1941, no. 222) intriguingly suggested that the costume of the sitter indicated that it was painted during Katherine's time as queen (1540–42). Possibly, as Ganz suggested, both the locket and the gold setting for the cameo were designed by Holbein himself, perhaps, if the sitter was Katherine, as a gift for the new queen. More importantly, Susan E. James and Jamie S. Franco in 'Susanna Horenbout, Levina Teerlinc and the Mask of Royalty' (*Jaarboek Koninklijk Museum voor Schone Kunsten Antwerpen*, 2000, p. 124), identified the sitter as Katherine Howard based on a supposed resemblance with another portrait painted by Levina Teerlinc.

As Starkey suggested, 'it would be unusual for someone [of evident youth] to sit for a miniature unless they had very high status'.[52] While the New York portrait is not a miniature, that does not take away from the fact that the sitter was evidently of high status to have been painted in the first place, especially when dressed in such lavish costume. If this portrait was painted during Katherine's queenship, it seems highly possible that it does represent her for there were no other royal women who could plausibly be identified as candidates for the identity of the sitter. The four previously mentioned royal women were significantly older than 16 or 17 in 1540–41: Mary Tudor was 24, Margaret Douglas 25, Frances Brandon 23 and Eleanor Brandon 21. The rich costume and expensive jewellery indicate that the sitter cannot have been a maiden or a lady-in-waiting, but in view of the fact that the new queen was reported to enjoy wearing French fashions, coupled with what is known of her detailed jewellery inventory, it is probable if not certain that the sitter is indeed Katherine, as suggested by Susan James and later Gareth Russell.[53]

This view is strengthened by the fact that Katherine was almost certainly born in 1523 or early in 1524, which would have made her 16 in 1540–41, and because of a mooted resemblance with a speculative engraving of the queen created by Francesco Bartolozzi after Hans Holbein the Younger. Apart from sitting in a strikingly similar position, both sitters have reddish-gold hair, pale skin, blue eyes, sensuous lips and a small neck. Holbein's image confirms reports of Katherine's appearance as beautiful, graceful and elegant. It also establishes that her appearance conformed to contemporary expectations of female beauty.

If the portrait does represent Katherine, then it must have been executed between July 1540, when she married Henry VIII, and October 1541, the latest possible date in view of the investigation into her sexual liaisons the following month. The suggestion seems to be that the sitter, whoever she was, was 16 but nearing her seventeenth birthday at the time of composition. If it is a likeness of Katherine, and it remains uncertain, then it would seem to indicate that she was born between July 1523 and October 1524, but it is difficult to know with certainty because the sitter remains unidentified. Further thoughts on the possible implications of the painting for Katherine's date of birth can be read in Appendix II. It is worth noting, however, that 'Catherine left no documentary proof that her portrait was ever painted during her lifetime, and, perhaps, we are searching for the impossible'.[54]

Although the tentative – and uncertain – identification of the New York portrait might allow us to perceive Katherine's possible appearance, her actual personality and characteristics are somewhat more difficult to determine. Surviving source material, preserved mainly by English chroniclers and foreign ambassadors at the king's court, contains little in relation to the queen aside from references to the splendid court ceremonies in which she played her part as well as, inevitably, the manner of her downfall. All that we know of her, especially with regard to her life before she married the king, is contained mostly in the legal documents compiled by the interrogators in the autumn of 1541 when she was accused of treason. The ambassadors at court were mostly uninterested in documenting Katherine as a private individual, although they did record gossip and rumour that circulated about her supposed pregnancies, for example. Unsurprisingly, writers who have utilised this mostly fragmentary material to theorise what Henry VIII's fifth queen must have personally been like have concluded that she was a 'juvenile delinquent';[55] 'an empty-headed wanton';[56] even, 'a natural tart who knew exactly what she was doing'.[57] One rather unfairly compared Katherine with her predecessor and cousin Anne Boleyn: 'Katherine Howard, another royal wife to die on adultery charges, mattered only a little longer than it took Henry to cheer up after he had her beheaded; by contrast, Anne triggered the English Reformation.'[58]

In the absence of extensive documentary evidence, it is understandable that historians have tended to speculate about Katherine's personality and motives, but it would seem logical to be upfront about the fact that such judgements are speculation and are not always supported by the extant record. The details recorded in the interrogations of 1541 remain open to interpretation and it is often uncertain whether – and to what degree – the details contained within them can be corroborated. The councillors who interrogated the queen and members of her household may have played on contemporary gender mores – not necessarily misogyny – in, for example, assuming that women were naturally prone to transgression and prone to entrapping men in sexual encounters, which may have assisted their largely negative construction of Katherine's life prior to her marriage.

It goes without saying that great care is needed in analysing these documents, especially with a view to forming a realistic picture of Katherine as an individual. It also seems excessively harsh to condemn her as selfish and greedy when her husband lavished jewellery and clothing upon her, while it also seems unfair to slander her as 'empty-headed' or stupid merely because she was not as educated as her cousin Anne Boleyn was. Rather, it would seem more realistic to view her as inexperienced at court, while her education was entirely representative of that customarily offered to early sixteenth-century gentlewomen. Jane Seymour, moreover, has never been criticised for her alleged stupidity, although the Spanish ambassador did note that she was said to show little wit.

When she became Queen of England in 1540, Katherine would have appreciated that she was now expected to devise a model of queenship, as her predecessors had done before her with varying degrees of success, which sought to honour her husband and glorify his ruling dynasty. In formulating her queenship, Katherine was required to negotiate early modern gender mores that featured culturally embedded perceptions of women, the inferior sex, as chaste, subservient, silent and unquestioningly accepting of male authority. Katherine's status as queen did not exempt her from these early modern gender codes, for as the wife of the king she was expected to visibly and publicly defer to her husband, the ruler of the kingdom, in all matters, whether ceremonial, political or religious. To act contrarily to these prescriptions was to risk upsetting not only the established framework of gender expectations but also the firmly established model of the 'body politic', in which all subjects within the kingdom were required to play a vital role in ensuring stability within the realm.

Early modern gender expectations were filtered and practised at court through the prism of ceremony, religious custom and political action. Women of all social ranks were expected to verbally express their inferior status using the 'rhetoric of submission'.[59] Contemporaries proclaimed women's inferior status in the form of constant reminders not to challenge the divinely ordained nature of that inferiority. In 1549, Sir John Cheke instructed Penelope Pie: 'Remember that as justice and fortitude are the more proper virtues of men, and the greater shame for men to lack them; so chastity, shamefacedness, and temperance are the more particular virtues of women, and the greater shame for women to offend therein.'[60] Undoubtedly, as the model of idealised womanhood, the queen consort was expected to actively uphold the virtues of 'chastity, shamefacedness, and temperance' favoured by Cheke in her interactions and activities at court. To act otherwise was to dishonour her husband and lord. Nevertheless, Henry VIII permitted his consorts to exercise religious and political influence, in the sphere of intercession, for example, as long as they did not overstep the – occasionally blurred – boundaries of sixteenth-century gender expectations. Thus, the Spanish ambassador recorded that Katherine 'took occasion and courage to beg and entreat the King for the release' of the poet and diplomat Thomas Wyatt in the spring of 1541, 'a prisoner in the said Tower [of London], which petition the King granted'.[61] The queen also subsequently and successfully pleaded for John Wallop, who had been detained for 'having said something in favour of Pope Paul'.[62]

In her intercessionary activities, Katherine behaved as a conventional and model queen consort. Intercession had emerged as an idealised queenly activity in the early Middle Ages, and originated from the consort's desire to emulate the heavenly intercessor, the Virgin Mary, Queen of Heaven. As Retha Warnicke noted, 'the intercession could well be interpreted as a tool for supporting the concept of patriarchal supremacy and the queen's subordination'.[63] Katherine of Aragon, Anne Boleyn and Jane Seymour had all attempted to fulfil the queenly role of intercessor on a number of occasions, with significantly varying degrees of success depending on the religious and political context in which they attempted to act. When she became Queen of England in 1536, it was sincerely hoped by supporters of the Lady Mary, Henry VIII's firstborn daughter, that Jane Seymour would seek Mary's restoration to royal favour by interceding with the king on her behalf. The Spanish ambassador Chapuys explained that 'she [Jane] was continually trying to persuade the King, her father, to restore the Princess [Mary] to his favor, as she formerly was', and the queen apparently promised Chapuys that 'she would work in earnest to deserve the honorable name which I had given her of pacificator'.[64]

It would be inaccurate to perceive Jane as the driving force behind Mary's restoration to court as a public symbol of her father's restored favour, however. As Henry's response to Jane's intercession on behalf of Mary in May 1536 (see below) demonstrated, the king was firmly in the driving seat when it came to the treatment of his eldest daughter, and only when she publicly proclaimed her submission to her father's policies was she permitted to return to court. According to custom, the king granted his queen's requests of intercession when they chimed with his political and religious interests within the context in which they were made, but if these requests were inappropriate or even hostile to those interests, he actively refused to grant them. Henry's hostile reaction to Jane's attempted intercession in the autumn of 1536 on the behalf of the dissolved abbeys, which had provoked rebellion in the north of England, can be understand within this context of royal intercessions:

> The Queen threw herself on her knees before the King and begged him to restore the abbeys, but he told her, prudently enough, to get up, and he had often told her not to meddle in his affairs, referring to the late Queen [Anne Boleyn], which was enough to frighten a woman who is not very secure.[65]

Henry had already demonstrated that he would vocally refuse to grant the intercessions of his consort if they did not suit his current political or religious interests. On the day of Anne Boleyn's execution, Chapuys recorded that Jane had at an unknown date 'suggested that the Princess [Mary] should be replaced in her former position; and the King told her she was a fool, and ought to solicit the advancement of the children they would have between them, and not any others'.[66] When he married Jane in May 1536, the king was fixated on siring what he perceived as a legitimate male heir to secure the continuation of the Tudor dynasty. In this context, Jane's intercession on the behalf of Henry's intransigent eldest daughter was foolish, especially since the king never wavered from his belief that the marriage to Katherine of Aragon had been unlawful and offensive to God.

Unlike Jane Seymour, there is no evidence that Katherine Howard ever attempted to intercede in matters that ran the risk of offending her husband.

It is likely that the king was aware in advance of her acts that she would publicly intercede for individuals such as Thomas Wyatt and John Wallop, but in graciously agreeing to pardon these offenders Henry was positively portrayed as a merciful and benevolent prince, while the generosity of his queen further glorified the ruling dynasty. Katherine's effectiveness in her albeit limited activities as an intercessor strengthened her suitability as queen consort, especially when coupled with her much-praised involvement in the extensive ceremonies of the court, perhaps evidenced most visibly during the northern progress of 1541.

Historians who have contrasted Katherine negatively with her older and more experienced queenly predecessors, especially in condemning Katherine for being a supposedly ineffective consort as she was apparently more concerned with the style as opposed to the substance of early modern queenship, have neglected to consider the possibility that Henry's own desires had changed regarding the style and performance of his consort's queenship. His responses to Jane Seymour's attempted political activities in the second half of 1536 surely indicate that, after his unsuccessful unions to the politically and religiously vocal Katherine of Aragon and Anne Boleyn, Henry was no longer interested in a queen who actively and publicly stepped outside of her demarcated sphere. Indeed, when he married Katherine Howard in 1540, Henry was surely desirous that his queen would primarily perform her expected function – childbearing – and only involve herself in the queenly functions of intercession and patronage as a secondary concern to her role as mother. Moreover, her contemporaries' responses indicate that Katherine undoubtedly conformed, at least outwardly, to early modern gender expectations, which surely attracted Henry to her in the first place. Lauren Mackay has convincingly noted that 'Henry's intention was to mould Catherine into the ideal Tudor queen, something that had eluded him for a number of years'.[67] This is the context in which Katherine's political activities should be interpreted, and it is unfortunate that so many historians have neglected to analyse the extant evidence within this context with a sensitivity to Henry VIII's changing perceptions and expectations of queenship in the early 1540s.

According to court observers, the summer of 1540 was the hottest in living memory, 'so that no raine fell from June till eight daies after Michaelmas', leading to 'sicknes among the people' and the deaths of cattle.[68] At court, following her marriage, the queen's family were in high favour with their monarch, and the Duke of Norfolk must surely have congratulated his niece on her personal success while emphasising to her the necessity of producing a male heir, for although Prince Edward was generally healthy a 'spare' was always necessary to fully safeguard against dynastic troubles which had plagued England intermittently since the mid fifteenth century. This had been made clear in 1502 when Arthur, heir of Henry VII, died suddenly at Ludlow Castle less than six months after his marriage to Katherine of Aragon. Only Katherine Howard herself knew whether her royal husband was physically able of fathering another son, for rumours had swirled since at least the time of his marriage to Anne Boleyn that the king was actually unable to perform sexually and his previous queens had been accused of rendering him impotent, thus reinforcing contemporary understandings which believed that women were capable of bewitching men and preventing them from fulfilling their sexual and reproductive duties.

Following the king's fifth marriage, he shortly afterwards set out on progress with his new queen, for he was eager to display her to his subjects in order to show off her beauty, youth and, most importantly in his eyes, her virtue. On 22 August, exactly two weeks after Katherine was first presented as queen to the court at Hampton Court, the royal couple departed from Windsor Castle to Reading, before travelling to Ewelm, Rycott, Notley, Buckingham, and Grafton (associated with the family of Elizabeth Woodville). In September, the court journeyed to Ampthill and to the More in Hertfordshire, the former residence of Cardinal Wolsey and later Katherine of Aragon.

The exact details of how Katherine and her new husband spent their time at these residences is unknown, but the French ambassador reported that there was nothing to speak of at court 'but the chase and the banquets to the new Queen'.[69] Henry appears to have been entirely besotted with his new wife. Although he was undoubtedly enchanted by her beauty, her youth and her pleasing personality, it was almost certainly her apparent fertility which demonstrated in his eyes her suitability as his consort. Her mother had given birth to at least ten children, six of whom had been fathered by Edmund Howard, and the king was surely well aware that three of those children were sons. Marillac confirmed Henry's love for the queen when he attended the court on progress: 'The new Queen has completely acquired the King's Grace and the other [Anne of Cleves] is no more spoken of than if she were dead.'[70] He also stated that the king caressed her openly more than he had his other queens.

Despite this marital happiness, damaging rumours about the queen had already begun to surface, threatening both her personal and political security months into her marriage. While the court was at residence in Grafton in late August, a Windsor priest had allegedly 'spoken unfitting words of the Queen's Grace, questioning her moral integrity'.[71] The exact circumstances that provoked this criticism remain unknown, but the likeliest of explanations is closely associated with the events of June 1540, when the king first openly demonstrated his love for Katherine and his desire to marry her while still married to Anne of Cleves. Citizens observed their monarch openly travelling to the residence of Bishop Gardiner to meet with his new love, and concluded that adultery was taking place to the dishonour of Queen Anne. Probably, therefore, the Windsor priest spoke openly against the queen because he believed that she had, through her beauty and charm, encouraged the king to commit adultery with her while still married to his fourth wife. Of course, his behaviour might be construed as conventional of early modern male observers, who believed that women were usually responsible for instigating sexual liaisons. There is no evidence to suggest that this priest was aware personally of the new queen's pre-marital liaisons, but it does indicate the dangers that the queen consort could find herself in if her sexual reputation was thought to be questionable.

It is interesting, however, to speculate that Francis Dereham may have had some connection with the affair. Following Katherine's appearance at court, Dereham had apparently vanished from the scene, leading her step-grandmother the dowager duchess to speculate as to his whereabouts. When she asked Katherine, she was informed that Katherine had no knowledge as to his whereabouts.[72] Despite the king's passion and his marriage to Katherine, Dereham commented at this time that, were the king to die, he believed he might still marry Katherine. If his remarks had been made public, and observers such as the Windsor priest had become aware of them, it might have been concluded that the new queen was unfit for her position since rumours linked her with the sexual and romantic attentions of other men. More simply, slandering powerful women through the use of sexual insults such as 'whore' was a common practice in early modern Europe that was utilised for political and religious reasons, namely to damage their reputations and that of their husbands irretrievably. If the Windsor priest was hostile to the Howards he could have sought to damage the queen's reputation by spitefully questioning her moral integrity.

How this gossip personally affected Katherine is unknown, but it is likely that both she and her family were perturbed if not overly concerned, since the position of the queen consort was expected to be safeguarded from any type of scandal, whether sexual or political. It also cast doubt on the king's honour, for as the author of the *Court of Good Counsell* (1607) noted, there was 'no greater plague [or] torment' than an 'untoward, wicked and dishonest wife'. Undoubtedly, women were believed to 'confirm' male honour and, if they were then associated with promiscuity and scandal, this damaged the reputation of their husbands.[73] Norfolk himself may have been greatly concerned, for without knowledge as to his niece's childhood it was probably the first time he had been acquainted with a connection between his niece and sexual immorality, whatever the degree of her blamelessness or otherwise.[74]

Although the matter was quickly dealt with, since the Windsor priest was warned to remain within his diocese and be 'more temperate in the use of his tongue', the slander upon her honour must have brought home to Queen Katherine the necessity of maintaining a modest and chaste appearance and the need for her past to be irrevocably forgotten. In an age in which powerful women were vulnerable to slander through the medium of sexual insults by those who opposed them for religious, political or dynastic reasons, Katherine's position as queen remained insecure and fragile. Only by bearing the longed-for second male heir would she survive as Henry's fifth queen consort.

7

QUEENSHIP, 1540–41

FROM HER MARRIAGE TO the king in July 1540, Katherine Howard was well aware that, amid the luxury and splendour of the court, political and religious rivals surrounded her and were eager to utilise scandalous gossip against her for their own advantages, in an age in which female consorts were vulnerable to accusations of promiscuity and misbehaviour as the downfall of Anne Boleyn in 1536 had so salaciously demonstrated. It was essential for Katherine to bear the king a second surviving son, for while only one prince lived the English succession would always remain somewhat uncertain should that prince suddenly die, as had happened in 1502 with Prince Arthur. Moreover, the man whom Katherine had married was intensely focused on ensuring the continuation of his dynasty and was hopeful that it would be destined for long-term success and glory well after his own death. In light of this, the brutal downfall of Anne Boleyn and the humiliating dismissal of Anne of Cleves made sense from Henry's perspective, for a fertile bride was essential in order to provide a satisfactory solution to the uncertainty that surrounded the future of the Tudor dynasty. Already in 1532 the king had lamented that 'I am forty-one years old, at which age the lust of man is not so quick as in lusty youth'.[1] His personal insecurities were evident in an insistent response to the imperial ambassador in 1533, when questioned as to whether or not he could sire a son with his new queen: 'Am I not a man like other men? Am I not? Am I not?'[2] In light of her predecessor's uncomfortable experiences and dismissal, after her virginity had been publicly questioned, Katherine cannot have failed to have been aware of the pressing expectations she faced regarding her duty to provide a second male heir following her marriage as Henry's queen.

Although the rumours alleging that the new queen was pregnant in the summer of 1540 turned out to be false, Katherine was acquainted with the

Tudor dynasty in a different form through her relations with Henry's three surviving children by his first three marriages. It is likely that of Henry's three children it was the Lady Mary, daughter of Katherine of Aragon, with whom the new queen first became acquainted, according to court reports and in view of Mary's own residence within the court. Following the downfall of Anne Boleyn, Mary had been pressured to agree with her father that her parents' marriage was invalid and consequently had been restored to favour, residing at court where she enjoyed amicable relations with Queen Jane. She had served as godmother at the christening of Prince Edward and her father took steps to negotiate a series of prospective marriage alliances with European princes, all of which ultimately came to nothing. The downfall and disgrace of the family of Mary's former governess, Margaret Pole, in 1538–39 personally endangered Mary's security, for she was regarded by some as a plausible heir to her father's throne and her dynastic status remained suspect.[3] Despite this, her position at court remained secure and she probably personally greeted Queen Katherine shortly after her new marriage. Most modern historians, however, have characterised relations between the two women as difficult, if not openly hostile.[4] At Christmas 1540 the Spanish ambassador, who had enjoyed a warm relationship with Mary for much of the preceding decade, reported that the queen sought to remove two of Mary's maids as punishment for her failure to treat Katherine with the same respect she had shown Jane Seymour and Anne of Cleves. Chapuys remained positive, however, stating that Mary had 'found means to conciliate her, and thinks her maids will remain'.[5]

In view of this, it has been conjectured by historians that 'it was almost inevitable that the two ladies should have clashed, for they were temperamentally the antithesis of each other'.[6] Apparently 'there seems to have been a wide temperamental gap between the two women despite their common taste for fine clothes and jewellery'.[7] Historians suspect that relations were not helped by the fact that the new queen was considerably younger than her stepdaughter. For all this speculation there is no supporting evidence. Although relations between the two may initially have been difficult because of a misunderstanding, it is problematic to assume that Mary openly resented her new stepmother, or that Katherine disliked the eldest daughter of her husband, when there is virtually no evidence to support this conclusion. If Mary did initially view Katherine somewhat negatively, it may not necessarily have been the new queen's youth or her temperament which offended Mary, for Anne of Cleves had been aged only five months older than Mary and sixteenth-century royalty was certainly not ignorant of mismatched alliances between sovereigns, often involving a mature groom and a much younger bride. Louis XII of France, for example, was thirty-four years the senior of his third wife, Mary Tudor, when they wed in late 1514.

A more reasonable explanation is that Mary might have been informed, perhaps by the ambassador Chapuys, of the damaging gossip circulating in England during the summer of 1540 regarding Queen Katherine, in which a Windsor priest had openly accused Henry's new wife of immorality. If Mary had become aware of this slander, she may have questioned the suitability of her father's new bride. Alternatively, she may have enjoyed warm relations with Anne of Cleves and subsequently resented Anne's displacement as queen. Perhaps more simply, as a devout Catholic, Mary may have personally objected to the dissolution of a marriage that, in her eyes, was binding until death parted the spouses. Other observers, however, suspected that Katherine, as 'a mere child', resented the affection shown towards Mary at court.[8]

If relations between the two may have been initially difficult, extant documentation indicates that shortly after their disagreement the two resolved any outstanding conflict and behaved cordially towards one another. At New Year 1541, Mary sent her new stepmother a gift, at which the king was said to show pleasure. Henry responded by sending his daughter two gifts from himself and Katherine.[9] In May 1541, Chapuys reported that Katherine had 'countenanced … with good grace' the king's decision to permit Mary to reside at court.[10] During her period as queen, Katherine granted Mary the gift of:

> A pomander with gold wherein is a clock enamelled with divers colours, garnished with xij small rubies, having a chain of gold hanging at it, containing viij pieces of gold of one fashion enamelled black, garnished with xvj small rubies and xvj small turquoises, xxiiij small pieces of gold, and xxxij pearls in links of gold of the same chain.[11]

Relations with the younger Lady Elizabeth, aged 7, may have been less complex. The queen similarly bestowed upon her stepdaughter gifts of jewellery.[12] In May, she journeyed to Baynard's Castle and Chelsea, perhaps with the intention of supervising the residence of Elizabeth.[13] Around the same time, the queen apparently encouraged a visit to the household of Prince Edward at Waltham in Essex, accompanied by Lady Mary and the king.[14] Katherine cannot have failed to have been aware, however, that while it was beneficial for her to enjoy warm relations with her stepchildren, it was more important that she bear her husband the king a second son.

While both her husband and her family prayed hopefully for the queen to fall pregnant, in the early months of her tenure as queen Katherine's jointure was settled on her, in January 1541. The queen received the castles, lordships and manors that had formerly belonged to Jane Seymour during her queenship, and was also granted the lands of Master Secretary Thomas

Cromwell, Walter Lord Hungerford (also executed on 28 July 1540) and Hugh, Abbot of Reading. Together these lands were extensive and made the new queen a wealthy landowner. She owned land in the counties of Berkshire, Hampshire, Surrey, Sussex, Dorset and Somerset.[15] Katherine also enjoyed the usage of a private barge when departing from Chelsea to Baynard's Castle and vice versa, with twenty-six bargemen commanded by Robert Kyrton and twenty gentlemen 'serving the train'.[16] The queen was supplied with a lavish and costly household, supervised by the Earl of Rutland as lord chamberlain, Sir Thomas Dennys as chancellor and Sir John Dudley as master of the horse. Her household cost the king £4,600 annually and comprised four gentlemen ushers, a cup bearer, a clerk, two chaplains, two gentlemen waiters, six great ladies, four ladies of the privy chamber, five maidens, twelve chamber yeomen, four footmen, seven sumptermen, two litter men and seventeen grooms.[17] Lavish gifts were offered to her after her marriage to the king. These included five books:

> 1. Item oone booke of golde ennamuled wherin is a clock. Upon every syde of which booke is thre diamondes, a litle man standing upon oone of them, foure turqueses and thre rubyes, with a litle cheyne of golde hanging at it ennamuled.
> 2. Item oone booke of golde ennamuled with blacke, garnesshed with xxvii rubyes, havyng also a cheyne of golde and perle to hange it by, conteignyng xliii peerlles.
> 3. Item oone other booke ennamuled with grene, white and blewe, havyng a feir sapher on euery syde and viii rubyes upon the same booke.
> 4. Item oone booke of golde ennamuled with blacke, white and red and garnesshed with viii small rubyes, havyng H.I. ennamuled with blacke, the backes of the same booke being glasse.
> 5. Item one booke of golde conteignyng xii diamondes and xl rubyes.[18]

These 'litle' books were presumably intended to be worn at the queen's girdle, and at least one of them had belonged to Katherine's predecessor for the 'H.I.' referred to the short-lived marriage of Henry and Jane Seymour. At a later date, further books were also bestowed on Katherine. These books were described thus:

> 1. Item oone masse booke coverid with purple vellat with claspes of copper.
> 2. Item oone other litle masse booke coverid with lether.
> 3. Item oone Newe Testament coverid with purple vellat gernysshid with silver and gilt with two claspes to the same of like silver and gilt.

4. Item oone litle Frenche booke coverid with crymsen vellat having two claspes of golde with these scripture 'Ihesus fiat uoluntas tua'.[19]

Henry and Katherine jointly owned a collection of Latin books that later descended to her kinsman Charles Howard, Earl of Nottingham in the seventeenth century; fourteen of these books were marked with the royal initials 'KH' (for 'Katherine' and 'Henry').[20] Rather than interpreting the gift of these books to Katherine as representing 'a humanistic educational programme' on the behalf of the king for his new wife, it would make more sense to perceive them in the context of Henry's public shows of magnificence,[21] in which he proclaimed his joy and gratitude that God had permitted him to marry this 'jewel of womanhood'. The queen would have used some of these books on a daily basis, specifically the 'litle masse booke coverid with lether' or the one 'coverid with purple vellat'. Olga Hughes has commented that the evidence of Katherine's ownership of books 'indicates Catherine could certainly read, although this should hardly be a surprising conclusion. It is extremely doubtful [that] Henry VIII, with his love of academic pursuits, would want an illiterate wife or allow his Queen Consort to be so ill-educated.'[22] One might argue that Hughes's conclusion is entirely logical, but as the analysis of the historiography of Katherine Howard at the beginning of this book made startlingly clear, many historians have doubted Katherine's intellectual capabilities and some have openly slandered her as 'empty-headed', 'foolish' or 'stupid', based on very little, if any, evidence. The evidence of her book ownership should serve to call such dubious conclusions into question.

As Queen of England, Katherine was expected to act as patron, as her predecessors had done, and to be accustomed to dealing with financial transactions and matters of property. During her period as queen, there is extant evidence for Katherine's desire to fulfil her traditional responsibilities as the king's consort. She leased the manor of Much Marcle to the gentleman Richard Scudamore of Wilton, Herefordshire, with note of surrender for renewal in 1557. In November 1540 at Windsor the queen wrote to Edward Lee, Archbishop of York, requesting him to grant the advowson of the archdeanery of York upon her unnamed chaplain, reminding him of a previous unsuccessful attempt on her behalf. The archbishop responded in early December by noting that he 'never granted advowson saving at the king's commandment, but one, which I have many times sore repented'. He did promise, however, the next position available to another of the queen's chaplains, Lowe, worth £40 per annum.[23] Although the evidence is inconclusive, Katherine may also have helped her page Anthony Stoughton in his quest to obtain the hospital of St John at Warwick in late December 1540, and may also have assisted her footman Laurence Lee in acquiring the keepership of seven woods in Rutland.[24]

The queen also participated in ceremonies that befitted her status as the king's wife. On 22 February 1541, she became a godparent alongside her stepdaughter Mary at the birth of Jane Seymour, daughter of Edward, Viscount Beauchamp and his wife Anne Stanhope. It is possible, although unproven, that she participated in a Maundy service in 1541. Her alleged first meeting with Thomas Culpeper took place in 1541 when Henry VIII held his Maundy on 14 April. This ceremony, in which the queen washed poor women's feet, had previously been performed by Anne Boleyn and Anne of Cleves.[25]

During the northern progress of 1541, Katherine participated in the court ceremonies at each town visited by the king and his court, including those at Lincoln and York. Henry evidently intended for her to be displayed as a public symbol of his happiness and, more broadly, the prosperity of the Tudor dynasty, especially when rumours circulated that the queen was thought to be pregnant. Katherine's role as patron was demonstrated in the winter of 1540, when Richard Jones dedicated his treatise *The Birth of Mankind, a Study of Childbirth* to 'our most gracious and virtuous Queen Katherine', completing his translation of the treatise from the Latin 'for the love of all womanhood, and chiefly for the most bound service the which I owe unto your gracious highness'.[26] This is the only extant evidence of a book being dedicated to her. Soon after Jones's dedication to the queen, Katherine and her husband presided over the Christmas festivities at court. Royal relatives, such as the queen's predecessor and now the king's 'sister' Anne of Cleves, were invited to court for the celebrations. On 3 January Anne, accompanied by Lord William Howard, personally visited Katherine and paid homage to her, having sent the king a New Year's gift of two horses with violet velvet trappings. She knelt before the queen and the queen responded by showing Anne 'the utmost kindness'. At this point the king entered the room and, following a bow, embraced and kissed his former wife. After the king retired to bed, Katherine and Anne danced together in the evening and dined together the next day alongside the king. Katherine generously gave her former mistress the gift of a ring and two small dogs which Henry had given to her as a present. Later that day Anne returned to her residence at Richmond.[27]

Katherine's activities in the spring of 1541 suggest her intent to adopt the traditional and customary role of the queen consort in her acts of intercession. Her actions were entirely traditional especially because 'churchmen stressed the queen-consort's duty to intercede with the king on behalf of the poor and oppressed'.[28] The queen has traditionally been credited with meeting with her tailor on 1 March and ordering him to send garments to Margaret Pole, Countess of Salisbury, a prisoner in the Tower of London on charges of treason. The countess was sent a furred nightgown, a kirtle of worsted, a furred petticoat, a satin-lined nightgown, a bonnet and frontlet, four pairs of hose, four pairs of shoes and a pair of slippers.[29] Whether Katherine herself personally asked her tailor to do so, or whether he was ordered to by others, is unclear. If she herself had personally acted, it is likely that she required the king's direct permission, for members of the Pole family had been arrested and executed only a few years previously for their involvement in the 'Exeter Conspiracy'.

Three weeks later, Katherine requested a pardon for the renowned court poet Sir Thomas Wyatt, who had also been imprisoned in the Tower, which was duly granted 'at the great and continual suit of the Queen's Majesty'. Sir John Wallop, charged with treason, was also pardoned at the same time as a result of the queen's intercession. Later that year, in October while in Lincolnshire on the royal progress, Katherine was successful in beseeching her husband to pardon Helen Page of Lyndesey for felony.[30] Her four recorded acts of intercession demonstrate Katherine's desire to take her position as queen and its accompanying responsibilities seriously.

Often dismissed as a senseless and irresponsible teenager who spent her days doing little but dancing and singing, the recorded evidence suggests a different picture of Katherine when read in the light of court customs and prevailing notions of queenship in the mid sixteenth century. Her desire to grant prisoners pardons and her bequests of jewellery upon her relatives and ladies suggest a kind and warm young woman who, although relatively inexperienced at court, was determined to take her duties as consort to the king seriously. These actions should also be interpreted in the context of Henry VIII's own changing perceptions of queenship. While the evidence for his preferences are sadly lacking, it is plausible that Katherine's recorded acts of intercession would have been discussed with her husband before she actually made them in public. In light of this it could be argued that, by the early 1540s, Henry placed greater importance than hitherto on his queen adopting the traditional role of intercessor, but this duty had clearly been valued by the king earlier in his reign in view of the recorded actions of Jane Seymour, for example, in seeking to intervene on behalf of certain individuals. Katherine's primary duty as queen remained childbearing, but her recorded intercessions in 1541 indicate Henry's desire for his queen, and by extension himself, to appear benevolent and merciful.

Possibly seeking to ensure that her former childhood companions such as Katherine Tylney remained silent about her sexual experiences, Katherine bestowed upon them positions at court. Gifts were also made to them: at Chenies Manor House in October 1541, Katherine gave jewellery, clothing and French hoods to Alice Restwold, who had previously served the dowager

Duchess of Norfolk.[31] Since her family would have warned her to conceal her pre-marital liaisons from the king, Katherine probably realised that it was imperative that she obtain the silence of those who had resided in her step-grandmother's household in order to ensure her own security. Only scant evidence survives about Katherine's relations with her ladies-in-waiting and maidens. As has been recognised, the queen's female attendants were expected to participate enthusiastically 'in all the activities connected to forming, maintaining, and exploiting patronage networks'.[32] Katherine's household included eight great ladies, nine ladies and gentlewomen attendant, five maidens, four gentlewomen of the privy bedchamber, and four chamberers.[33] In total twenty-six staff served in Katherine's household compared with only sixteen in that of Katherine of Aragon.[34] As well as giving gifts of jewellery to her stepdaughters, the queen bestowed beads on Lady Carew, Lady Rutland, Lady Surrey and Lady Margaret Douglas.[35]

Because she was queen for a comparatively short period of time, little evidence exists about Katherine's interactions with her ladies. As with Jane Seymour, who occasionally made gifts of jewellery to favourite ladies, Katherine's relations with them appear to have been professional and cordial, although loyalty and trust may not have been inspired as had been the case with her predecessors Katherine of Aragon and Anne Boleyn. But there is no extant evidence to support the sweeping claim that 'there were plenty of others among the Queen's immediate household who also cordially disliked their Howard mistress ... Catherine, in life as well as in death, became the victim of that malice'.[36] In contrast, Katherine's ladies only moved against her at the time of her downfall when they were required by the Crown to provide what proved to be damning evidence against their mistress, whether willingly or reluctantly, for they had little choice but to co-operate regardless of their personal feelings. That Katherine was close to her female family members and provided them with respectable positions at court there is no doubt, for at time of the queen's downfall the prosecutors utilised these women's intimate connections with the queen against Katherine: four Howard women were accused of abetting or concealing Katherine's pre-marital and extramarital affairs.[37]

Like her ancestor Anne of York and her cousin Anne Boleyn, Katherine actively sought to promote and raise her family's fortunes through her patronage as queen. Nicola Clark has recently concluded that the Howards 'were not automatically united and did not consistently function as a coherent unit, but neither were they ever wholly disunited'.[38] Indeed, for the Howard women 'kinship connections of all kinds were of vital importance ... Like most other aristocratic women of this period, the evidence shows that they valued both natal and marital connections throughout their lives, and often passed on these relationships to the next generation, creating matrilineal kinship bonds that were distinct from the usual patriarchal line of inheritance.'[39]

In August 1541, Katherine appointed Francis Dereham as her private secretary. Possibly the king encouraged her to do so, if Dereham approached the king directly. There is extant evidence that Dereham relations were viewed favourably by the Crown. In December 1540, the king had granted to Thomas Dereham and his wife – possibly the parents of Francis – the house of Westdereham Monastery with reservations for twenty-one years; lands in Westdereham and Roxham, Crimplesham (where Francis had been born) and Wyram; lands in Faltewell and Estholme; and tithes of corn, hay, and woods on the premises.[40] Following Katherine's appointment at court, Dereham had departed for Ireland, where he seems to have engaged in piracy. After her step-granddaughter's marriage to Henry VIII, the dowager Duchess of Norfolk encouraged Dereham to seek a position within the queen's household. Almost certainly she was neither aware of the full extent of Dereham's sexual relations with Katherine nor his relentless pursuit of her within the duchess's household. Although he openly confronted Katherine with rumours of an engagement to Thomas Culpeper, the queen consented to 'be good unto him' because of her step-grandmother's request.[41] In August 1541, the queen found a place for Dereham within her household as private secretary and as an usher of the chamber. She warned him to 'take heed what words you speak',[42] since her reputation had already been slandered by hostile observers the previous summer and because she quite reasonably feared Dereham's aggressiveness and reckless speech. Moreover, the king's actions in the spring of 1536 had demonstrated how savagely he responded to court rumours that suggested the queen possessed a sexual life that involved other men, whether before or after her marriage. Katherine, surely, would have been cognisant of that context on a daily basis. As with her decision to favour others who had lived in the dowager duchess's household, Katherine seems to have believed that she could ensure Dereham's silence by appointing him to her household where she could monitor his activities.

Although Katherine sought to placate potentially threatening acquaintances such as Francis Dereham with appointments within her household, she continued to be troubled by the behaviour of Dereham. Soon after his appointment as private secretary in the summer of 1541, he openly boasted to his friend Robert Davenport that:

Many men despised him by cause they perceived that the Queen favoured him insomuch that one Mr John, being gentleman usher with the Queen, fell out with him for sitting at dinner or supper with the Queen's council after all others were risen, and sent one to him to know whether he were of the Queen's council, and the said Dereham answered the messenger – Go to Mr John and tell him I was of the Queen's council before he knew her and shall be there after she hath forgotten him.[43]

This report seems to shed light on Dereham's aggressive, even violent, temperament, and his possessiveness towards Katherine. In remarking that 'an the King were dead I am sure I might marry her', his behaviour was highly dangerous, for were the king to become aware of his comments, he would face charges of treason for predicting the king's death. Dereham himself showed no respect towards the queen or consideration of her feelings. His behaviour was irresponsible, for 'in a culture … where a woman's honour was construed in purely sexual terms, loose talk could cause cruel damage'.[44] Believing that she had consented to his almost certainly unwelcomed sexual advances, Dereham continued to believe that, when the king died, Katherine would eagerly return to him as his 'wife'.

Dereham's allegations were especially foolish in the light of the concerns of Henry VIII regarding treasonous behaviour. The 1534 Treason Act condemned those who maliciously desired the death of the sovereign through 'words or writing, or by craft imagine'. By prophesying that once the king had died, Dereham would be able to marry his young queen, he placed both himself and Katherine in serious danger. Later on, the queen was to be accused of offering Dereham a place within her household in order to continue her 'abominable' lifestyle of lust which, the councillors believed, she had shamelessly enjoyed with him during her adolescence. Three weeks before her execution in 1536, Anne Boleyn had allegedly engaged in a dangerous conversation with Henry Norris in which she accused him of seeking 'dead men's shoes' – that is, once the king had died, Norris hoped to marry Anne. Dereham's behaviour was a re-enactment of the 1536 conversation between Anne and Norris, a conversation that had led to the ruin and deaths of both individuals. The behaviour of her former suitor meant that Katherine found herself in a vulnerable position by the summer of 1541.

After a relatively successful first few months as queen, Katherine's relationship with her husband, which seems to have been promising, was placed in some difficulties by the king's dangerous illness at the end of February 1541. Marillac informed the French king that Henry had suffered a tertian fever, and had simultaneously endured:

A mal d'esprit having conceived a sinister opinion of some of his chief men, in his illness … most of his Privy Council under pretence of serving him, were only temporizing for their own profit, but he knew the good servants from the flatterers … Under this impression he spent Shrovetide without recreation, even of music … and stayed in Hampton Court with so little company that his Court resembled more a private family than a king's train.[45]

Chapuys was later to write that at Lent, because of his illness, the king refused to see his queen for a period of ten or twelve days, 'during which time there was much talk of a divorce, but owing to some surmise that she was with childs or else because the means for a divorce was not arranged the affair slept'.[46] For various reasons Chapuys's suggestion that Henry seriously considered annulling his marriage to Katherine in the spring of 1541 is dubious. Firstly, the French ambassador, who was well informed, made no mention at the time of the queen or an annulment in his reports to the King of France when discussing Henry's illness. Secondly, in March 1541 Henry publicly arranged for Katherine to pass through London as queen in which she was saluted and warmly greeted by the citizens of the city. Thirdly, the queen's personal activities in the spring, in which she was involved with the pardoning of several criminals as well as her visits with the king to the royal children, indicate that the king warmly expected her to continue her duties appropriately as his consort. With the benefit of hindsight, Chapuys – writing eight months later in the wake of Katherine's downfall – probably misinterpreted the king's decision to part from his wife as sinister evidence of his intent to separate from her pending the annulment of their marriage. As evidence of the couple's continuing happiness together, on Katherine's first passage on the Thames as queen on 19 March, Henry arranged for the Tower cannons to salute her and she was escorted, along with her husband, by the lord mayor of London, aldermen, and craftsmen in barges decorated with banners. Charles Wriothesley viewed these festivities as 'a goodlie sight'.[47]

Nevertheless, the rumour noted by Chapuys that the queen was pregnant in the spring of 1541 is intriguing, for Marillac also indicated that Katherine was believed to have conceived, writing in April:

This queen is thought to be with child, which would be a very great joy to this king who it seems believes it, and intends, if it be found true, to have her crowned at Whitsuntide. Already all the embroiderers that can be got are employed making furniture and tapestry, the copes and ornaments taken from the churches not being spared. Moreover, the young lords and gentlemen of this Court are practising daily for the joists and tournaments to be then made.[48]

Since there is no other evidence of Katherine's pregnancy, either at this time or later, it is difficult to credit both gentlemen's reports, for foreign ambassadors were customarily deceived by the king's councillors about matters pertaining to pregnancy and fertility. By custom the English queen did not publicly announce a pregnancy, which meant that resident ambassadors were reliant on court rumours and court ceremonial to provide 'evidence' of a royal pregnancy. If the king had been suffering with a life-threatening illness early that year it is difficult to believe that he had recovered sufficiently to father a child on his consort. Potentially Marillac was deceived by councillors close to the king, who untruthfully informed the ambassador that their monarch's marital relations were so happy that he had managed to father an heir on his present queen. Alternatively, Katherine may have believed herself to be pregnant when in fact she never was. At the time of her downfall later that year, it was rumoured that physicians had confirmed that the queen was unable to bear children.[49] More possibly, the physical effects of the sexual abuse she had suffered earlier on may have damaged her, rendering her unable to have children.[50] Despite the reports of both Marillac and Chapuys, there is no evidence that Katherine became pregnant during her tenure as queen consort. More probably the reason for this was her husband's impotence, from which he had suffered increasingly from the period between Jane Seymour's death and Anne of Cleves's rejection.

It should be considered why the king failed to discern that his wife was not a virgin at the time of his marriage to her. During this period the modern fixation with the hymen was not necessarily relevant in determining virginity, for other attributes were believed to offer evidence of virginity. A woman's behaviour and dress, the colour of her urine, and the direction in which her breasts pointed were viewed as valid indicators of virginity.[51] Jane Seymour's downcast eyes and modest gestures, for instance, were viewed commendably by Henry because they signified that Jane was a virginal maid. From the classical period writers had debated whether or not the hymen existed at all. Socrates, writing in 200 AD, argued that it was non-existent.

Katherine's own panic and concern, if she had believed herself to be pregnant and was subsequently proved wrong, can only be guessed at, for the dangerous game of fertility politics which threatened the security of Henry's queen consorts now threatened to turn against her. There is some evidence that the queen became concerned, even pensive, about her relations with her husband around this time. On 26 May Chapuys reported that Katherine had been melancholy owing to a rumour that the king desired to annul his marriage to her and remarry Anne of Cleves.[52] Although Henry assured her that these rumours were false and that he loved her, Katherine's position remained fragile, for ten months into her marriage she had still not managed to conceive the long-desired second male heir. While she continued to perform her duties admirably as queen, she also faced concerns about the behaviour of Dereham, whose threatening behaviour within her household further endangered her already insecure position.

Only in the context of these pressing dynastic and political concerns can Katherine's involvement with her husband's gentleman of the chamber and her relative, Thomas Culpeper, in the spring and summer of 1541 be satisfactorily and clearly understood, rather than advocating the traditional view which suggests that the queen, by nature a supposedly lusty young woman, sought night-time meetings with this handsome young man in order to enjoy sexual relations. However, Katherine's relative inexperience at court and her position as queen meant that her liaisons with Culpeper were interpreted negatively in the eyes of political enemies at court who sought to bring down the ambitious Howards through the slander of female sexuality.

8

THE CULPEPER AFFAIR

IN APRIL 1541, SHORTLY after her husband's serious illness, Katherine began an association with Thomas Culpeper that was eventually to prove fatal. Modern historians have disputed the nature of the relationship between the queen and a handsome young gentleman who served her husband the king within the intimate faculty of gentleman of the privy chamber. As has been seen, Culpeper had enjoyed a successful career at court before Katherine's arrival and marriage to Henry VIII. A favourite of the king, as a 'handsome youth' he also seems to have been something of a ladies' man. Why he became involved with Queen Katherine in the spring of 1541 is a subject of mystery that continues to divide historians. Before moving to an analysis of their ultimately fatal liaison, it is worth noting at this point that there is actually scarcely any evidence to support the theory that Katherine and Culpeper were lovers or that she desired him either sexually or platonically. The discussion of the extant historiography in the opening chapter of this book, however, sheds light on the reluctance of modern historians to acknowledge the scarcity of the evidence for a love affair between queen and servant, perhaps because of its salacious or romantic appeal coupled with the prevailing, if misguided, perception of Katherine as the wife who 'cheated' on Henry VIII and paid for it with her life. Such lingering beliefs have proved difficult to challenge even in a more modern context.

Most modern historians continue to believe that Katherine and Culpeper, two allegedly lusty individuals, were naturally attracted to one another and, shortly after the queen's marriage, foolishly and recklessly began to meet at night-time for the purpose of enjoying sexual fulfilment with one another.[1] As a consequence, they conclude that while Katherine's execution can be interpreted as a tragedy, it was in a sense entirely deserved because of her reckless conduct. These historians have failed to answer one salient, but often neglected question: assuming, according to their interpretation of the evidence, that Katherine and Culpeper were lovers in the physical sense, why would they have risked their lives and status merely for sexual gratification? Katherine surely would have been fully aware of the bloody end suffered by her cousin Anne Boleyn in 1536, when that queen was accused and found guilty of adultery and incest on the basis of extremely questionable evidence.

Proponents of the adultery argument often suppose that Katherine was stupid and reckless enough to fling caution aside in pursuit of sexual gratification with Culpeper, but that explanation does not make sense of the available evidence, namely Katherine's essentially dismissive attitude towards Culpeper, as when she instructed Lady Rochford to inform Culpeper that she would not meet with him again. The available evidence does not indicate that Culpeper enjoyed significant financial or material rewards as a 'thank you' for committing adultery with the queen. Why, then, would he have risked his life to meet with her in secret solely for adultery? It would have been astonishingly reckless and – as events proved – fatal behaviour on the part of both individuals, who surely could not have hoped to conceal a sexual liaison from the court for long. Other historians who believe that Katherine and Culpeper did not likely consummate their union nevertheless suggest that love existed between the pair.[2]

A feminist interpretation has also been advocated, which argues that, as an aggressive courtier, Culpeper manipulated the young queen into granting him sexual favours in return for keeping quiet about her pre-marital liaisons.[3] Warnicke has proposed that 'Culpeper … exchanged information about her with Dereham'.[4] The difficulties in relation to understanding Katherine's relations with Culpeper arise from the problematic nature of the evidence. As has been succinctly observed about the sex lives of individuals living in the early modern period, 'we usually acquire information … only when they are publicized as a result of someone behaving in a fashion which is considered scandalous, or has caused outrage'.[5] The confusing mixture of hearsay, rumour and contradiction that comprise the indictments produced against the queen and her associates further obscures the degree of understanding and insight one can hope to gain in learning of the events of 1541. It is therefore necessary to recognise that the basis of what we know about the affair stems entirely from indictments produced against the couple with an expectation that they would almost certainly be attainted for treason.

It is impossible to know how well acquainted Katherine was with Culpeper prior to her marriage to the king. Her mother was a member of the Culpeper family, meaning that the queen and Thomas were related by blood. Culpeper basked in the king's favour and it is plausible that during

Henry's courtship of Katherine in the spring and summer of 1540 the king acquainted his new love with those at court whom he favoured. One of those would undoubtedly have been Culpeper, who had served Henry as a gentleman of the privy chamber for several years prior to 1540. According to the queen's confession in November 1541, when Dereham arrived at court he questioned Katherine about rumours he had heard about her and Culpeper:

> If I should be married to Mr. Culpepper, for so he said he heard reported. Then I made answer, What should you trouble me therewith, for you know I will not have you; and if you heard such report, you heard more than I do know.[6]

It is unclear whether these rumours were in circulation after their initial meeting on Maundy Thursday in 1541. As will become evident, members of Katherine's household were clearly aware of her meetings with Culpeper, despite the concerted efforts made by both the queen and Lady Rochford to keep the interviews secret. Some historians, however, have suggested that Dereham confronted Katherine shortly after his return from Ireland in the spring of 1540. One such is Josephine Wilkinson, who speculated that Culpeper was 'the young man with whom Katherine entered into a relationship during the early months of 1540'.[7] That conclusion, however, is problematic when one considers Katherine's alleged response to rumours of a liaison between her and Culpeper in 1540: 'If you heard such report, you heard more than I do know.' No other contemporary evidence prior to Katherine's marriage indicates any form of relationship with Culpeper, and it is worth bearing in mind that Dereham's alleged accusation that Katherine was going to marry Culpeper only surfaced in November 1541, when not only her household but the court as a whole knew of Katherine's clandestine meetings with Culpeper before and after the summer progress.

It may be significant that Katherine's secret liaisons with Culpeper began in the spring of 1541 shortly after her husband was taken seriously ill and at about the same time that Dereham began openly boasting of his former intimacy with the queen. After warning Dereham to be careful with his speech, Katherine lent him £3 and £10 on two separate occasions.[8] Despite her attempt to mitigate the damage caused by Dereham's recklessness, it is entirely plausible that other residents at court would have learned of the salacious gossip about the two, one of whom may have been Culpeper, who had previously been associated with both the queen and Dereham, if one gives credence to the rumours of a betrothal between Katherine and Culpeper as reported by Dereham. It is possible that Culpeper initially instigated the affair by approaching Lady Rochford, beseeching her to assist him in meeting with the queen. Lady Rochford, according to both the queen and her ladies-in-waiting, encouraged the affair and was responsible for arranging the practicalities of it, in terms of the rooms in which queen and servant could converse, but if Culpeper had first approached Lady Rochford then Katherine would only have been aware of Lady Rochford's encouragements to her. Culpeper may have assumed that, as an experienced courtier and lady of the bedchamber, coupled with her kinship ties to the Howard family, Lady Rochford would be an ideal candidate to approach in order to aid him with meeting with the queen in private.

Significantly, according to Culpeper's later admission, the couple first met on Maundy Thursday, which fell on 14 April 1541; this meeting occurred only four days after the French ambassador had reported that the queen was believed to be pregnant and the court was in the midst of preparations for the impeding birth.[9] It is possible that both the king and his councillors remembered this timing at the time of the queen's downfall and interpreted this first meeting in a sinister light. According to Culpeper's report, the queen summoned Culpeper to her presence via her servant Henry Webb. She there gave him 'by her own hands a fair cap of velvet garnished with a brooch and three dozen pairs of aglets and a chain'. Katherine then warned Culpeper to hide the items to prevent anyone seeing them. When Culpeper questioned her behaviour, she rebuked him: 'Is this all the thanks ye give me for the cap? If I had known ye would have [said] these words you should never have had it.'[10] When analysing this evidence, it seems to suggest that Katherine initiated the meeting between the two. By Katherine's admission, however, it was Lady Rochford who encouraged her to meet with Culpeper, promising that he 'meant nothing but honesty'. She also advised the queen to 'give men leave to look' on her, 'for they will look upon you [Katherine]'. Katherine's own feelings towards Culpeper are uncertain, but she responded to Lady Rochford's suggestions with the retort that she did not wish to be involved with 'such light matters'.[11]

Although the queen had generously provided Culpeper with several small gifts at their meeting in April, they did not next meet until three months later during the summer progress. This in itself should caution against interpreting their relationship as the amorous love affair that it has so often and uncritically been presented as. In sixteenth-century England, there was an 'expectation concerning virtuous female behaviour [that was] impressed upon the consciousnesses of all well-educated ladies … [which] was that they should avoid trivial flirtatious relationships, not merely carnal liaisons, with all men except their husbands'.[12] The difficulty with interpreting Katherine's relationship with Culpeper as either a 'flirtatious relationship' or 'carnal liaison' (to paraphrase Warnicke's article quoted above) is that both parties denied engaging in sexual intercourse. Culpeper subsequently admitted that he intended to do 'ill' with the queen, but it remains unclear whether this goal was ever shared, or even considered, by Katherine in the course of their meetings with one another. Another problem with interpreting their relationship as an amorous love affair is the lack of evidence to support the lingering popular notion of Katherine as a promiscuous young woman who found sexual relations pleasurable and fulfilling. It is possible, if unproven, that having escaped the coercion (if not abuse) at the hands of both Manox and Dereham after her appointment at court that Katherine developed an aversion to sex. Unfortunately, the frequent references to Katherine in modern historical accounts as a 'tart' or 'whore', coupled with the titillating portrayals of her in film and television productions such as *The Tudors*, have encouraged the dominant perception of her as an adulteress, but the lack of extant evidence to support this interpretation of her character is another example of how she has been slandered since her execution.

Since Katherine did not seek to renew Culpeper's acquaintance until three months after their April meeting, her infrequent meetings with him, at which Lady Rochford was often present, accompanied with the occasional exchange of gifts, does not suggest an amorous affair between the two, nor does it indicate that she instigated it or even necessarily controlled it. One possibility is that Lady Rochford helped to facilitate a friendship between the two based on kinship which saw Culpeper become the young queen's confidant and companion.

Notably, the game of courtly love flourished at the Tudor court and was viewed as a popular social convention in which young, well-born ladies participated with handsome knights in witty exchanges. First originating in the love lyrics of eleventh-century French troubadours and codified at Eleanor of Aquitaine's court, courtly love was variously perceived to be a genuine way of life or merely a pleasant literary convention. The theme of courtly love may have first become extent in the Latin writings of Ovid and later flourished in twelfth-century Provence.[13] The knight was expected to serve his lady, obey her commands, and gratify her whims. Obedience and loyalty to the high-ranking lady was viewed as critical, while the lady was regarded as being unavailable by virtue of her status and was consequently inclined to be remote, haughty and imperious. The constant presence of Lady Rochford might suggest that the relationship between the queen and Culpeper was nothing more than a game of courtly love, for a go-between was customarily expected to deliver letters between the two and plead the knight's case for him to his lady. Lady Rochford encouraged Katherine to consider Culpeper's suit, while persuading her that he would not be the only handsome gentleman to 'look' on the queen. Perhaps most significantly, these courtly love exchanges were expected to remain secret.

Usually, in exchanges of courtly love, it was expected that the male lover suffered from love sickness, encouraging him to write emotional letters to his lady and lament his piteous lot.[14] In view of this it may be significant that in April Culpeper was believed to be 'at Greenwich ... sick'. The lady in question was often married, meaning that the relationship had to be conducted in an atmosphere of secrecy and danger, with a need for absolute discretion in order to preserve the lady's honour.[15] From the late fourteenth to the sixteenth century reading and talking about love, casting, playing and emulating the lover constituted a form of polite recreation for 'social play' and 'social display'.[16] However, the repartee of courtly love threatened highborn women's personal security and the honour both of themselves and of their family, for prevailing domestic codes associated female chastity with silence and self-effacement which the game of courtly love appeared to threaten.[17] The contemporary *Book of the Courtier* warned of the need for female discretion: 'And therefore muste she keepe a certaine meane verie hard, and (in a manner) derived of contrary matters, and come just to certaine limittes, but not to passe them.'[18]

Although Renaissance courts may have provided an ideal setting for the flourishing of courtly love between the sexes, some male contemporaries, dictated by their cultural perceptions of female sexuality, viewed such exchanges pessimistically and fearfully. The downfall of Anne Boleyn in 1536 clearly demonstrated 'the dalliance prescribed by courtly codes of female behaviour was seen to threaten the chastity prescribed by domestic codes'.[19] Katherine was surely aware that, as an aristocratic woman and as the Queen of England, her actions could be misinterpreted by those hostile to her queenship or the influence of her family. If the queen engaged in the convention of courtly love, it may have been because she believed that she was merely playing a part in a game which had flourished in Renaissance courts for centuries. Other ladies within her household, including Lady Margaret Douglas and her own cousin Mary Howard, had engaged in similar pastimes encouraged at the Tudor court.[20] The ideals of courtly love, contained within love poems and novels in particular, continued to be transmuted into practice well into the late sixteenth century at the court of Elizabeth I.[21] Literature on courtly love was reshaped in order to allow an ideal form of love to exist without violating accepted norms of aristocratic society, and refused to endorse adultery as an ideal type of love.[22]

The giving of gifts to Culpeper indicated Katherine's desire to become better acquainted with him, for although he was kin to her, because he served within the household of her husband she probably knew very little of him. However, because he was viewed warmly and was held in high favour at court it is likely that she believed it would be useful to be acquainted with this respected courtier who was, after all, a member of her family. Because lurid evidence of Katherine's involvement with Culpeper survives only in a negative sense firstly in the indictments presented against both individuals and secondly in the dubious gossip forwarded by international ambassadors to their monarchs, scepticism is required when interpreting what is known of this relationship. These individuals, particularly the ambassadors, had very little contact with the queen, yet they accepted negative gossip related to her and preserved it as fact. During Katherine's period as queen, no mention, in fact, of her supposed affairs with either Dereham or Culpeper was related by resident ambassadors such as Marillac or Chapuys before her actual downfall in November 1541. Had there even been a hint that she was conducting a sordid and amorous affair with either gentleman behind her husband's back, they would surely have eagerly revealed it to their monarchs, who would have delighted in the humiliation of their rival, the King of England. That there was no mention of the queen in much of their reports warns against accepting later 'evidence' of an adulterous affair supposedly carrying on at this time. Moreover, no evidence indicates that the queen – or Culpeper – was bribing members of her household to keep silent about their secret meetings in the summer of 1541. Ultimately, it remains impossible to know what was said to Lady Rochford by both individuals, and whether financial rewards were offered to her as a reward for facilitating the meetings.

A later chronicle, *The Chronicle of King Henry VIII of England* (more commonly known as the *Spanish Chronicle*) was written and published by an unknown Spaniard, perhaps a merchant, living in London several years after the events which he describes.[23] Historians have responded negatively to this source because of its manifest inaccuracies, perceiving it to encompass 'garbled street gossip, strongly laced with the picaresque'.[24] Most notably, the author identified Katherine as the king's fourth consort, rather than his fifth.[25] Although the chronicler could not have been aware of the intricacy and reality of court politics by virtue of his isolated position within the city, his evidence pertaining to Katherine's affair with Culpeper may have some basis in fact, although most historians have tended to dismiss his version of events without considering the other evidence he provided in an appropriate social and cultural context. The chronicler evidently made it his business to learn as much about Katherine's affair with Culpeper as possible, which was not surprising in the context of sixteenth-century political culture: 'Individuals eagerly sought intelligence about the monarchy, the events at court, and other titillating

matters.'[26] However, whether the chronicler's reports about Katherine's relations with Culpeper can be validated depends on whether these reports can be
confirmed by other evidence, which is difficult with regard to the indictments
produced against the queen and her acquaintances. More potently, rumours
about the queen's affair may be 'more likely to provide a deeper understanding of cultural attitudes than reliable facts about those defamed'.[27]

Relying on gossip circulating within the city of London, the Spanish chronicler reported that, before Katherine's marriage to the king, Culpeper had
been in love with her, and the queen had looked favourably upon him. As
with most of his contemporaries, the chronicler adhered to prevailing gender
assumptions which assigned women the blame for sexual transgression:'The
devil tempted her [Katherine].'[28] It is problematic, however, to interpret the
mostly negative evidence produced against the queen and her husband's attendant as convincing evidence of an adulterous affair. As other noblewomen,
including the king's niece, Lady Margaret Douglas, and the queen's cousin,
Lady Mary Howard, participated in social and literary courtly love exchanges
with other gentlemen, Katherine might have believed that, following Queen
Anne Boleyn's example, her political position as queen and her social position
as mistress of her household permitted her to engage in similar exchanges. She
failed, however, to recognise the dangers a young woman faced by involving
herself too closely in these affairs, for women were warned to guard their
honour and virtue against the threats presented by carnal love.

Much of what the chronicler suggests in his account can apparently be
corroborated by extant evidence. Suggesting that Katherine wrote a letter in
reply to an amorous one written by Culpeper is significant, for the chronicler
believed that the queen's letter promised the courtier 'to have patience, and
she would find a way to comply with his wishes'.[29] At some point during the
early summer of 1541 the queen may have penned a letter to Culpeper.[30] On
30 June the court had set off on a northern progress with the intention of
quashing the threat of a rebellion headed by disgruntled conservatives, as well
as intending to meet with the Scottish king, James V, in a lavish rendezvous at
York. The poor weather did not augur well for the progress, nor did rumours
that the queen was ill.[31]

On 29 July the court reached Lodington, where it was later reported that
one of Katherine's ladies, Margaret Morton, carried a sealed letter without superscription from the queen to Lady Rochford, to whom Katherine
responded that she was sorry that she could write no better. Lady Rochford
promised an answer the following morning, 'praying her Grace to keep it
secret and not to lay it abroad'.[32] It is almost certain that Katherine's note was
the letter penned to Thomas Culpeper written about this time. However, it

is unknown whether the queen herself actually composed this piece. Because no other extant evidence of her handwriting survives, it is usually believed that she was illiterate. Other queen consorts, who were married to the English king for similarly short periods, including Jane Seymour and Anne of Cleves, nonetheless have examples of their signatures surviving. Moreover, it has been noted that the first couple of words of the letter are penned in a different hand to the rest of the letter.[33] If Katherine had commissioned Lady Rochford to complete a letter to Culpeper, what follows may not be indicative evidence of Katherine's personal feelings about the affair. That she probably wrote the first couple of words is likely given the impersonal and restrained address and nature of the subject matter that would have been expected of her royal status. The letter is as follows:

Master Culpeper,

I heartily recommend me unto you, praying you to send me word how that you do. It was showed me that you was sick, the which thing troubled me very much till such time that I hear from you praying you to send me word how that you do, for I never longed so much for [a] thing as I do to see you and to speak with you, the which I trust shall be shortly now. The which doth comfortly me very much when I think of it, and when I think again that you shall depart from me again it makes my heart to die to think what fortune I have that I cannot always be in your company. It my trust is always in you that you will be as you have promised me, and in that hope I trust upon still, praying you then that you will come when my lady Rochford is here for then I shall be best at leisure to be at your commandment, thanking you for that you have promised me to be so good unto that poor fellow my man which is one of the griefs that I do feel to depart from him for then I do know no one I dare trust to send to you, and therefore I pray you take him to be with you that I may sometime hear from you one thing. I pray you to give me a horse for my man for I have much ado to get one and therefore I pray send me one by him and in so doing I am as I said afor, and thus I take my leave of you trusting to see you shortly again and I would you was with me now that you might see what pain I take in writing to you.

Yours as long as life endures

Katheryn

One thing I had forgotten and that is to instruct my man to tarry here with me still for he says whatsomever you bid him he will do it.[34]

The survival of this letter strengthens the evidence presented by the Spanish chronicler in relation to this affair, for he too had recognised the passive nature of the queen's response to Culpeper in promising to fulfil 'his wishes'. This letter cannot be taken as evidence of a love letter evidencing Katherine's true feelings in relation to Culpeper, as many historians still continue to believe it is. As has been wryly noted, 'it is an odd specimen of the romance genre'.[35] Before proceeding to an analysis of Katherine's letter, it would be useful to first consider the context and nature of letter-writing in early modern England.

Historians have questioned whether early modern English letters are able to allow 'direct unmediated access to inner emotions' hundreds of years after they were first penned.[36] The content and structure of letters was crafted, in the same manner that church court depositories were manipulated, with specific models for letter-writing in circulation. Cultural archetypes were utilised to structure languages of feeling, meaning that 'the rhetoric of love-letters was … paralleled in epistolary fiction, romances and letter-writing manuals'.[37] Moreover, 'acts of writing and reading the familiar letter involve making and inferring meanings that may be pertinent to a single reading only as well as constructing meanings that might shift with the circumstances in which the letter might be read'.[38] The same applied to letters crafted at the early modern French court: 'Far from providing a transparent portrayal of events or sentiments, letters offered a complicated conjunction of meanings shaped by compositional forms and conventions and the conditions of their expedition and reception'; 'letter writers negotiated established ways of representing personal identity, and, by extension, how they thought about and represented themselves'.[39] The flourishing of courtly love at the English court allowed young noblewomen to write letters in which they used crafted expressions gleaned from texts such as novels and poems to convey a sense of identity and fulfil a particular purpose. This literary context means that it would be naïve to believe that Katherine's true sentiments could be transparently deduced from this letter alone.

In the first two sentences, the writer asks how Culpeper is, concerned that he is ill because she seeks to meet with him as soon as possible. Certain phrases utilised in this letter, such as 'at your commandment', were utilised in contemporary guides to letter-writing.[40] The language itself is somewhat melodramatic. The writer fears that if she cannot meet with Culpeper her heart will 'die' with sorrow at her ill fortune at being parted from him. The long, even laborious sentences indicate a well-thought-out, even calculated, approach; in contrast with shorter sentences that might convey a sense of urgency or restlessness. The letter contains very little in the way of love or passion, meaning that it is questionable why modern historians continue to persist in identifying this piece as a love letter. This becomes especially significant when the letter is interpreted in the context of the 'flowery' style of Tudor letters that historians have recognised. John Creke, for example, wrote in his letter to Thomas Cromwell:

> My love toward you resteth in no less vigour than it did at our last being together. My [hear]t mourneth for your company and Mr. Wodal's as ever as it did for men … I never had so faithful affection to men of so short acquaintance in my life; the which affection increaseth as fire daily. God knoweth what pain I receive in departing, when I remember our gosly walking in your garden; it make me desperate to contemplate.[41]

No one has ever suggested, however, that Creke was homosexual or was involved sexually with Cromwell, despite phrases such as 'My love toward you' and 'I never had so faithful affection to men'. Sixteenth-century letters should not naïvely be read as offering 'a transparent portrayal of events or sentiments', for their meanings were 'complicated' and 'shaped by compositional forms and conventions and the conditions of their expedition and reception'.[42]

The abiding theme of Katherine's letter is a desire to meet with Culpeper as soon as possible, a point repeatedly emphasised: 'I never longed so much for a thing as I do to see you and to speak with you, the which I trust shall be shortly now'; 'when I think again that you shall depart from me again it makes my heart die'; 'praying you that you will come when my lady Rochford is here', 'trusting to see you shortly again'.

Although the writer repeated her desire and intent to meet with Culpeper again, she did not specify for what reason. Probably, rather than instigating the affair as has been commonly believed, the queen's emphasis on meeting with Culpeper stemmed from her wish to placate his desire to meet with her; she promised to meet with him because of his continual demands to see her. This essentially passive tone is corroborated by the Spanish chronicler's belief that Katherine, in her letter, had assented to 'comply with his wishes'.[43] It is significant that Lady Rochford, as an intermediary, was specifically mentioned, perhaps because the queen desired her older relative – an experienced courtier – to chaperone her meetings with Culpeper. Similarly, Katherine's cousin Mary had acted as chaperone 'divers times' during the exchanges of courtly love between Lady Margaret Douglas and Lord Thomas Howard.[44]

Whether the letter was as significant as evidence produced against Katherine and Culpeper as most modern historians suggest is uncertain, for no mention of it as a document of evidence survives in the later indictments drawn up by the prosecutors. Other detail indicates that the letter cannot be viewed

necessarily as a love letter professing passion and desire. Despite the belief of
writers that the ending 'yours as long as life endures' convincingly establishes
Katherine's passionate love for Culpeper, it is more likely that the writer chose
to use an ending quite commonly used in practice by the nobility. For example, the Duchess of Norfolk had finished a letter written to Thomas Cromwell
with the promise 'by yours most bounden during my life',[45] but there was
no hint of scandal suggesting that the duchess and Cromwell had been conducting a sordid adulterous affair. Moreover, in the context of the practice of
early modern letter-writing, as has been suggested, the sentiments expressed
in this letter cannot necessarily be taken at face value as a genuine and realistic
indication of the writer's true feelings.[46] As Daybell cautions in relation to letters, they were 'subject to generic and linguistic conventions; texts that were
socially and culturally coded'.[47] Elite women, as Daybell suggests, often had
access to published guides by Erasmus and Angel Day, and many women followed the style and conventions they had seen in other letters, meaning that
many letters were formulaic. It would therefore be foolish to read too much
into this letter, in the context of the nature of early modern letter-writing,
but it does establish the writer's intent to meet with Culpeper. The abiding
impression from the letter is that the queen wanted strongly to meet with
Culpeper, although her reason for doing so was not specified, perhaps because
it was feared that the letter would fall into the wrong hands. Certain phrases
in the letter, such as 'at your commandment', were usually utilised in contemporary guides to letter-writing. Culpeper, for example, used this phrase in an
earlier message to Lady Lisle. It is impossible on the basis of the letter alone
to conclude that the queen was involved in an adulterous relationship with
Culpeper, especially when both the literary context in which such letters were
written and the highly stylised expressions used by sixteenth-century authors
means that the nature of Katherine's letter is much less clear-cut than earlier
historians believed.[48]

Why Jane, Lady Rochford chose to involve herself in the affair is uncertain and has perplexed most historians for decades. Her recent biographer
disposes of the theory that she became involved because she was involved
in financial difficulties and hoped to profit economically by assisting with
Katherine's exchanges with Culpeper, arguing instead that 'since she [Jane]
had just obtained her jointure settlement and was richer than ever before in
her own right, Jane did not need to endanger her life for money'.[49] There
is no extant evidence during the early months of Katherine's marriage, or
during her time as a maiden to Queen Anne of Cleves, to indicate that she
was particularly close to Lady Rochford, although the two were bound by ties
of kinship, Lady Rochford being the widow of Katherine's cousin George

Boleyn. Lady Rochford's feelings towards Katherine remain unknown, which is unfortunate because an awareness of her stance towards the queen might explain her motivations for assisting, even encouraging, Katherine to meet with Culpeper. Most writers adhere to the belief that Lady Rochford involved herself in the affair because she had lived a life starved of affection, worsened by her supposedly loveless marriage to George, and assisted Katherine's meetings with Culpeper in order to enact her own fantasies.[50] Others suggest that she was actually insane.[51]

No convincing evidence exists to suggest that Lady Rochford had been an especially notorious or meddlesome woman before her involvement with Katherine, since most historians do not now accept the traditional suggestion that she acted as the crucial witness in the charges of adultery and incest made against her husband and Anne Boleyn in 1536.[52] What remains clear is that Lady Rochford encouraged Katherine to meet with Culpeper on the grounds that, as queen, male courtiers would naturally look upon her. Furthermore, she allegedly promised not to reveal details of the meetings between the queen and Culpeper, 'to be torn with wild horses'. To have spoken such a statement seems to imply that Katherine possessed some kind of psychological hold over Lady Rochford, thus ensuring her silence about the affair, but if Lady Rochford was being bribed – or potentially blackmailed by Culpeper – then her avowals of silence, in an attempt to convince Katherine, might appear to make sense. In view of the political dangers to Katherine's reputation, were details to emerge of her meetings with Culpeper and the topics of their conversation – including the Dereham affair – it was absolutely necessary for Lady Rochford to reveal nothing of what had happened during the northern progress, and financial rewards may well have ensured her silence.

The likeliest explanation for Jane's conduct is that she had been directly approached by Culpeper in the spring of 1541, who sought to obtain her assistance in meeting with the queen, for he seems to have desired to become better acquainted with Katherine. One difficulty with accepting the theory of courtly love as an explanation for the nature of Katherine's relationship with Culpeper is the inherent risks involved and the lack of obvious gain for either party. In her response to David Starkey's suggestion that Katherine and Culpeper *were* conducting a game of courtly love between April and September 1541, Joanna Denny asked: 'But how likely is it that Culpeper the rapist would have settled for a juvenile romance of whispered endearments and pretty promises?'[53]

While it remains uncertain whether Culpeper actually had committed rape earlier in his career, Denny's question remains a pertinent one. It is possible, as historians have traditionally assumed, that Culpeper and Katherine were attracted to one another, but it remains unknown whether they committed, or ever intended to commit, adultery; neither of their confessions in late 1541 support the popular belief that theirs was a carnal relationship, because both denied committing adultery.

An alternative, and perhaps more convincing, explanation of their relationship can be reached by placing the timing of their meetings in a wider political and dynastic context. As has already been noted, their first meeting occurred shortly after Henry VIII was seriously unwell and his life despaired of, at around the same time that Dereham began boasting of his former relations with the queen and at a time when court rumours circulated that she was with child. The latter point might be thought to have placed her in a strong position, but the first two circumstances undermined her, firstly because her position remained uncertain if the king died, and secondly because rumours of sexual scandal circulating from Dereham threatened her reputation. As was noted earlier, there had already been at least one rumour in the summer of 1540 that Katherine was an unsuitable consort for the king, because of her pre-marital sexual history. An alternative explanation of their relationship, placing it in the context of the timing of their meetings, proposes that Culpeper learned about Katherine's pre-marital past and used it to manipulate her to grant him political and financial rewards for his silence. This explanation would make sense of the great lengths both parties went to in order to meet both before and during the northern progress, while also accounting for Katherine's evident desire, as expressed in her letter, to ensure that Culpeper remained as he had 'promised' her – i.e. that he did not reveal what he might have heard, or knew, about her.

Either at their first meeting or at some point after, and it is impossible to know when, Culpeper's motives became darker than they might at first have been. It is surely significant that he first sought to meet with the queen when she was both being harassed by Dereham and having to cope with the serious illness of her husband, thus placing her in a vulnerable political and personal position. Although he may not have been the violent rapist reported by rumour, as an ambitious and power-seeking member of the king's household he could have believed that establishing a hold over the queen would be an effective means of acquiring greater power at court, especially in the wake of Henry's illness and perhaps with an expectation that the king might shortly die, thus leaving Katherine in the financially and socially lucrative position of dowager queen. Probably, Culpeper bribed Lady Rochford to help him meet with Katherine.

Although the queen may initially have responded to Culpeper's entreaties because of her awareness that, as a gentleman of the king's privy chamber, it was worth cultivating his goodwill if not his friendship, she quickly discovered that Culpeper's motives may have focused on acquiring political power and influence through establishing influence with her. The letter penned to Culpeper in the summer of 1541 focuses not on passion or romance, its urgent even desperate tone suggesting a need for placation. If Katherine continued to give Culpeper gifts, it may have been because she was attempting to placate him. Margaret of Anjou famously bequeathed gifts to her enemy Richard, Duke of York as 'a form of reassurance and pacification, a message that the queen was aware of York's concerns'.[54] Arguably Katherine was acting in a similar manner. As noted in the introduction of this book, Ives accused the queen of irresponsibly ignoring court protocol,[55] but if she felt threatened by Culpeper's knowledge of her pre-marital affairs, Katherine's actions become more understandable. Historians have frequently condemned the queen as foolish or reckless in deciding to meet with her husband's attendant during the summer progress, but they have not perhaps adequately considered her motives for doing so. As Warnicke suggested in her biographical entry on Katherine, it is possible to make sense of the queen's actions during the summer of 1541 if one considers the likelihood that Katherine 'was trying to ensure his [Culpeper's] silence through a misguided attempt at appeasement'.[56]

Although Culpeper later blamed Jane Rochford for 'having provoked him much to love the queen',[57] it is interesting that Katherine and her ladies swore that Lady Rochford had initially encouraged her to meet with Culpeper, promising her that handsome gentlemen would look upon her. Yet Katherine would probably not have been aware, unless Jane informed her, that Culpeper had first met with Lady Rochford and asked her to arrange a meeting with the queen. Thus, in the queen's eyes, it was her lady of the bedchamber who had instigated the whole affair, although Lady Rochford had probably been acting on the wishes of Culpeper. Lady Rochford's behaviour condemned her in the eyes of her contemporaries, especially because of her association with a man executed on criminal charges of treason and incest. Because of who her husband had been, it was easy to believe in her guilt. Her own behaviour was foolish, for she should have been aware, having resided at court for lengthy periods during the last twenty years, that young women who met with gentlemen who were not their husbands were viewed with suspicion and hostility. Tellingly, it was later reported of Lady Rochford that 'all her life [she] had the name to esteem her honour little and thus in her old age had shown little amendment'.[58]

That Katherine desired for meetings with Culpeper to be conducted appropriately, assisted by Lady Rochford as the queen's chaperone, is evident given that no hint of scandal attached to the affair during its actual period. Only later, in the advent of Katherine's downfall, did her ladies suddenly and helpfully remember that Katherine had been missing from her bedchamber during the early hours of the morning, and testified that she had been explicitly showing her love for Culpeper by giving him amorous looks when looking out of the window. As has already been recognised in relation to this affair, much of the later evidence may have been embroidered and distorted with the benefit of hindsight, but the fact remains that Katherine met with Culpeper only on a handful of occasions and eventually ordered Lady Rochford to instruct him not to request further meetings with her, which is hardly indicative of a romantic love affair. It is surprising that some modern historians, who have recognised and appreciated the problematic nature of the testimonies of 1541, nevertheless accepted it at face value.[59]

It is unlikely that Katherine would willingly and recklessly have endangered her own position as queen and jeopardised her family's security by engaging in adultery with her husband's attendant. Her own activities demonstrate her desire to provide the Howards with greater wealth and influence at court, and it is doubtful whether she would have subsequently sought to ruin them and the rewards they had acquired through her marriage through her own actions. Anne Boleyn's example surely would have served as a warning to the queen, and Lady Rochford's own position as widow to a man executed alongside Queen Anne might have been thought to confirm Katherine's awareness that caution was essential, in a context in which early modern polemicists frowned upon young women meeting in secret with men who were not their husbands. Moreover, the belief that the queen was an oversexed adolescent who threw caution aside in fulfilling her carnal desires with the handsome Culpeper is problematic in view of what this study has indicated, for it is possible, if not certain, that she had, at an early age, formed an aversion to sex and may have equated it with violence and dishonour. That Katherine knew that sexual relations with Culpeper were impossible and dangerous is proven by her comment that only if she had still been in the maidens' chamber might she 'have tried' him.[60]

These meetings were to be viewed in a hostile light because of how they could be interpreted and represented by unsympathetic male observers. Male awareness of the fragility of their potency, coupled with an anxiety about female power within sexual dynamics, encouraged noblemen to view powerful women negatively, especially because it continued to be believed that women brought about their impotence and destroyed their manhood.[61] Because of prevailing gender expectations, young women were encouraged to avoid flirtatious relationships with all men except their husbands, because it threatened beliefs regarding virtuous female behaviour.[62] Katherine's secret meetings with Culpeper, in which adultery almost certainly did not take place, compromised her reputation, for they conflicted with domestic codes which associated female chastity with silence and self-effacement.[63] Culpeper himself played on these courtly norms to provide an effective background for manipulating the queen.

The suggestion that Katherine and Culpeper could not merely have been exchanging in the pastime of courtly love because 'she could have talked to him, although admittedly not for such long periods, within the normal confines of the court if that was all she wanted'[64] ignores the nature of their meetings. If Culpeper had discovered sensitive information about the queen that could politically ruin her and her family, she would have been well aware of the need to converse with him in private, almost certainly to gain his promise that he would reveal nothing of her pre-marital liaisons. In her letter, the queen explicitly wrote that: 'It my trust is always in you that you will be as you have promised me.' She probably and understandably believed that it was safer for her to meet with Culpeper in secret, aided by an experienced female courtier who could deflect controversy from the affair. The necessity for secrecy was evidenced in the pair's meeting at Lincoln in early August. The queen admitted that they had met 'in a little gallery at the stairs' head' near the back door, before journeying to Lady Rochford's chambers.[65] Although Lady Rochford, three months later, admitted to the prosecutors that the couple might have participated in sexual intercourse, Katherine's chamberers Katherine Tylney and Margaret Morton supplied no such evidence, although they reported that the queen had spent two nights in Lady Rochford's chambers. Lady Rochford actually admitted earlier that she had heard and seen nothing of what had passed between the two.[66] Margaret Morton fancifully claimed several months later that, at Hatfield, 'I saw her [Katherine] look out of her chamber window on Master Culpeper after such sort that I thought there was love between them.'[67] But, tellingly, this did not spur her to accuse the queen of improper behaviour or adultery at this time, and it is questionable whether one's inner motivations and thoughts can be transparently revealed from a facial expression remembered only several months later.

Lady Rochford's involvement in the affair as chaperone was crucial. While Culpeper reported that she had encouraged him in his love for the queen, Katherine later suggested that Jane 'would at every lodging search the back doors' for secret meeting places, which the queen may have assented to in the belief that their use for meetings was innocent, for Lady Rochford had sworn 'upon a book' that Culpeper 'meant nothing but honesty'. When confronted with Lady Rochford's reports of Culpeper's love and desire to meet with her, Katherine, recognising the dangers attached, sighed: 'Alas, madam, will this never end? I pray you, bid him desire no more to trouble me or send to me.'[68] That Culpeper was in love with Katherine and wished to meet with her to tell her, in person, of his love for her is at first glance plausible, for extant documentation reported that Culpeper 'was very much in love with her' but 'had committed no treason'.[69] Katherine sought to placate him by agreeing to meet with him, but she was understandably fearful because of her awareness of how these meetings could be misinterpreted. Conducting her meetings in a climate of male suspicion of female sexuality alongside the menace of Francis Dereham at court, Katherine was unsurprisingly 'skittish and jittery', fearful 'lest somebody should come' in.[70] Although Hall later reported that Katherine had met with Culpeper 'alone' at Lincoln in August, he did not specify their actual activities. He did state that the queen provided him with 'a Chayne, and a riche Cap', but whether Katherine bestowed these upon Culpeper as a reward for his good service to her husband the king, or whether they were a token of friendship between the two, Hall did not specify.[71]

That Katherine and Culpeper did not commit adultery or seek the destruction of King Henry, as was later alleged, is clear from a detailed reading when the interrogations are read in the appropriate social and cultural context. The court reached Lincoln by early August, and on 9 August the king and queen 'came riding into their tent, which was pitched at the furthest end of the liberty of Lincoln, and there shifted their apparel, from green and crimson velvet respectively, to cloth of gold and silver'.[72] They were welcomed by the city dignitaries and church bells were rung in celebration of the royal arrival. Henry and Katherine entered the magnificent eleventh-century cathedral 'under the canopy to the Sacrament and made their prayers while the choir sang *Te Deum*'.[73] On 12 August the royal progress departed for Gainsborough Old Hall, 18 miles north of Lincoln.[74]

At Lincoln, Katherine and Culpeper conversed for four hours regarding their former experiences – in Culpeper's words, 'their loves before time' – and Culpeper's treatment of Elizabeth Harvey, a former maiden to Anne Boleyn. Indicating her detachment from Culpeper and her recognition that she could not be inappropriately involved with him, the queen encouraged him to resume his relations with Elizabeth by giving her 'a damask gown' and warning Culpeper that 'he did ill to suffer his tenement [Elizabeth] to be so ill repaired and that she, for to save his honesty, had done some cost over it'. During this interview, according to Culpeper, 'she [Katherine] had bound him both then and now and ever that he both must and did love her again above all other creatures'. Katherine was aware of Culpeper's deceit, however, for at their next interview at Pontefract on 31 August, she accused him thus: 'I marvel that ye could so much dissemble as to say ye loved me so earnestly and yet would and did so soon lie with another.' Aware of the dangers of the meetings, Katherine proceeded to restrain herself and showed Culpeper 'little favour'.[75] This may also have been because of his increasingly controlling behaviour, which would have reminded her of the dangers Dereham posed in her household. As the Queen of England, it was essential for her to behave virtuously and to avoid social exchanges that could give rise to suspicions of sexual misbehaviour, as the downfall of Anne Boleyn in 1536 had so brutally demonstrated.

It is significant that, while Lady Rochford chaperoned these meetings, Katherine admitted to her that if these conversations 'came not out, she feared not for nothing'.[76] She was demonstrably aware of how her enemies could misinterpret her secret exchanges with Culpeper. But, in referring to the actual subject matter of the conversations, Katherine may have been alluding to a possible discussion of Dereham which she could have had with Culpeper. Four days before her meeting with Culpeper at Pontefract, Katherine had appointed Dereham to the position of secretary within her household, in an attempt to silence his arrogant boasts of his previous relationship with her. Warning him to 'take heed what words' he uttered, Katherine offered him £13 in total, probably in a desperate attempt to prevent him from jeopardising her security. If, as Culpeper reported, Katherine was fearful and anxious during their meetings, it is possibly because she lived in dread of Dereham and his aggressive behaviour. If Culpeper was aware of her pre-marital sexual liaisons, her fear is entirely understandable because it would have meant that two men in close proximity to her household, coupled with female attendants such as Katherine Tylney – some of whom had been acquainted with her in the household of the dowager Duchess of Norfolk – had the means of politically ruining her and effecting her disgrace.

Culpeper later recalled that he had kissed the queen's hand, 'saying he would presume no further', and Katherine later admitted that Culpeper had touched no part of her body except her hand.[77] After their final meeting at York in September, when Katherine may have voiced her warning to Culpeper that 'whensoever he went to confession he should never shrive him of any such things as should pass betwixt her and him, for, if he did, surely the King, being Supreme Head of the Church, should have knowledge of it', Katherine sent word via Lady Rochford to Culpeper that she did not wish to see him again: 'I pray you, bid him desire no more to trouble me or send to me.' When Culpeper proved reluctant, Katherine dismissed him as a 'little sweet fool', in which she vocally restrained and distanced herself from him, while showing disdain for 'such light matters'.[78]

In the increasingly dangerous climate of Dereham's aggressive threats and boasting of his former liaisons with the queen, Katherine became more sensitive to the perils of her meetings with Culpeper and sought to put an end to them, especially if his manipulative behaviour endangered her security. At York, the king and queen were welcomed by 200 gentlemen wearing coats of velvet and 4,000 yeomen, who generously bestowed £900 upon the king.[79] Although Henry had hoped to meet at York with his nephew James V, King of Scots, by 26 September the French ambassador reported that the Scottish king was no longer expected.[80]

The circumstances in which Katherine and Culpeper met, during which she expressed her desire that he would be as he had 'promised' her, while assuring him that she was at his 'commandment', indicates that Culpeper most likely discovered unwelcome knowledge about the queen that subsequently caused concern to her. It is surely not a coincidence that their initial meeting took place shortly after Dereham's open declarations of his intimacy with Katherine. That Culpeper could have initially approached Lady Rochford, a senior attendant of the queen, with a view to arranging an interview with Katherine, is suggested by the evidence. In November 1541, the queen revealed that:

> My lady Rocheford hath sondry tymez made instans to her to speke with Culpeper declaryng hym to beare her good wyll and favour ... my lady of Rocheford affyrmyng that he desiered nothyng elles but to speke with her and that she durst swere uppon a booke he ment nothyng but wodin.[81]

When she agreed to meet with Culpeper, Katherine insisted that Lady Rochford attend their interviews as chaperone, and admonished her when she moved away: 'For Goddes sake madam even nere us.'[82] Eventually, she instructed Lady Rochford to inform Culpeper that she would not meet with him again.[83] Culpeper's possessive attitude emerged when he responded that 'he wold take no suche aunswer'.[84] No evidence indicates that the queen and Culpeper were engaged in an adulterous or romantic affair; in this context it is incredible that the majority of modern historians have accused her of cuckolding the king whether for sexual satisfaction or as a means of conceiving a child to pass off as the king's own.

It is possible that some modern historians have argued that Katherine actually considered passing off Culpeper's bastard as the king's child on the grounds that her position remained fragile until she had delivered a son, which was the primary duty of the early modern queen consort. Court observers keenly watched the queen for signs of pregnancy. Since the English consort did not customarily announce her pregnancy to the court, observers relied on ceremonial gestures and rituals as confirmation of a royal pregnancy. This dependence on court protocol and ceremonial led to confusion and uncertainty surrounding the rumoured pregnancies of Henry VIII's previous consorts: whether Anne Boleyn was actually pregnant in 1534 remains a mystery, mostly due to the contradictory court reports. When Henry and Katherine visited York in mid September, the French ambassador wrote to François I that:

> [Henry] is furnishing a great lodging of an old abbey, on which 1,200 or 1,500 workmen are night and day building, painting, &c., and adding tents and pavilions. Besides, he has had brought from London his richest tapestry, plate, and dress, both for himself and his archers, pages, and gentlemen, with marvellous provision of victuals from all parts. This seems to betoken some extraordinary triumph, like an interview of kings or a coronation of this Queen, which is spoken of to put the people of York in hope of having a Duke if she were to have a son.[85]

Marillac's report seems to suggest that the queen would have been honoured with a coronation if had she delivered a son, but whether she was actually widely believed to be pregnant in the autumn of 1541 remains uncertain. In the wake of her downfall two months later, her physicians allegedly confirmed, according to court gossip, that she was biologically unable to produce surviving children. Perhaps Katherine's rumoured pregnancy and the promise of a coronation in York, both of which promised royal favour to this northern city, was intended to maintain a degree of social and political stability in a troubled region of Henry's realm. Memories of the Pilgrimage of Grace of 1536 would not yet have faded from the king's mind. Marillac's report, however, should be read in the context of this wider and enduring court obsession with the childbearing role of the queen consort. From her marriage to Henry in July 1540 to her arrival in York in September 1541, Katherine was the subject of contradictory and confusing court gossip and rumour that focused on whether or not she was believed to be with child. The proliferation of these rumours sheds light on how contemporaries perceived that it was vital that Katherine give birth to a son, a 'spare', should anything befall the king's heir Edward.

After fourteen months of marriage, the queen had not managed to conceive a second son to secure the Tudor succession if the king's son by Jane Seymour, Prince Edward, were to fall ill and die, as had occurred in 1502 when Henry VII's heir Arthur unexpectedly died. Having set aside his first wife, executed his second wife for adultery and incest, lost his third wife in childbed and discarded his fourth wife on the grounds that she had bewitched him into impotence, Henry was surely fearful that his fifth marriage was, once more, contrary to God's will because it had not produced the longed-for second son.

Anxious about her future as Queen of England, Katherine ended her meetings with Culpeper while Dereham continued to threaten her personal and political security. She may have hoped that the end of the Culpeper affair would allow her to regain a sense of safety as the king's consort in the knowledge that he was placated by her agreement to meet with him in secret. But, on the court's return to London that autumn, a malicious allegation regarding Katherine's pre-marital past, made while she was on progress, would destroy any hopes she harboured regarding her future as queen.

9

DISGRACE AND DEATH

THE ROYAL COURT RETURNED slowly back to London, passing through Kettleby, Collyweston and Ampthill. On 26 October, they reached Windsor. The king might have been somewhat worried to learn that his son Edward was suffering from a quartan fever, which the French ambassador described as strange given the prince's young age. It was reported 'that the prince was so fat and unhealthy as to be unlikely to live long'.[1] It is somewhat ironic, given the upcoming events, that Prince Edward's life was feared of at this time, and probably brought home to Henry the continuing uncertainty of the English succession. Whether or not he had come to privately doubt his queen's capacity to bear a second son is unknown, but given that rumours were to circulate weeks later that Katherine's physicians had admitted that she could not bear children, it is probable that the king was anxious about whether his fifth wife had been a suitable choice as consort in terms of her childbearing potential. Nevertheless, publicly the king continued to express love and happiness with his queen. Arriving at Hampton Court on 29 October, Henry was reported to believe that 'after sundry troubles of mind which have happened unto him by marriages, [he had] obtained ... a jewel. For womanhood and very perfect love towards him'; Katherine demonstrated 'virtue and good behaviour' and would be 'to his quietness' and likely to bring 'forth the desired fruits of marriage'.[2] On All Saints Day, Henry also thanked God with 'humble and hearty thanks for the good life he led and trusted to lead' with Katherine. But the king's newfound happiness was to be abruptly destroyed.

During the court's summer progress, Thomas Cranmer, Archbishop of Canterbury, had been approached by a young woman, Mary Lascelles, who had resided in the household of the dowager Duchess of Norfolk in the company of the young Katherine Howard. When Cranmer confided to Henry the details of Mary's allegations, the king agreed that a secret investigation into the queen's conduct should take place, led by the Earl of Southampton, Lord Russell, Sir Anthony Browne and Thomas Wriothesley. Mary was the sister of John Lascelles, a courtier and religious activist who had at one point served Thomas Cromwell. A devout evangelical, Lascelles had urged 'not to be rashe or quike in mayntenyng the scrypture, for yff we wolde lete [Gardiner and Norfolk] a lone and suffer a lettell tyme they wolde (I doubte not) ower throwe them selves, standyng manyfestlye a nenst god and theyr prynce'.[3] In the autumn of 1540, Lascelles had learned that Katherine's uncle, the Duke of Norfolk, was opposed to the idea of reading the Bible in the vernacular. The duke apparently boasted that 'he had never read the Scriptures nor ever would, and it was merry in England before this new learning came up'.[4] While it would be incorrect, therefore, to assume that the evangelical Lascelles's dislike of the uneducated duke motivated him to seek the queen's downfall, it is possible to argue that 'Lascelles … continued to brood on the religious situation, doubtless earnestly praying for divine guidance as to whether and how to undermine the influence of the Howard clan'.[5]

When John visited his sister Mary in Sussex in 1541 he encouraged her to seek a place in the queen's household. Mary refused her brother's suggestion, reporting that she found the queen 'light' in living and 'conditions'. When questioned by the Earl of Southampton, Mary confessed that 'misconduct' had taken place some three or four years previously between Katherine and Henry Manox, although she had berated Manox for his arrogance in seeking to corrupt one of the dowager duchess's relatives while criticising Katherine's behaviour, spitefully suggesting that 'she will be nought within a while'.[6] But Manox had aggressively and callously refused to desist in seducing Katherine, instead bragging about his manipulation of her: 'I know her well enough, for I have had her by the cunt, and I know it among a hundred.' He reported that 'she loves me, and I love her, and she hath said to me that I shall have her maidenhead, though it be painful to her, and not doubting but I will be good to her hereafter'.[7] Whether Katherine had promised Manox anything of the sort is highly unlikely, for she was well aware of the lineage of her family and therefore refused to associate herself with a lowly musician. Manox may well have invented these details to justify his pursuit of Katherine. When investigated, Manox confirmed Mary's allegations, but swore 'upon his damnation and most extreme punishment of his body, he never knew her [Katherine] carnally'.[8]

Portrait of a Lady. Dated
c. 1540–45, it is
possible that this is a
portrait of Katherine
Howard after her
marriage to Henry VIII.
© Metropolitan Museum
of Art, New York

Unknown woman, formerly identified
as Katherine Howard. This late
seventeenth-century oil on panel painting
probably depicts Elizabeth Seymour, sister of
Jane, or a niece of Henry VIII, perhaps Lady
Margaret Douglas or Frances Brandon. Versions
of this portrait are also held at the Toledo
Museum of Art and at Hever Castle. © National
Portrait Gallery, London

Henry VIII. The king was 49 years old and in increasingly poor health when he married Katherine in 1540. © Bridgeman Images

Thomas Howard, 3rd Duke of Norfolk. The duke was the uncle of both Anne Boleyn and Katherine Howard. © Bridgeman Images

Anne Boleyn. Henry VIII's second wife was the first Queen of England to be executed, in 1536; her young cousin Katherine Howard suffered the same fate in 1542. © Bridgeman Images

Jane Seymour. Henry VIII married his third wife, Jane Seymour, at Whitehall Palace on 30 May 1536. Jane gave birth to the long-desired male heir, Edward, on 12 October 1537, but she was never crowned. She died twelve days after her son's birth and was buried at St George's Chapel, Windsor. © Royal Collection Trust/Her Majesty Queen Elizabeth II, 2018

Anne of Cleves. Katherine briefly served as Henry VIII's fourth wife in 1540. © Bridgeman Images

Left: Hampton Court Palace. Katherine was proclaimed queen at Hampton Court on 8 August 1540, and it was at the palace in November 1541 that Henry VIII learned of her pre-marital liaisons. According to legend, Katherine ran down what is today known as the Haunted Gallery in a desperate attempt to speak to her husband. © Historic Royal Palaces

Right: Lincoln Cathedral. Henry and Katherine visited the cathedral in August 1541 as part of their northern progress. © Author's collection

Below: The Old Bishop's Palace, Lincoln. Henry and Katherine may have stayed here in August 1541. © Author's collection

Left: York Minster. Henry and Katherine visited York in September 1541. The French ambassador wrote that York was rumoured to be hosting 'a coronation of this Queen … if she were to have a son'. If true, the coronation would have taken place at York Minster. © Author's collection

The Great Hall, Gainsborough Old Hall. After their stay in Lincoln, Henry and Katherine visited Gainsborough Old Hall, home of Thomas Burgh. Thomas's son Edward was briefly married to Katherine Parr, who became Henry VIII's sixth wife in 1543. © Bridgeman Images

Chenies Manor House, home of John Russell, later first earl of Bedford. Henry and Katherine stayed here in October 1541 on their return journey to London. © Bridgeman Images

The Chapel Royal of St Peter ad Vincula, Tower of London. Katherine's remains were interred here after her execution. © Historic Royal Palaces

Memorial to Katherine Howard at the Chapel Royal of St Peter ad Vincula, Tower of London. © Historic Royal Palaces

Dereham, who had been continuing to cause trouble in the queen's household through his foolish behaviour, was later questioned after both Manox and Mary Lascelles testified to his pursuit of Katherine. He openly and without shame confided that 'he hath had carnal knowledge with the Queen, lying in bed by her in his doublet and hosen divers times and six or seven times in naked bed with her'. Another of Katherine's acquaintances, Alice Restwold, alluded to the 'puffing and blowing' between Katherine and Dereham.[9] Perhaps significantly, none of these individuals suggested that Dereham had forcefully pursued Katherine with the pursuit of sexual pleasure. As has been indicated, the language utilised by men and women during this period to describe sexual experiences was vastly different.[10] No mention was made of how Katherine herself felt during, and reacted to, the sexual experiences of her adolescence, which is not surprising in the context of the time, for interrogators in criminal cases involving sexual crimes often did not believe in the need to record how women felt during sex, believing instead that they usually consented to sexual relations.[11]

Two days later, Cranmer interviewed Katherine herself after initially approaching the queen with her uncles, Audley and Winchester. She had been confined to her chambers and was informed that 'there is no more time to dance'.[12] Undoubtedly shocked and horrified by the unwelcome news that Mary Lascelles had provided details about her adolescence in the dowager duchess's household, Katherine was found by the archbishop in an appalling state. He feared that she would fall into a frenzy, and believed that her state 'would have pitied any man's heart to see'.[13] Cranmer proceeded to emphasise her demerits, on the orders of the king, but then decided to offer her mercy in an attempt to exact a confession. This initially seemed effective, since 'for a time she began to be more temperate and quiet, saving that she still sobbed and wept'. But Cranmer was to be disappointed, for Katherine's composure once again deserted her shortly afterwards and she 'suddenly fell into a new rage, much worse than before', before admitting to the archbishop that:

> The fear of death grieved me not so much before, as doth now the remembrance of the king's goodness; for when I remember how gracious and loving a prince I had, I cannot but sorrow; but this sudden mercy, and more than I could have looked for, showed unto me, so unworthy at this time, makes my offences to appear before my eyes much more heinous than they did before.[14]

She nevertheless was able to confess to Cranmer that Manox had inappropriately fondled the 'secret parts' of her body and Dereham, after his 'many persuasions', had succeeded in seducing her. According to Gilbert Burnet, the seventeenth-century bishop of Salisbury, Katherine made the following confession in relation to her liaison with Dereham:

> First, I do say, that Deram hath many times moved unto me the question of matrimony; whereunto, as far as I remember, I never granted him more than before I have confessed: and as for these words, *I promise you, I do love you with all my heart*, I do not remember that ever I spake them. But as concerning the other words, that I should promise him by my faith and troth, that I would never other husband but him, I am sure I never spake them.[15]
>
> [...]
>
> Examined whether I called him husband, and he me wife. I do answer, that there was communication in the house that we two should marry together; and some of his enemies had envy thereat, wherefore, he desired me to give him leave to call me wife, and that I would call him husband. And I said I was content. And so after that, commonly he called me wife, and many times I called him husband. And he used many times to kiss me, and so he did to many other commonly in the house. And, I suppose, that this be true, that at one time when he kissed me very often, some said that were present, *they trowed that he would never have kissed me enough*. Whereto he answered, *Who should let* [prevent] *him to kiss his own wife?* Then said one of them, *I trow this matter will come to pass as the common saying is. What is that?* quoth he. *Marry,* said the other, *That Mr. Deram shall have Mrs. Katherine Howard. By St. John,* said Deram, *you may guess twice, and guess worse.* But that I should wink upon him, and say secretly, *What and this should come to my lady's ear?* I suppose verily there was no such thing.
>
> As for carnal knowledge, I confess as I did before, that divers times he hath lien with me, sometime in his doublet and hose, and two or three times naked: but not so naked that he had nothing upon him, for he had always at the least his doublet, and as I do think, his hose also, but I mean naked when his hose were put down. And divers times he would bring wine, strawberries, apples, and other things to make good cheer, after my lady was gone to bed. But that he made any special banquet, that by appointment between him and me, he should tarry after the keys were delivered to my lady, that is utterly untrue. Nor did I ever steal the keys myself, nor desired any person to steal them, to that intent and purpose to let in Deram, but for many other causes the doors have been opened, sometime over night, and sometime early in the morning, as well at the request of me, as of other. And sometime Deram hath come in early in the morning, and ordered him very lewdly, but never at my request, nor consent.
>
> And that Wilks and Baskervile should say, what shifts should we make, if my lady should come in suddenly. And I should answer, that he should go

into the little gallery. I never said that if my lady came he should go into the gallery, but he hath said so himself, and so he hath done indeed.

As for the communication of my going to the court, I remember that he said to me, that if I were gone, he would not tarry long in the house. And I said again, that he might do as he list. And further communication of that matter, I remember not. But that I should say, it grieved me as much as it did him, or that he should never live to say thou hast swerved, or that the tears should trickle down by my cheeks, none of them be true. For all that knew me, and kept my company, knew how glad and desirous I was to come to the court.

As for the communication after his coming out of Ireland, is untrue. But as far as I remember, he then asked me, if I should be married to Mr. Culpepper, for so he said he heard reported. Then I made answer, What should you trouble me therewith, for you know I will not have you; and if you heard such report, you heard more than I do know.[16]

In vocalising her memories of the liaison with Dereham, Katherine admitted that they had referred to one another as husband and wife, but she denied ever saying that she loved him. When Dereham 'lewdly' arrived in the chamber early in the morning, Katherine denied that he did so at her request or with her consent. Dereham believed that she 'would never other husband but him', but Katherine evidently did not agree with Dereham's version of events regarding their relationship: 'I am sure I never spake them.' That is, although Dereham believed that he was married to Katherine, she did not believe that they were actually joined in wedlock. It may be significant that, while denying that she loved Dereham or ever agreed to marry no other man but him, she assured him that she 'was content' to refer to him as husband and for him to describe her as his wife. It is impossible to know exactly what she meant by 'content': possibly it meant that she willingly agreed to Dereham's suggestion of their terms of address for one another, but it is also possible that she consented to his request in a bid to please or placate him. When she received an appointment at court in the autumn of 1539, she was 'glad and desirous' because it meant that she would no longer have to be in the company of Dereham.

She then beseeched the king to grant her mercy on account of her youth, 'ignorance and frailty', although admitting that she deserved 'extreme punishment'.[17] It is important to remember, however, that for a woman to have had sexual experiences before she married the king was not, at this stage, a criminal offence. Chapuys reported at this time that the queen's household was discharged, her brother Charles Howard was forbidden from the king's chamber, and Dereham had been sent to the Tower on account of the king's belief that he had actually been betrothed to the queen before her marriage, rendering her subsequent marriage to Henry invalid.[18] It emerged that Katherine's brother Charles had been clandestinely involved with the king's niece Margaret Douglas. On 11 November, the French ambassador wrote that 'her [Katherine's] brother, gentleman of this King, is banished from Court without reason given'.[19] There is no evidence that Katherine was questioned about her brother's relationship with Margaret Douglas, which would seem to suggest that she had been unaware of it.[20] Marillac also reported the rumour that 'physicians say she [Katherine] cannot bear children'.[21]

Although Dereham admitted that a marriage contract had existed between him and Katherine, which could account for his later admissions that he was indeed married to her, the queen disagreed that she had been pre-contracted to Dereham, although it is possible – if unproven – that this might have spared her life. Most modern historians suggest that Katherine did not acknowledge such a pre-contract due to her refusal to accept that she had never, in consequence, been Queen of England.[22] However, in view of the reality of Katherine's sexual relations with Dereham in 1538–39 it is more likely that the queen believed that no pre-contract had existed since she had never consented to Dereham's sexual advances. The Catholic Church specifically required that vows for marriage should only be freely given and not coerced in order for them to be valid.

On 11 November, the Privy Council learned that the king wished to send his wife to Syon Abbey, where she would be housed 'moderately, as her life has deserved, without any cloth of estate'. Although it was confirmed that Katherine would continue to be served 'in the state of a Queen', she was permitted only the use of three chambers, 'hanged with mean stuff', and the services of four gentlewomen, including her half-sister Isabel, Lady Baynton, and two chamberers.[23] Her clothing as prisoner was also much plainer than that worn during her tenure as queen. As Maria Hayward highlighted, with the exception of Anne Boleyn, the clothing of high-ranking imprisoned Tudor women was regulated and limited. Katherine was deprived of her jewellery and some of her clothing, and was instructed to wear French hoods without 'stone or pearl in the same'. She was not permitted to wear cloth of gold, cloth of silver or cloth of tissue once she was imprisoned.[24]

Marillac reported that the king was 'as gay as ever he saw him' and alluded to rumours that the king would take back Anne of Cleves in the wake of Katherine's disgrace.[25] Surely Henry was not happy, because Katherine's downfall appears to have devastated him on both a personal and a political level. Not only had his queen failed to secure the English succession by bearing him a second son, but evidence had emerged that she had become sexually experienced at an early age and had failed to inform him of it at the time of their marriage. Prevailing cultural and social beliefs may have governed the king's fear that, because Katherine had lost her virginity several years previously, his wife had conducted amorous affairs as queen behind his back.[26] The king may also have genuinely believed that his wife might have revealed damaging information about his sexual habits and his impotence to her suspected lovers, as Anne Boleyn had allegedly done in 1536.

In the indictment drawn up against her, Katherine was accused of leading the king 'by word and gesture to love her' and had jeopardised the succession at risk 'to the most fearful peril and danger of the destruction of your [Henry's] most royal person and to the utter loss, disherison and desolation of this your Realm of England'. This damning indictment of Katherine's behaviour played on, and was informed by, contemporary fears of female sexuality, for women were believed to possess the ability to manipulate and control male sexuality, bewitching men into loving them, and destroying their manhood, which as a fragile achievement was always open to threat and dishonour.[27] Early modern men, perhaps including Henry, feared and doubted their ability to rule their wives, especially on a sexual level, since wives gained a personal knowledge of their husbands' bodies and could subsequently dishonour their husbands on a sexual level by exposing their manhood to risks and dangers.[28] Early modern men often feared being cuckolded, and because masculine identity was constructed largely on the basis of the control of female sexuality, it was essential that women's sexual lives were rigorously controlled, prescribed and regulated.[29]

During the course of his interrogation, Dereham voiced the suspicion that Culpeper had succeeded him in Katherine's affections. The council were immediately alerted to the possibility that the queen had committed adultery with her husband's gentleman of the privy chamber, alluding to their suspicion in a letter written to William Paget, the English ambassador in France: '[Now may you] see what was done before the marriage. God knoweth what hath been done sithence.'[30] They also feared the nature of Katherine's relations with Dereham during her period as queen, for his appointment to the position of private secretary was perceived in the worst possible light. However, because they were unaware of, or failed to appreciate, Katherine's unwilling relations with Dereham during her adolescence, they were unable to believe the likeliest scenario that she had only appointed him on the advice of her step-grandmother, and hoped to silence him about their former relations by appearing to show him favour.

Katherine admitted that Culpeper had touched no part of her body except her hand, and confirmed that she had met with him three times during the summer progress at Lincoln, Pontefract and York with the assistance of

Lady Rochford. She confessed that she bestowed gifts of a cap, chain and a cramp-ring upon him. But the queen refused to admit that adultery had taken place between the two. When examined, Culpeper reported that he intended 'to do ill with her', which together with Katherine's confession effectively disposes of the popular belief that theirs was a sexual relationship. He believed that the queen sought 'in every house [to] seek for the back doors and back stairs herself'. Marillac later reported that 'although he [Culpeper] had not passed beyond words; for he confessed his intentions to do so, and his confessed conversation, being held by a subject to a Queen, deserved death'.[31]

As with Dereham's admission, the interrogators did not concern themselves with whether or not the queen herself shared the alleged desire of Culpeper. When subjected to questioning, Lady Rochford reported that she had heard and seen nothing at the interviews between the queen and Culpeper, although she later opined that the couple had known each other carnally but admitted that Katherine had daily asked for Culpeper since her 'trouble'.[32] Perhaps she wished to discover what Culpeper had confessed to the interrogators and whether or not it concerned her relations with Dereham. The queen's ladies, Katherine Tylney and Margaret Morton, testified that the queen had spent two nights in Lady Rochford's chamber during the summer progress, but they admitted that they were unaware of who she had been meeting there. Margaret later added that the queen had forbidden Mrs Loffkyn and her other ladies to enter her bedchamber unless called, and later threatened to dismiss Mrs Loffkyn from her household. She reported that every night the queen's chamber door was locked.[33]

Only when evidence had emerged that the queen had not been a virgin at the time of her marriage to Henry did her ladies voice the suspicion that she had subsequently conducted an adulterous liaison behind her husband's back. Tellingly, no suspicion of the queen's behaviour during the summer progress had been raised by her ladies or other officials, which cautions against accepting these interrogations at face value and indicates that these revelations only occurred when it became known that the queen had engaged in pre-marital sexual liaisons. As with Anne Boleyn, Katherine's ladies turned against her when faced with the prospect of the king's wrath and possibly even punishment for what the interrogators termed misprision of treason. Consequently, her actions may well have been interpreted in the worst possible light. Her meetings with Culpeper were thought to constitute treason, although it was never resolved whether theirs had been a sexual relationship, a platonic affair or whether it arose in a climate of political intrigue in the queen's household. As has been succinctly noted, 'the only indiscretion proved against Catherine Howard was that she had, quite understandably, failed to inform her royal lover that her life before her marriage had not been as pure as might have been expected of a queen'.[34] On 22 November, Katherine's title of queen was stripped from her.

Describing her as a prostitute, Katherine's uncle the Duke of Norfolk sought to placate Henry by distancing himself from his 'abominable' niece, 'mine ungracious mother-in-law, mine unhappy brother ... with my lewd sister of Bridgewater', all of whom were accused of aiding the queen in her abominable lifestyle and concealing it from the king. He regretted that Katherine had shown him 'small love'.[35] Although the purpose of writing such a letter was to save himself from the threatened destruction of his family, the evidence seems to indicate that Norfolk was genuinely unaware of his niece's sexual experiences during her adolescence in the household of the dowager duchess. His horror and disgust at the revelation that she had not been a virgin at her marriage is evident, and surely confirms that, had he been aware of her pre-marital escapades, he would never have sought a place for her at court in the household of Anne of Cleves. Inviting Katherine to court threatened the dishonour of the Howard family and it is inconceivable that the proud and ambitious duke would have taken the risk of doing so if he had known of his niece's pre-marital relationships.

It is worth considering why it was at this point that Mary Lascelles fatally voiced her opinion to her brother that Katherine was light in both her living and conditions, provoking John to inform the archbishop about the queen's sexual past. There is no evidence that she was personally hostile to Katherine, for she attempted to portray herself positively by confessing that she had sought to persuade Manox to desist from seducing the young Katherine. Whether or not she had in fact done so is unknown. On the other hand, as has been noted, John was distrustful and resentful of the Howards on account of their political influence and their religious conservatism. Although he was to insist that he had only revealed information about the queen's past in order to avoid a charge of misprision of treason, it is possible that he delighted in the chance to ruin the Howards.[36]

Although Mary may not have knowingly revealed this information about Queen Katherine in a spiteful attempt to destroy her reputation, the fact that she did do so had fatal consequences for Katherine and her family. The early modern slander of highborn women often had damaging consequences, for in focusing overwhelmingly on sexual sins dishonour dismantled the trappings of these women's rank and the credit of their marriages.[37] Only in the context of early modern beliefs about gender, sexuality and honour can John's decision to reveal information about Katherine's past and the negative reception it received at court be fully understood. The early modern period witnessed a

growing obsession with the dangers associated with womanhood and a visible
fear of women's intentions and behaviour, focusing on their principal vices
that included voracious sexuality, scolding, and wilful pride and vanity which
endangered male livelihood.[38] Honourable women retained their honour
through avoiding sexual sin and maintaining a modest and chaste appearance.[39]
In view of this it is significant that Katherine was condemned for feigning
chastity and using modest gestures to ensure that the king would 'love her' by
behaving in a 'pure and chaste' manner.[40] The men accused with Katherine
of sexual crimes adhered to prevailing gender and cultural prejudices which
fixated on the lasciviousness of women. Manox and Dereham both swore that
she had consented to their advances while Culpeper blamed the queen for
enticing him, through Lady Rochford, to meet with her in private because
she was dying for his love.[41] Culpeper's admission was at odds with Katherine's
own recorded remarks about him.

Other Howard relatives were subsequently interrogated and punished for
their role in concealing their knowledge about Katherine. Four Howard
women, including the queen's step-grandmother Agnes, her aunts Katherine,
Countess of Bridgewater and Lady Margaret Howard, and her sister-in-law
Anne were punished for concealing information about Katherine's relations with Manox and Dereham.[42] By 1 December the Privy Council had
confirmed the need to interrogate Agnes, dowager Duchess of Norfolk, and
arranged for Katherine's former acquaintances Joan Bulmer and Robert
Damport to be examined regarding the queen's pre-marital sexual experiences.[43] The dowager Duchess of Norfolk believed that the queen and
Dereham should not die for what had passed several years before under her
roof, but confirmed her sorrow for the king, who had taken the matter 'heav-
ily'.[44] She also admitted that she had hidden £800 in her house, falling on her
knees and weeping 'most abundantly' before her examiners.[45] Lady Margaret,
when interrogated, reported that she had been aware of the affair between
Dereham and her niece, although the Countess of Bridgewater and Anne
Howard denied knowledge of Katherine's sexual relations with Dereham.
Katherine's uncle Lord William Howard also admitted knowing about his
niece's sexual past, although he had earlier admonished her and her acquaintances for being 'mad wenches' who 'must thus fall out' because they were
unable to be merry.[46] Although the evidence against the queen and her associates proved that she had not been a virgin when she married Henry in 1540,
the king in his grief and dismay was certain that she had committed adultery
with both Dereham and Culpeper after her marriage. This was despite the
fact that Katherine, Dereham and Culpeper were 'falsely accused of crimes
they never committed, and condemned on the most tenuous, distorted and

vicious evidence possible – testimony which today would be thrown out of court as totally false and unacceptable'.[47]

The Spanish ambassador Chapuys reported at this time that the king had 'wonderfully felt the case of the Queen, his wife, and has certainly shown greater sorrow at her loss than at the faults, loss, or divorce of his proceeding wives'. Cynically, he attributed this to the fact that Henry did not yet have a new wife to replace Katherine, meaning that 'it is like the case of the woman who cried more bitterly at the loss of her tenth husband than at the deaths of all the others together'.[48] Despite his personal sorrow, Henry proceeded to exact his vengeance on both Dereham and Culpeper. His honour required it, for being deemed a cuckold was perhaps the most damaging threat to early modern masculinity. Both men may have been tortured during the interrogations, since the documents against them contain suggestive phrases such as 'this much we know for the beginning' which could support such a conclusion, although it remains uncertain whether torture – technically illegal – was employed during the examinations.[49] On 1 December both men were tried for treason at the Guildhall in London. The French ambassador voiced the opinion that 'many people thought the publication of these foul details strange, but the intention is to prevent it being said afterwards that they were unjustly condemned'.[50] Culpeper, after initially pleading not guilty, changed his plea to guilty during the trial. Both were found guilty and were sentenced to a traitor's death. The Duke of Norfolk, who was present at the trial, was seen to laugh loudly during the proceedings 'as if he had cause to rejoice'.[51]

On 10 December both men were executed at Tyburn. Because of his intimacy with the king, Culpeper's sentence was commuted to decapitation. Modern historians continue to believe that this closeness to the king accounts for why Dereham was forced to suffer the penalty of hanging, drawing and quartering, but an alternative interpretation is possible when considering his sexual relations with Katherine. Since the queen had reported that Dereham had forcibly raped her, it is possible that the king ordered that Dereham should suffer a traitor's death because rape was viewed at this time as a theft of male property. The prevailing custom in medieval England had been to execute those who raped virgins, especially those who sexually assaulted minors.[52] Because those who sexually molested pre-pubescent girls suffered the death penalty, it is possible that Dereham suffered a worse death than Culpeper because of his molestation of the teenaged Katherine, which became doubly heinous in the eyes of the king when Dereham returned to court in 1541 and, Henry suspected, swiftly resumed his former relationship with the queen. In the absence of any other evidence to indicate why Dereham was forced to suffer a traitor's death rather than decapitation, this suggestion is reasonable. Alternatively, it is possible that Culpeper's favour with the king permitted him the kinder death. The English merchant Richard Hilles later opined to Henry Bullinger that 'people did not inquire much, as it is no new thing to see men hanged, quartered or beheaded for one thing or another, sometimes for trifling expressions construed as [being] against the king'.[53]

On 22 December Katherine's relatives were tried and found guilty of misprision of treason. The indictment read as follows:

> Jurors further find that the said Katherine Tylney, Alice Restwold, wife of Anthony Restwold, of the same place, Gentleman; Joan Bulmer wife of William Bulmer, of the same place; Gentleman; Anne Howard, wife of Henry Howard late of Lambeth, Esq.; Robert Damporte late of the same place, Gentleman; Malena Tylney late of the same place, widow; and Margaret Benet, wife of John Benet, late of the same place; Gentleman; knowing the wicked life of the Queen and Dereham, did conceal the same from the King and all his Councillors. And that this said Agnes, Duchess of Norfolk, with whom the Queen had been educated from her youth upward; William Howard, late of Lambeth, uncle of the Queen and one of the King's Councillors; Margaret Howard, wife of William Howard; Katherine, Countess of Bridgewater, late of Lambeth, otherwise Katherine the wife of Henry, Earl of Bridgewater; Edward Waldegrave late of Lambeth, Gentleman; and William Asheley, late of Lambeth, in the county of Surrey, knowing that certain letters and papers had been taken from a chest and concealing the information from the King... Katherine Tylney, Alice Restwold, Joan Bulmer, Anne Howard, Malena Tylney, Margaret Benet, Margaret Howard, Edward Waldegrave, and William Asheley are brought to the Bar by the Constable of the Tower, and being severally arraigned as well upon the Surrey Indictment, as the Indictments for Kent, and Middlesex, they pleaded guilty. JUDGEMENT: they shall be severally taken back by the Constable of the Tower, and in the same Tower, or elsewhere, as the King shall direct, be kept in perpetual imprisonment and that all their goods and chattels shall be forfeited to the King, and their lands and tenements seized into the King's hands.[54]

Perhaps surprisingly, Henry Manox was not convicted of misprision of treason or for his sexual relations with Katherine before she had been seduced by Dereham. Rather than suffering the fate of Dereham, he escaped prosecution and eventually moved to Hemingford in Huntingdonshire, dying in 1564, thirty years after his ultimately tragic relations with the one-time Queen of England.[55]

Katherine's brothers also escaped punishment. Henry Howard received a gift of £10 '*intuitu charitatis*' a few weeks after his sister's death.[56] Charles left court in disgrace on account of his relationship with Margaret Douglas and departed for Europe. He returned to England in 1544 and joined the army of Edward Seymour, Earl of Hertford that was sent to invade Scotland. Charles was later knighted by Hertford and he may have died in France at an unknown date.[57] Katherine's brothers were later seen to ride about the town in their finest attire, in order 'to show that they did not share the crimes of their relatives'.[58] In the wake of her downfall, Katherine's relatives were desirous of publicly demonstrating that they shared none of her guilt.

Following the executions of Dereham and Culpeper, the bill of attainder against Katherine and Lady Rochford was introduced in parliament in January 1542. The attainder recorded that:

> Katharine Howard whom the King took to wife is proved to have been not of pure and honest living before her marriage, and the fact that she has since taken to her service one Francis Dereham, the person with whom she 'used that vicious life before,' and has taken as chamberer a woman who was privy to her naughty life before, is proof of her will to return to her old abominable life. Also she has confederated with lady Jane Rocheford, widow, late wife of Sir Geo. Boleyn, late lord Rocheford, to 'bring her vicious and abominable purpose to pass' with Thos. Culpeper, late one of the King's Privy Chamber, and has met Culpeper in 'a secret and vile place,' at 11 o'clock at night, and remained there with him until 3 a.m., with only 'that bawd, the lady Jane Rocheford.' For these treasons, Culpeper and Dereham have been convicted and executed, and the Queen and lady Rochford stand indicted. The indictments of such as have lately suffered are hereby approved, and the said Queen and lady Rochford are, by authority of this Parliament, convicted and attainted of high treason, and shall suffer accordingly; and the said Queen, lady Rocheford, Culpeper, and Dereham shall forfeit to the Crown all possessions which they held on 25 Aug. 33 Hen.VIII. The Royal assent to this Act shall be given by commission.[59]

Lord Chancellor Audley, however, warned that the queen should not be proceeded against too hastily for she was 'an illustrious and public' person and so her case should 'be judged with … integrity'. He recommended that Katherine should be allowed to speak in her own defence to the peers of the realm.[60] The Earl of Southampton, Archbishop Cranmer, the Duke of Suffolk and the Bishop of Westminster later met with the queen, who confirmed her guilt and asked for the king to bestow some of her clothes upon her ladies for she had no other way of paying them for their service. On 11 February the attainder against the queen and Lady Rochford became law. It was made a criminal offence for any future consort who was not a virgin to conceal her sexual past from the king. Unlike Anne Boleyn, Katherine was never granted a trial in which to state her case before the peers of the realm. Although acts of attainder had been consistently used by earlier monarchs such as Richard III and Henry VII, to deny the queen consort the opportunity to stand trial meant that Katherine's downfall was distinguished from that of Anne Boleyn in 1536. Whether the decision of Henry and the Privy Council not to proceed with a trial was fair remains uncertain for, as would later be stated by the defenders of Mary Queen of Scots, 'it is against all law and reason to condemn any living creature without first hearing them in their defence'.[61] It is perhaps for this reason that it has been stated with regard to Katherine that she was 'led like a sheep to the slaughter, without being permitted to unclose her lips in her own defence'.[62]

Chapuys heard at this time that Katherine, still imprisoned at Syon Abbey, was 'making good cheer, fatter and handsomer than ever, taking great care of her person, well dressed, and much adorned; more imperious and command-ing, and more difficult to please than she ever was when living with the King, her husband'.[63] Surely Chapuys was deceived, for her uncle heard that she was tormented and sorrowful, and Marillac also reported that she wept and cried, tormenting herself regularly. Katherine's life was about to end brutally on the assumption that she had intended to commit adultery with Culpeper, if she had not already done so, and because her pre-marital relationship with Dereham meant that she had deceived the king about her virginity. She cannot but have been aware that during her short life she had been surrounded by avaricious and arrogant men who sought to exploit her to further their own influence and gain a measure of control over her. Fear of female sexuality and family dishonour governed her downfall in 1541–42, which was insti-gated when Mary Lascelles opined that Katherine was dissolute. Her failure to provide the king with a second son confirmed the king's belief that he had erred grievously in selecting her as a consort. Rumours circulated at this time that she was unable to bear children. Henry VIII seems to have shared the contemporary cultural and social beliefs regarding pregnancy and fertility, which meant that Katherine was held responsible, as were three of the king's previous four wives, for failing to bear her husband a son. Faced with a brutal fate, it is hardly likely that she was 'making good cheer' as Chapuys believed, but it is also possible that in her isolation she was still unaware of the sentence of death against her.

On 10 February Suffolk and Southampton arrived at Syon Abbey to escort the queen to the Tower of London, where her accomplice Lady Rochford already resided. Lady Rochford had suffered a mental breakdown after being incarcerated at the Tower, which meant that she was placed in the care of Lady Anne Russell, whose job it was to nurse Lady Rochford back to health. The Spanish ambassador Chapuys recorded that:

> On the afternoon of the 10th, the Queen after some difficulty and resist-
> ance was conducted to the Tower by the river. The Lord Privy Seal, with a
> number of privy councillors and a large retinue of servants, went first in a
> large oared barge; then came a small covered boat with the Queen and four
> ladies of her suite, besides four sailors to man the boat. Then followed the
> duke of Suffolk in a big and well-manned barge, with plenty of armed men
> inside. On their arrival at the Tower stairs the Lord Privy Seal and the duke
> of Suffolk landed first; then the Queen herself, dressed in black velvet, with
> the same honors and ceremonies as if she were still reigning.[64]

Chapuys had also heard that Lady Rochford 'had shown symptoms of mad-
ness' in the wake of her mental breakdown, but whether she was actually
insane as historians have traditionally suggested remains uncertain.[65] When the
lords arrived to escort Katherine, she broke down and had to be forcibly conducted into the barge waiting for her. Late on the evening of 12 February, both
she and Lady Rochford were informed that they would die on the morrow.[66]
Famously, it was reported by Chapuys that Katherine spent her last hours
practising how to lay her head on the block in order to die well. It was commented that, although the English people were by now somewhat familiarised
with the sight of blood, they experienced 'feelings of national abasement' as
'they beheld another queen ignominiously led to the scaffold'.[67] Some observers were in doubt as to whether or not Katherine was guilty, for the Lord
Chancellor admitted that 'some do suppose her to be innocent'.[68]

On the morning of her death, Katherine swore to her confessor
Dr Longland, Bishop of Lincoln, that:

> As to the act, my reverend lord, for which I stand condemned, God and his
> holy angels I take to witness, upon my soul's salvation, that I die guiltless, never
> having so abused my sovereign's bed. What other sins and follies of youth I
> have committed I will not excuse; but I am assured that for them God hath
> brought this punishment upon me, and will, in his mercy, remit them, for
> which, I pray you, pray with me unto his Son and my Saviour, Christ.[69]

Although Anne Boleyn's admission of innocence before the Sacrament on the eve of her death has been seen as compelling evidence by historians that she was guiltless of the crimes attributed to her, Katherine's act of doing so has not prevented them from judging her to have been guilty.

The following morning at nine, Katherine and Lady Rochford were conducted to the scaffold within the Tower of London. The foreign ambassadors were present, although both Katherine's uncle Norfolk and the Duke of Suffolk were absent.[70] Marillac described the queen as 'so weak that she could hardly speak', which is plausible given earlier reports that she had been in a fragile state during her imprisonment. Chapuys confirmed that neither Katherine nor Lady Rochford spoke much on the scaffold.[71] Hall reported that both women confessed their offences and died repentant.[72] A merchant, Ottwell Johnson, who was present, later wrote to his brother John that the queen and Lady Rochford 'made the most godly and Christian end that ever was heard tell of … uttering their lively faith in the blood of Christ only, and with godly words and steadfast countenances, they desired all Christian people to take regard unto their worthy and just punishment for their offences against God', and admitted that they had sinned traitorously against the king and deserved to die by the laws of the realm.[73] The queen's head was removed with a single stroke before Lady Rochford was also decapitated. It is a myth that she admitted on the scaffold her sinfulness in providing false evidence of incest between her husband and Queen Anne, although it was felt that she spent too long in recounting the 'several faults which she had committed in her life'.[74] Both women were later buried in the Tower chapel of St Peter ad Vincula. Katherine's remains have never been found, although the remains of a woman aged between 30 and 40 found in the 1861 excavation led Dr Doyne Bell to presume that they belonged to Lady Rochford, who was aged around 37 at her execution.[75]

Retha Warnicke noted that 'Catholic polemicists, especially [Nicholas] Sander, defamed Anne Boleyn and Katherine Howard in order to attack the characters of Henry [VIII] and Elizabeth [I] because the king removed England from the Roman confession and the queen established a Protestant church'.[76] One effective means of defaming Katherine's reputation was to present her as performing rebelliously on the scaffold in the final moments before her death. Early modern authors believed that the executed individual should demonstrate meekness and an acceptance of death in order to attain salvation. Even if the individual was actually innocent of the crimes for which they had been accused, condemned and brought to execution, it was nonetheless expected that they would publicly proclaim their sinfulness and their deservedness of death as the will of God. Because they were critical of his decision to break with the Roman Catholic Church and establish the Church of England as a means of attaining an annulment of his first marriage to Katherine of Aragon, polemicists hostile to Henry VIII chose to defame his wives, including Katherine Howard, in representing the king as foolish, vulnerable to political manipulation, and easily led by lust. One means of slandering Katherine was in representing her conduct at her execution as rebellious, in defiant opposition to early modern expectations of how the accused individual should respond to their death sentence.

Johnson's characterisation of the queen's death as conventional and in line with contemporary expectations of the good death stands in marked contrast to the version offered by the unknown Spanish chronicler. Accepting the official stance of Katherine's adulterous relationship with Culpeper, the chronicler reported that the queen confessed that she would rather have been married to Culpeper 'than be mistress of the world, but sin blinded me and greed of grandeur'. Her final words were: 'I die a Queen, but I would rather die the wife of Culpepper.'[77] Elsewhere, Edward Hall recorded that 'these two Ladies were behedded on the Grene, within the Tower with an axe, and confessed their offences, and died repentaunt', while Charles Wriothesley noted that 'the sayd Quene ... was beheaded within the Tower on the grene, and my Lady of Rochforde also', and the ambassador Chapuys opined that 'neither she [Lady Rochford] nor the Queen spoke much on the scaffold; they only confessed their guilt and prayed for the King's welfare'.[78] None of these accounts suggest a rebellious death on the scaffold.

Katherine Howard had been queen consort for little over sixteen months when her title of queen was stripped from her in November 1541, and died on the scaffold in her eighteenth year. Although both her interrogators and her husband believed that she had intended to commit, or actually had committed, adultery with Thomas Culpeper during her queenship, the evidence available from the indictments surely demonstrates that Katherine was not unfaithful to her husband in the physical sense and the question of intent remains uncertain, but the evidence argued in this biography has indicated that she was not in love with Culpeper and her approach to him was reactive, even passive. Only when it emerged that Katherine had not been a virgin at the time of her marriage did her ladies step forward and provide eventually damning evidence that she had secretly met with, and perhaps committed adultery, with Culpeper on the northern progress. It has already been noted that if this was true, it is strange that they did not come forward when these events were allegedly happening in the summer of 1541, and instead waited to confess that their mistress was an adulteress, for there is no evidence that Katherine bribed any of them.

Although by her own admission Katherine had indiscreetly agreed to meet with Culpeper several times during the spring and summer of 1541 with the assistance of Lady Rochford, there is no convincing evidence to indicate that her meetings with him, from her perspective if not his, were motivated by love or passion. It was perhaps only under the threat, and perhaps use, of torture that Culpeper stated that that he had intended to know the queen carnally. Moreover, as has been noted, Katherine was never given a trial and the opportunity of defending herself before the peers of the realm, in direct opposition to the processes involving the other decapitated sixteenth-century queens: Anne Boleyn, Lady Jane Grey and Mary, Queen of Scots. Whether this was because such a trial would have been thought to compromise the honour of her husband is uncertain.

As queen, Katherine had worked hard to fulfil the traditional duties of queenship, acting as intercessor, patron and a good wife to her husband, while consolidating her family's influence at court and rewarding her supporters. This study has reinterpreted her queenship and suggests that the prevailing modern image of her as a party-loving, hedonistic 'juvenile delinquent' could not be further from the truth, for it rests on no extant evidence whatsoever.[79] Instead, she took her duties seriously and genuinely sought to be a good wife to her king. In the end, however, Katherine was accused, condemned and executed firstly because she had concealed her pre-marital sexual liaisons from the king and secondly because her meetings with Culpeper were interpreted as evidence of adultery. Her downfall played on, and was informed by, contemporary gender mores and beliefs about female sexuality, while the allegations made against her in the autumn of 1541 arose in a climate of religious conflict and political dislike of the Howard family.

Even if Mary Lascelles had not chosen to report Katherine's scandalous past to her brother, perhaps quite by chance, in 1541, it is likely that Katherine would never have been entirely safe as queen. Hostile individuals aware of her pre-marital liaisons surrounded her at court, and she was well aware of the dangers involved in meeting with Culpeper. As he began to manipulate and control her, she belatedly broke off meetings with him as a misguided attempt at preserving her own security, but to no avail. Katherine never consented to sexual relations with Culpeper because of her probable association of sex with dishonour, and because of her awareness of the connection between adulterous queens and disgrace.

To summarise the eventually fatal liaisons of Katherine's life: Henry Manox persuaded her to grant him sexual intimacies at about the age of 13, in which she apparently allowed him to fondle her privately; Francis Dereham seduced her at the age of 15, probably with the intention of marrying her and gaining an envied blood relationship with the Howards; and Thomas Culpeper almost certainly manipulated her after he learned of her liaisons with Manox and Dereham, while blaming her for the meetings on the grounds that she was supposedly dying of love for him and had coerced him into meeting with her.

Katherine's actions during the 1541 progress indicate that she was well aware of the dangers involved because of the dishonourable interpretation that could be placed on her encounters with Culpeper. Her meetings with her husband's gentleman of the privy chamber arose in a climate when the king's life was despaired of and Dereham was openly boasting of his former intimacy with the queen, and both circumstances placed Katherine in a vulnerable political and personal position. In the absence of any convincing evidence that Katherine committed adultery or treason against her husband, it is possible to regard her as a victim of both her husband's paranoia and the political climate of distrust and fear associated with the Tudor succession. The French ambassador noted in the aftermath of Katherine's execution that 'it is not yet said who will be Queen; but the common voice is that this King will not be long without a wife, for the great desire he has to have further issue'.[80] It is to be hoped that this biography, in interpreting Katherine's life in the context of early modern gender relations and in approaching her queenship in the political and religious context of her husband's obsession with the continuation of the Tudor dynasty, thus rendering her, as a childless consort, vulnerable to political and sexual intrigues at court, will go some way to restoring Katherine's unfairly tarnished reputation as Henry VIII's slandered queen.

APPENDIX I

KATHERINE HOWARD IN
FILM AND TELEVISION

ALTHOUGH KATHERINE HOWARD DID not feature in the Reformation controversies that were associated with the king's annulment of his first marriage to Katherine of Aragon and subsequent marriage to Anne Boleyn, her life and that of her successor Katherine Parr were of interest to both Catholic and reformed authors, who either praised or criticised Henry for his marital choices, depending on their religious interests. Generally the religious perspective has been absent in screen adaptations of the king's final two marriages.

The first actress to portray Katherine Howard's life in detail was Binnie Barnes in the 1933 historical comedy *The Private Life of Henry VIII*, which starred Charles Laughton as the Tudor monarch. Unlike in other television adaptations, the fifth marriage dominated the film. The 30-year-old Barnes, who was almost double Katherine's age, represented her as a beautiful, ambitious and witty debutante. Adopting the ambitious role usually associated with Anne Boleyn – as in, for example, the two film adaptations of the novel *The Other Boleyn Girl* – Barnes's Katherine met her doom when she rashly began an affair with her husband's attendant, Thomas Culpeper. Their executions shortly followed the discovery of their illicit liaison.

A BBC adaptation, *The Six Wives of Henry VIII*, aired in 1970 and featured the late Keith Michell as Henry VIII; Michell subsequently reprised the role in the film *Henry VIII and His Six Wives* (1972). Again a mature actress was selected to play Katherine Howard, but in contrast to the vivacious and witty Katherine of *The Private Life of Henry VIII*, Angela Pleasence portrayed her as scheming, manipulative and devoid of charm. Henry's attraction to her seems to have been based largely on her youth and seeming ability to sympathise with his medical ailments. In one respect, the adaptation was accurate:

contemporary observers at court reported the king's desire to fondle his consort as frequently as possible, which was represented in the television series. Pleasence's Katherine was aware of the dangers that could ensue if her king discovered her past, but nonetheless embarked on an affair with Culpeper in the aftermath of a disastrous wedding night, when she experienced shock at realising that Henry was not the virile man she had expected. She threatened to have Francis Dereham, her childhood lover, killed off if he did not keep silent about their affair. Her motives for seeking Culpeper's company were ambiguous, but possibly she hoped to fall pregnant by him. When Katherine's uncle discovered his niece's illicit past, he elected to inform the king, thus sacrificing both Katherine and Lady Rochford, who had assisted her with the Culpeper liaison, to the enemies of the Howards. The devastated king berated the duke for humiliating him, while the unfortunate Katherine prepared for her execution while imprisoned in the Tower of London.

Pleasence's portrayal may have been influenced by Lacey Baldwin Smith's biography of Katherine, which had been published the previous decade. Baldwin Smith characterised her as a materialistic, insubstantial and foolish adolescent with an inability to inspire loyalty in her adherents. He also asserted that she and Culpeper committed adultery after her marriage to Henry. Pleasence's Katherine conformed closely to Baldwin Smith's image, a conformity that extended to choices of costume (Baldwin Smith believed that the portrait thought to depict Elizabeth Cromwell actually represented Katherine Howard, and a similar costume worn by that portrait's sitter was featured in the 1970 TV series).

Two years after the BBC adaptation, the film *Henry VIII and His Six Wives* was aired. Unlike the previous two adaptations, the film's characterisation of Katherine Howard probably corresponded more closely to historical reality. Lynne Frederick, who was 18, was chosen to represent Katherine, having previously played another doomed royal, Grand Duchess Tatiana of Russia in *Nicholas and Alexandra* (1971). She portrayed the queen as a kind-hearted if ineffectual courtier who captivated the ageing king with her beauty, charm and seeming innocence. In this regard, it is significant that, in the wake of the historical Katherine's downfall, she was charged with misleading the king as to her virginity by adopting gestures and behaviour associated with virtuous maidens. Unlike the BBC adaptation, Dereham did not feature in the 1972 film, while Culpeper's association with the queen was presented more ambiguously. When Henry discovered his wife's unchaste childhood, he wept, while the distraught Katherine experienced a nervous breakdown when interrogated by the Archbishop of Canterbury. Her youth and innocence were emphasised in the scaffold scene, which, again, did not feature her accomplice Lady Rochford.

The next full-feature adaptation of Katherine's marriage to Henry occurred in the 2003 television series *Henry VIII*, starring Ray Winstone as the king and featuring Emily Blunt as Katherine. She lacked the ruthlessness and vindictiveness of Pleasence's performance, while the innocence and sweet nature of Frederick's portrayal were also largely absent. Instead, the series placed emphasis on the hedonist Katherine's recklessness, while highlighting her beauty and sex appeal. As in the 1970 adaptation, the guileless Katherine was placed by her relatives at court with a view to securing Henry VIII's attention; the ageing monarch subsequently proclaimed his love for her and offered her marriage. Modern historians are sceptical of this traditional factional interpretation; court gossip circulated that the king himself chose to wed Katherine because he had fallen in love with her.

In the 2003 series, Katherine decided to seduce her husband's handsome attendant Culpeper and invited him with sexual intimacies. In this regard, Blunt's performance more closely corresponded with Pleasence's scheming seductress than it did with Frederick's naïve teenager. When Henry discovered his wife's affair, he physically manhandled her and threatened to kill her, before ordering the execution of Culpeper, which was observed by the queen. Later, she followed to the scaffold and a dramatic scene took place, whereby she wept and pleaded for her life before being decapitated. Blunt's performance, in almost every respect, departed from historical accuracy.

Several years later, the third and fourth seasons of the acclaimed Showtime series *The Tudors* included Tamzin Merchant as Katherine. In an entirely fictional scene Katherine was introduced to Charles Brandon, Duke of Suffolk, and Sir Francis Bryan as a sexually active, knowing woman who had grown up in a household closely resembling a brothel. Later, she debuted at court and captivated the restless Henry with her free spirit and sexual experience, which runs entirely counter to the historical Henry's belief that his fifth wife was virginal and sexually inexperienced. Profoundly concerned about his dynasty, it seems highly unlikely that Henry VIII would have ever considered marrying a woman with a dubious sexual reputation.

In *The Tudors* the unpopular Katherine was duly proclaimed queen at court, but irritated her husband's courtiers and displeased his eldest daughter Mary, with whom she regularly quarrelled. This idea may have been influenced by the imperial ambassador's report that Katherine had expelled several of her stepdaughter's maids as punishment for Mary's rude behaviour, but he duly noted that the two behaved cordially towards one another thereafter. Continuing the brothel atmosphere that characterised the dowager Duchess of Norfolk's household, the court was featured as a sexual hothouse in which the king's grooms looked lustily upon the vivacious Katherine, but her eye soon fell on the handsome, if cruel, Thomas Culpeper, who had earlier raped a park-keeper's wife.

As in the 1970 adaptation, Katherine's friends were shown to be a danger to the queen because of their knowledge of her pre-marital activities. The embittered Lady Rochford assisted Katherine's affair with Culpeper, while sleeping with him herself. Eventually, the liaison was discovered. Although Katherine ran screaming through the court in a bid to secure her husband's mercy, she was subsequently imprisoned and executed alongside Lady Rochford. Anne Boleyn's ghost, in the closing episode of the series, voiced sympathy for her tragic cousin, but the lasting impression of Merchant's Katherine is a spoiled, hedonistic and unintelligent woman, unable to inspire loyalty or affection in her friends or attendants. In this respect, Merchant's portrayal fit Baldwin Smith's characterisation of the queen, and was not informed by modern historical research that took a more sympathetic view of Katherine.

It is perplexing that the majority of actresses selected to play Katherine have been older than the historical figure, whether by a few or by several years. Binnie Barnes was 30 years old, Angela Pleasence 29, Emily Blunt 20 and Tamzin Merchant 22. Lynne Frederick most closely resembled the historical Katherine, for she was not yet 18 when *Henry VIII and His Six Wives* aired. In 2001, David Starkey's documentary *The Six Wives of Henry VIII* appeared. Michelle Abrahams starred as an older Katherine, but Starkey's emphasis was on the factual record as opposed to a dramatic or fictionalised version of Katherine's life. In his documentary Starkey did not consider whether Katherine's relationship with Culpeper was a love affair or whether it amounted to something else entirely. Abrahams's portrayal of Katherine is arguably one of the more forgettable versions.

None of the television portrayals of Katherine Howard considered the idea that her illicit liaisons were involuntary, nor did they factor into their interpretations Katherine's age and inexperience when involved with Manox (who did not feature in any of the adaptations) or Dereham. Moreover, the relationship with Culpeper was characterised either as a love affair or as a sexual relationship facilitated by Lady Rochford, rather than as blackmail, as has recently been argued by modern historians. *The Tudors* followed the traditional notion that the queen had a poor relationship with her stepdaughter, while *The Six Wives of Henry VIII* and *Henry VIII and His Six Wives* both featured the discredited notion that Katherine was manipulated by her relatives and the conservative political faction at court into seducing the king. The historical Katherine's activities as a patron and intercessor were, predictably, ignored in favour of featuring her in the titillating guises of a seductress and adulteress.

Appendix II

Katherine Howard's Age

BIOGRAPHERS OF KATHERINE HOWARD usually fall into one of two camps when it comes to her date of birth: those favouring a date of 1521 and those who prefer 1525. It is interesting that the former date is mainly preferred by earlier historians, including Lacey Baldwin Smith, Antonia Fraser and David Starkey.[1] Alison Weir proposed a birth date of 1525 in her 1991 biography of Henry VIII's six queens, a date subsequently adopted by Joanna Denny and Josephine Wilkinson.[2] This biography has indicated that both dates are almost certainly incorrect, and it has been argued that Katherine was more plausibly born between 1522 and 1524, probably in 1523.

Undoubtedly, when she was born is highly important for it influences our interpretation of her adolescent relationships in the household of her step-grandmother, the dowager Duchess of Norfolk. It also influences how her relationship with Henry VIII, whom she married in 1540, is perceived. In any discussion of Katherine Howard's age, it is worth paying attention to Henry's own marital and sexual preferences, a much-debated issue that perhaps, strangely, neglects the issue of age. In this context, it is possible to determine which women would have appealed to the king as prospective candidates for the role of queen.

Henry VIII was not yet 18 when he married Katherine of Aragon, who was 23, in 1509. Sixteenth-century women could legally marry at 12 years old, but it was rare for them to marry at so young an age. Women from the lower classes married, on average, at 25 or 26, and even among the nobility women tended to marry at about 20, or in their late teens.[3] Anne Boleyn's mother, for example, was probably married by the age of 19 or 20, and Lady Jane Rochford, wife of George Boleyn, was about 19 at her marriage. During his marriage to Katherine of Aragon, Henry was involved in liaisons with Bessie Blount (who was born by 1500, if not before, and was therefore at least 19 when she gave birth to the king's son in 1519) and Mary Boleyn, who had probably been born by 1501 and was therefore in her early twenties.

In about 1527 Henry fell passionately in love with Anne Boleyn, the younger sister of his previous mistress Mary. A strong argument can be made that Anne was probably six years younger than most historians have assumed. In 1527, she was probably 20 years of age. A variety of palace officials, servants and the likes of Cardinal Reginald Pole all characterised her as young. Gareth Russell has also recognised that not once, during the six arduous and time-consuming years in which Henry fought to secure from the pope an annulment of his first marriage, was Anne's age queried as a barrier to marriage. Undoubtedly, had she been as old as 30 or 31 during Henry's courtship, questions would have been raised as to whether she was a suitable partner for childbearing.[4]

When Anne married the king in late 1532, she was probably 25 and, according to an attendant of her stepdaughter Mary, the disgraced queen was not yet 29 when she was executed in May 1536.[5] Why would such a specific statement have been made if it was not based on at least some knowledge of Anne's age? Her successor Jane Seymour was, according to the imperial ambassador Eustace Chapuys, a little over 25 when she became Henry VIII's bride in 1536, suggesting that she was about 26 or 27.[6] At her funeral the following year, there was a female mourner for every year of Jane's life: 29 in all. Probably, according to the contemporary tradition of marking one's age, this referred to Jane dying in the twenty-ninth year of her life, rather than having died at the age of 29; this suggests that she was born in about 1509.

In 1540, Henry married Anne of Cleves, a 24-year-old German noblewoman. It was rumoured before his marriage to Anne that Henry had been romantically interested in Anne Basset, a former maiden of Jane Seymour. Mistress Basset was born in 1521 and so would have been 16 or so when the king's eye fell on her, however briefly. Before the negotiations to marry Anne of Cleves, Henry had expressed an interest in marrying the 17-year-old Christina of Milan.

Plainly, Henry's preference was for women in their late teens or early twenties. Bessie Blount and Mary Boleyn, his two most well-known mistresses, were in their late teens, Mary perhaps her early twenties. Katherine of Aragon and Anne of Cleves were both in their early twenties, while Henry first became interested in Anne Boleyn when she was about 20, although she was in her mid twenties when they married. Jane Seymour, on the other hand, was probably 27. The glaring exception to this rule was Katherine Parr, who was 31 when she married Henry VIII in 1543, but she had already been married twice previously and there does not appear to have been any expectation on the

king's behalf that she would provide him with children, unlike all of his previous marriages. It was highly unusual for a noblewoman to remain unwed by
her late twenties or early thirties. Indeed, so anomalous was the as-yet unwed
Jane Seymour's position in early 1536 that the imperial ambassador openly
questioned both her virginity and her morals.[7] Jane, at 27, was still unmarried.

When Katherine Howard caught the king's eye in late 1539 or early 1540,
contemporary observers not only praised her attractiveness, but they also commented on her youth. According to Richard Hilles, she was a 'young girl', while
the French ambassador referred to her as a 'young lady'. The anonymous author
of *The Chronicle of Henry VIII* expressly stated that she was about 15 when Henry
fell in love with her, and also referred to her as a 'mere child'. George Cavendish,
in his verses about Katherine's life, mentioned youth ten times. Plainly, the implication was that Katherine's youth and beauty were noticeable.

In the late twentieth century, modern historians assumed that Katherine
was born in 1520–21 because of a portrait housed in the Toledo Museum of
Art, with versions also at the National Portrait Gallery and Hever Castle. The
well-dressed sitter is, according to an inscription in the painting, in her twenty-
first year. Quite why this portrait was identified as a portrait of Katherine
remains unclear. This biography has refuted the notion that the portrait depicts
Katherine during her tenure as queen, and Russell also recently suggested that
the sitter may be Frances Brandon or Elizabeth Cromwell, younger sister of
Jane Seymour. The Metropolitan Museum of Art portrait, dated 1540–45, may
depict Katherine, but the possible identification is tentative. It was suggested
earlier in this book that the Metropolitan portrait may represent Henry's fifth
queen and may date to July 1540–October 1541; if the sitter was in her seventeenth year, this would indicate a birth date between July 1523 and October
1524. The unknown Spanish chronicler's claim that Katherine was about 15
when she met the king – presumably in late 1539 or early 1540 – would
seem to suggest a birthdate of 1524, whereas the French ambassador's report
that Dereham 'violated' Katherine until her eighteenth year, perhaps in reference to the summer or autumn of 1541, would suggest a birthdate of 1523.
A birthdate in the second half of 1523 or sometime in 1524 would make
sense of the commencement of music lessons in the autumn of 1536, perhaps
in the expectation of an appointment in the household of the queen, at that
time Jane Seymour. Maidens were usually aged in their mid teens when they
were appointed to office. It may be of significance that the codicil to her step-
grandfather Sir John Legh's will was added in late August 1523, perhaps shortly
after the birth of a Howard child.[8] In view of the available evidence, there is a
good chance that the Howard child born in August 1523 was Katherine, but
it remains uncertain.

When she was appointed a maiden of honour to Anne of Cleves in late 1539, Katherine joined her cousin Katherine Carey and Mary Norris, who were born in 1524 and 1526, respectively. Undoubtedly, had she been born as early as 1520, Katherine's family would have attempted to arrange for her to serve Anne Boleyn or Jane Seymour in the years 1533–37. There is no evidence that they did so. It is probably significant that she only began receiving music lessons from Henry Manox and Master Barnes in late 1536, when she was likely in her early teens.

The French ambassador Marillac reported in December 1541 that Dereham 'violated her at the age of 13 until 18'.[9] However, there is no evidence that Katherine's liaison with Dereham lasted five years, and it was probably less than two years in duration, having been dated to 1538–39. Warnicke has convincingly suggested that Marillac 'could have heard the ages, 13 and 18, and attached them to the facts that he knew. Learning that she was abused at 13 and not knowing about Manox, Marillac would have identified Dereham as the perpetrator.'[10] It is significant that Katherine and Dereham were suspected of continuing their relationship during her tenure as queen. According to the 1523 birth date she would have been 18 in 1541, when Dereham was appointed to her household.

The contradictory comments of the French ambassador and the unknown author of *The Chronicle of Henry VIII* clearly indicate that there was a degree of confusion about Katherine's exact age; possibly neither man knew for certain when she was born. However, Cavendish's ten references to her youth in his verses is probably significant, as are the other reported remarks about her young age when she became queen. That she was not born earlier than 1523 is a reasonable assumption in view of the ages of her fellow maids of honour, the date at which she began receiving music lessons (probably in readiness for her anticipated appointment to the queen's household) and the evidence of her grandparents' wills. Her step-grandfather John Legh's will did not refer to Katherine or her younger sister, but the will of John's wife Isabel, which was written in 1527, referred to all three Howard girls. Whether this constitutes evidence that Katherine and Mary were born between 1523 and 1527, however, is unclear, but at the very least it seems to suggest that they were either not yet born or were very young when John's will was penned.

The traditional argument that Katherine was born as early as 1520–21 has been proven to be shaky and based on a dubious portrait identification. Most modern historians now believe that the portrait is not of the queen, but probably depicts one of the king's nieces or Elizabeth Cromwell, younger sister of Jane Seymour. It is probably significant that the three most recent biographers of Katherine – myself, Josephine Wilkinson and Gareth Russell – all advocate a later birth date.[11] Wilkinson agrees with Joanna Denny that Katherine was born in 1525, probably the latest possible date for her birth. Russell suggests 1522 or 1523. The evidence – albeit fragmentary – analysed in the course of this chapter seems to suggest that Katherine Howard was born in the second half of 1523 or sometime in 1524. Sixteenth-century children were occasionally named for the saint on whose feast day they were born; St Katherine's Day is 25 November.[12] Whether this suggests that Katherine was born in November 1523 is impossible to say, but the considerable – albeit fragmentary – evidence available to historians probably indicates that she was born no earlier than 1523 and no later than 1525. This would mean that she was about 17 when she married Henry VIII and had probably not yet attained the age of 19 when she was executed in early 1542.

NOTES

Abbreviations

Cal. SP. Spanish	*Calendar of Letters, Despatches and State Papers Relating to Negotiations between England and Spain, Preserved in the Archives at Simancas and Elsewhere* (eds G.A. Bergenroth, P. de Goyangos, Garrett Mattingley, R. Tyler et al., London, 17 vols, 1862–1965).
Cal. SP. Ven.	*Calendar of State Papers Relating to English Affairs in the Archives of Venice and in the other Libraries of Northern Italy* (eds L. Rawdon Brown, Cavendish Bentinck et al., London, 7 vols, 1864–1947).
LP	*Letters and Papers, Foreign and Domestic, of the Reign of Henry VIII. Preserved in the Public Record Office, the British Museum, and Elsewhere in England* (eds J.S. Brewer and R.H. Brodie, London, 21 vols, 1862–1932).

References to works cited are given in full at first mention and are abbreviated thereafter.

Introduction

1　Holly K. Kizewski, 'Jewel of Womanhood: A Feminist Reinterpretation of Queen Katherine Howard', Lincoln Masters Thesis, University of Nebraska (2014), p. ii; accessed online at digitalcommons.unl.edu/cgi/viewcontent.cgi?article=1073&context=hist orydiss.

2　Martin Hume (ed.), *The Chronicle of Henry VIII of England: Being a Contemporary Record of Some of the Principal Events of the Reigns of Henry VIII and Edward VI* (London, 1889).

3　Ibid., p. 75.

4　Ibid., pp. 76–77.

5　Ibid., pp. 82–83.

6　Ibid., pp. 86–87.

7　Edward Herbert, *The Life and Raigne of King Henry the Eighth* (London, 1649).

8　Ibid., p. 474.

9　Nicholas Harpsfield, *A Treatise on the Pretended Divorce between Henry VIII and Catharine of Aragon* (ed. Nicholas Pocock, London, 1878), p. 278.

10　George Cavendish, *The Life of Cardinal Wolsey and Metrical Visions* (ed. Samuel Weller Singer, London, 1825), pp. 64–70.

11　Nicholas Sander, *Rise and Growth of the Anglican Schism* (eds Edward Rishton and David Lewis, London, 1877), pp. 153–54.

12　Agnes Strickland, *Memoirs of the Queens of Henry VIII, And of His Mother, Elizabeth of York* (Philadelphia, 1853), pp. 279–80.

13　Ibid., p. 280.

14　Ibid., pp. 310–11.

15　Ibid., p. 325.

16　Henry Herbert, *Memoirs of Henry the Eighth of England: With the Fortunes, Fates, and Characters of His Six Wives* (New York, 1860), pp. 413, 431.

17　Martin Hume, *The Wives of Henry the Eighth and the Parts They Played in History* (New York, 1905), pp. 351, 371–72, 396.

18　Lacey Baldwin Smith, *A Tudor Tragedy: The Life and Times of Catherine Howard* (London, 1961), p. 9.

19　Ibid., p. 10.

20　Ibid., p. 45.

21　Ibid., p. 54.

22　Ibid., p. 61.

23　Ibid., p. 189.

24　Eric Ives, 'Marrying for Love: The Experience of Edward IV and Henry VIII', *History Today* 50.12 (2000).

25　Alison Plowden, *Tudor Women: Queens and Commoners* (Stroud, 2002), p. 96.

26　Tracy Borman, *Elizabeth's Women: The Hidden Story of the Virgin Queen* (London, 2010), p.72, 74 for 'empty-headed'.

27　Alison Weir, *The Six Wives of Henry VIII* (London, 1991), pp. 9, 462.

28　Antonia Fraser, *The Six Wives of Henry VIII* (London, 1992), pp. 388, 427.

29　Derek Wilson, *The Queen and the Heretic: How Two Women Changed the Religion of England* (Oxford, 2018), p. 65.

30　David Loades, *Catherine Howard: The Adulterous Wife of Henry VIII* (Stroud, 2012).

31　David Loades, *The Tudor Queens of England* (London, 2009), p. 139.

32　Ibid.

33　Ibid., p. 153.

34　Ibid., p. 154.

35　Anne Crawford (ed.), *Letters of the Queens of England* (Stroud, 2002), p. 207.

36 Ibid., pp. 207–08.
37 Loades, *Tudor Queens*, p. 152.
38 Joanna Denny, *Katherine Howard: A Tudor Conspiracy* (London, 2005), p. 88.
39 Ibid., pp. 116, 123.
40 Ibid., pp. 148–49.
41 Ibid., p. 198.
42 David Starkey, *Six Wives: The Queens of Henry VIII* (London, 2004), pp. 644, 646.
43 Ibid., p. 654.
44 Ibid., pp. 674–75.
45 Ibid., p. xxv.
46 Karen Lindsey, *Divorced, Beheaded, Survived: A Feminist Reinterpretation of the Wives of Henry VIII* (Cambridge, MA, 1996), p. 169.
47 Retha M. Warnicke, *Wicked Women of Tudor England: Queens, Aristocrats, Commoners* (New York, 2012), pp. 45, 76.
48 Josephine Wilkinson, *Katherine Howard: The Tragic Story of Henry VIII's Fifth Queen* (London, 2016), p. 44.
49 Ibid., p. 125.
50 Gareth Russell, *Young and Damned and Fair: The Life and Tragedy of Catherine Howard at the Court of Henry VIII* (London, 2017), p. 380.
51 Kizewski, 'Jewel of Womanhood', p. 1.
52 Baldwin Smith, *A Tudor Tragedy*, p. 186.

Chapter 1

1   George Cavendish, *Thomas Wolsey Late Cardinal his Life and Death* (ed. Roger Lockyer, London, 1962), p. 10.
2   Cal. SP.Ven. ii.1287.
3   Sebastian Guistinian, *Four Years at the Court of Henry VIII* (trans. R. Brown, 2 vols, London, 1854) i.85–90f.; LP II 395.
4   See, for example, Starkey, *Six Wives*, pp. 88–89.
5   Cited in Agnes Strickland, *Memoirs of the Queens of Henry VIII* (Philadelphia, 1853), p. 279.
6   R. Virgoe, 'The Recovery of the Howards in East Anglia, 1485–1529', in E.W. Ives, R.J. Knecht and J. J. Scarisbrick (eds), *Wealth and Power in Tudor England* (London, 1978), pp. 5–16; D. Head, 'The Life and Career of Thomas Howard, Third Duke of Norfolk: The Anatomy of Tudor Politics', PhD dissertation, Florida State University (1978), pp. 28–40.
7   Baldwin Smith, *A Tudor Tragedy*, p. 16.
8   M.J. Tucker, *The Life of Thomas Howard, Earl of Surrey and Second Duke of Norfolk, 1443–1524* (London, 1964), p. 72; J. Gairdner, '"The Spousells" of the Princess Mary, 1508', *Camden Miscellany* IX (New York, 1965); A.R. Myers, 'The Book of Disguisings for the Coming of the Ambassadors of Flanders, December, 1508', *BIHR* 54 (1981), pp. 120–9.
9   D. Head, 'The Life and Career', p. 167.
10 *Letters and Papers, Foreign and Domestic of the Reign of Henry VIII* (eds J.S. Brewer, J. Gairdner and R.H. Brodie, London, 21 vols, 1862–1932) ½, no. 2684 (2); Michael A.R. Graves, 'Thomas Howard, Third Duke of Norfolk (1473–1554)', *Oxford Dictionary of National Biography* (2004); accessed online at www.oxforddnb.com/view/10.1093/ref:odnb/9780198614128.001.0001/odnb-9780198614128-e-13940.
11 C. Rawcliffe, *The Staffords, Earls of Stafford and Dukes of Buckingham, 1394–1521* (Cambridge, 1978), p. 43; see B.J. Harris, *Edward Stafford, Third Duke of Buckingham,*

1478–1521 (Stanford, 1986), H. Miller, *Henry VIII and the English Nobility* (Oxford, 1986).

12 Denny, *Katherine Howard*, p. 261.

13 Cal. SP. Span., IV, 694, p. 295.

14 Ibid.,V, ii, 104, p. 269.

15 LPI 698, 2246.

16 *Archaeologia Cantiana: Being the Transactions of the Kent Archaeological Society*, vols IV, XXII (London, 1861, 1917), p. 319.

17 LPII 2246; II, ii, 'The King's Book of Payments', p. 1463.

18 Starkey, *Six Wives*, p. 645.

19 LP, xii. 463, 466.

20 Muriel St Clare Byrne (ed.), *The Lisle Letters* (Chicago, 6 vols, 1981), pp. 373–76.

21 *Surrey Archaeological Collections*, LI, pp. 85–88; *Visitations of Surrey*, H.S., XLIII, p. 21; *Inquisitions Post Mortem – Henry VII*, I, p. 820. See Denny, *Katherine Howard*, pp. 6–8.

22 *Surrey Archaeological Collections*, LI, pp. 87–88.

23 Ibid., p. 87, seems to suggest that Henry was the eldest son since he was named first in John Legh's will of 1523, before his two brothers.

24 Gerald Brenan and Edward Statham, *The House of Howard* (New York, 2 vols, 1907), I, p. 166, n. 1.

25 Pamela Y. Stanton, 'Arundell, Sir Thomas (*c.*1502–52)', *Oxford Dictionary of National Biography*; accessed online at www.oxforddnb.com/view/10.1093/ ref:odnb/9780198614128.001.0001/odnb-9780198614128-e-725; Douglas Richardson, *Magna Carta Ancestry: A Study in Colonial and Medieval Families* (ed. Kimball G. Everingham I, Salt Lake City, 2011), p. 44.

26 For Anne's age, LP XV 22; for Margaret, LPXVI 868.

27 *Surrey Archaeological Collections*, LI, pp. 85–90; which shows that, in John Legh's will of 1523, none of the Howard daughters were mentioned, but in his wife Isabel's will in 1527, all three daughters were named, with Isabel naming Mary as her goddaughter, which was probably after John's death. It has been argued that 'infant girls did not warrant mention as beneficiaries in a will' (Baldwin Smith, *A Tudor Tragedy*, p. 194), but this fails to take into account the fact that Isabel Legh decided to include all three girls, while other infant females from the Legh family were included in the earlier will. See *Visitations of Cornwall* (ed. J.L. Vivian), pp. 4–5; H. Howard, *Memorials of the Howard Family* (1834), pp. 1–26; Baldwin Smith, *A Tudor Tragedy*, pp. 194–96. The unknown author of *The Chronicle of Henry VIII of England*, p. 75, suggested that Katherine was about 15 in 1539–40. See later in this chapter. Mary Howard married Edmund Trafford some years later, and he was born in 1526. The fact that he was born in this year, and that Mary was apparently still unwed at the time of her sister's marriage to the king, suggests that she was the youngest Howard daughter. For a Lambeth birth, see LPXVI 1395 (indictment against the queen). Some suspected that Katherine was born at Oxenhoath in Kent; see Brenan and Statham, *House of Howard*, I, pp. 268–69. See Conor Byrne, 'Katherine Howard's Age' (2017); accessed online at conorbyrnex.blogspot.co.uk/2017/06/ katherine-howards-age.html.

28 Richardson, *Magna Carta Ancestry*, p. 108.

29 Cal. SP. Span., V, i, p. 165, p. 468. Denny, *Katherine Howard*, pp. 10–11.

30 LPIV 3731–2; Henry Ellis (ed.), *Original Letters Illustrative of English History*, third series, (London, 4 vols, 1846), I, pp. 160–63.

31 LPV 166, 15.

32 Brenan and Statham, *House of Howard*, I, pp. 268–69.

33 Cited by Jeremy Goldberg, 'Girls Growing Up in Later Medieval England', *History Today*, 45.6 (1995).

34 Olwen Hufton, 'What is Women's History?', *History Today*, 35.6 (1985).

35 If one accepts the disputed 1507 birthdate for Anne Boleyn, it follows that she was 6 years old when she was sent abroad to France to serve within the household of Mary Tudor and later Claude of France. See Retha M. Warnicke, *The Rise and Fall of Anne Boleyn: Family Politics at the Court of Henry VIII* (Cambridge, 1989), Ch. 1.

36 Nicola Clark, 'Dynastic Politics: Five Women of the Howard Family During the Reign of Henry VIII, 1509–47', PhD Thesis, Royal Holloway College, University of London (2013), pp. 241–42.

37 Barbara J. Harris, *English Aristocratic Women, 1450–1550: Marriage and Family, Property and Careers* (Oxford, 2002), p. 32.

38 Ibid.

39 Barbara J. Harris, 'Women and Politics in Early Tudor England', *The Historical Journal* 33 (1990), pp. 262–63.

40 Warnicke, *Wicked Women*, p. 50.

41 See Appendix II: Katherine Howard's Age.

42 Cited by Denny, *Katherine Howard*, pp. 15–16.

43 Strickland, *Memoirs*, p. 282.

44 Graves, 'Thomas Howard'.

45 Ibid.

46 Catharine Davies, 'Agnes Howard [née Tilney], Duchess of Norfolk (*b.* in or before 1477, *d.* 1545), Noblewoman', *Oxford Dictionary of National Biography* (2004); accessed online at www.oxforddnb.com/view/10.1093/ref:odnb/9780198614128.001.0001/ odnb-9780198614128-e-70806. See also Warnicke, *Wicked Women;* Baldwin Smith, *A Tudor Tragedy*, pp. 46–48.

47 Warnicke, *Wicked Women*, p. 57. Baldwin Smith agrees, noting that 'how many people were involved in such an organization it is impossible to say, and very likely the old lady of Norfolk was not sure herself'; *A Tudor Tragedy*, p. 47.

48 Harris, 'Women and Politics', p. 260. See also Barbara Harris, 'The View from My Lady's Chamber: New Perspectives on the Early Tudor Monarchy', *Huntingdon Library Quarterly* 60 (1997), pp. 215–47.

49 Clark, 'Dynastic Politics', p. 6.

Chapter 2

1   *Calendar of State Papers Relating to English Affairs in the Archives of Venice, Volume 5: 1534–1554* (ed. Rawdon Brown, 1873), pp. 531–67.

2   Sander, *Anglican Schism*, pp. 8, 15.

3   S. Giustinian, *Four Years at the Court of Henry VIII* (trans. R. Brown, 2 vols, London, 1854), I, pp. 181–82.

4   Cal. SP. Ven., II, 479; LP III i, 1284.

5   Mark Breitenberg, 'Anxious Masculinity: Sexual Jealousy in Early Modern England', *Feminist Studies* 19 (1993), p. 388.

6   Linda A. Pollock, 'Childbearing and Female Bonding in Early Modern England', *Social History* 22 (1997), p. 300.

7   Anne L. Barstow, *Witchcraze: A New History of the European Witch Hunts* (San Francisco, 1994), p. 136.

8   Cal. SP. Ven., II, 248, 529, 560.

9   Cal. SP. Ven., IV, 105.

10 Lois Honeycutt, 'Medieval Queenship', *History Today*, 39.6 (1989).

11 Warnicke, *Rise and Fall*, p. 177.

12 Sander, *Anglican Schism*, p. 8.

13 BL Sloane MSS.

14 J.G. Nichols (ed.), *Inventories of the Wardrobes, Plate, Chapel Stuff, etc., of Henry Fitzroy, Duke of Richmond and of the Wardrobe Stuff at Baynard's Castle of Katharine, Princess Dowager* (London, 1855), LXI, p. xv. See also M.J. Lechnar, 'Henry VIII's Bastard: Henry Fitzroy, Duke of Richmond', PhD Dissertation, West Virginia University (1977).

15 Raphael Holinshed, *Chronicles of England, Scotland and Ireland* (ed. Henry Ellis, 6 vols, 1807–08).

16 George Cavendish, *The Life of Cardinal Wolsey* (ed. S. W. Singer, 2 vols, 1815), IV, p. 108.

17 Lancelot de Carles, *La Grande Bretagne devant L'Opinion Francaise* (ed. G. Ascoli, Paris, 1927), lines 53–54.

18 William Forest, *The History of Grisild the Second: A Narrative in Verse of the Divorce of Queen Katherine of Aragon* (ed. M. D. Macray, London, 1875), pp. 52–53.

19 J.W. Luce (ed.), *The Love Letters of Henry VIII to Anne Boleyn: With Notes* (London, 1906), p. iii.

20 G.E. Cockayne, *The Complete Peerage* (eds V. Gibbs, H.A. Doubleday, D. Warrand, T. Lord Howard de Walden and G. White, 13 vols, London, 1910–59), IX, pp. 219–22.

21 Ibid., xii, pp. 249–57.

22 Warnicke, *Rise and Fall*, p. 88.

23 Cal. SP. Span., IV, i, pp. 189–90.

24 Edward Hall, *A Chronicle containing, the History of Henry the Fourth and the Succeeding Monarchs to the End of the Reign of Henry the Eighth, carefully collected with the editions of 1548 and 1550* (ed. Henry Ellis, London, 1809), p. 760; *Correspondence du Cardinal du Bellay*, I, pp. 108, 110; LPIV, iii, 6011.

25 See Warnicke, *Rise and Fall*, pp. 1–3.

26 LPIV, iii, 6199.

27 David Starkey, 'From Feud to Faction: English Politics 1450–1550', *History Today*, 32.11 (1982).

28 See Harris, 'Women and Politics', pp. 259–81.

29 Barbara Harris, 'The View from My Lady's Chamber: New Perspectives on the Early Tudor Monarchy', *Huntingdon Library Quarterly* 60 (1997), p. 220.

30 See Laura Gowing, 'Women's Bodies and the Making of Sex in Seventeenth-Century England', *Signs* 37 (2012); Laura Gowing, 'Women, Status and the Popular Culture of Dishonour', *Transactions of the Royal Historical Society* 6 (1996), p. 225.

31 Gowing, 'Women, Status', p. 234.

32 Barstow, *Witchcraze*, p. 136.

33 Hume, *Chronicle of Henry VIII of England*, pp. 8, 44.

34 Cal. SP. Ven., 1527–33, pp. 294–95.

35 LPV 1059.

36 Charles Wriothesley, *A Chronicle of England During the Reigns of the Tudors, from 1485 to 1559* (ed. William Douglas Hamilton, 2 vols, 1875–77), I, pp. 17–18.

37 *Hall's Chronicle*, p. 233.

38 Cited by Denny, *Katherine Howard*, p. 57.

39 Cal. SP. Span., IV, ii, 934, p. 429; V, i, 122, p. 355.

40 See, for example, Anne Somerset, *Ladies in Waiting: From the Tudors to the Present Day* (London, 1984), pp. 9–33. Whether Mary Boleyn actually resided in her sister's household is uncertain. After her second marriage was made public in the summer or autumn of 1534, she was banished from court.

41 Byrne, *Lisle Letters*, II, pp. 528–31.

42 See Conor Byrne, 'Katherine Howard's Age' (2017); accessed online at conorbyrnex. blogspot.co.uk/2017/06/katherine-howards-age.html.

43 LPIX 308.

44 Warnicke, *Rise and Fall*, p. 146; Baldwin Smith, *A Tudor Tragedy*, p. 31.

45 LPVI 1528.

46 Hamilton, *A Chronicle of England*, I, pp. 27–29.

47 LPVIII 1105.

48 Warnicke, *Rise and Fall*, p. 171.

49 Cited by H.F.M. Prescott, *Mary Tudor* (London, 1952), p. 307.

50 See Eric Ives, *The Life and Death of Anne Boleyn: 'The Most Happy'* (Oxford, 2005), pp. 190–91.

51 LPV 907.

52 George Cavendish, *The Life of Cardinal Wolsey and Metrical Visions* (ed. Samuel Weller Singer, London, 1825), p. 42.

53 Lancelot de Carles, in G. Ascoli, *La Grande-Bretagne devant L'Opinion Francaise* (Paris, 1927), lines 209–13.

54 Harris, 'My Lady's Chamber', p. 247.

55 LPVII 556; Byrne, *Lisle Letters*, II, p. 175.

56 Cal. SP. Span., V, p. 90.

57 There is some dispute about the queen's second pregnancy. See Ives, *Anne*, pp. 191–92; Warnicke, *Rise and Fall*, pp. 173–77; G.W. Bernard, *Anne Boleyn: Fatal Attractions* (London, 2010), pp. 74–75.

58 LPVII 476.

59 Cal. SP. Span., V, p. 127.

60 LPVIII 111, 174, 327, 355.

61 LPVIII 263.

62 LPIX 802.

63 LPX 142.

64 Anthony Fletcher, 'Men's Dilemma: The Future of Patriarchy in England 1560–1660', *Transactions of the Royal Historical Society* Sixth Series 4 (1994), p. 80.

65 LPX 282.

66 *Hall's Chronicle*, p. 818.

67 Hamilton, *A Chronicle of England*, I, p. 33.

68 De Carles, *Poeme sur la Mort d'Anne Boleyn*, lines 317–26, in Ascoli, *La Grande Bretagne devant l'Opinion Francaise*.

69 LPX 283.

70 James Anthony Froude, *History of England from the Fall of Wolsey to the Death of Elizabeth* (New York, 1870), III, p. 21.

71 Brenan and Statham, *House of Howard*, I, pp. 183–84.

72 LPX 726.

73 LPX 873.

74 Starkey, *Six Queens*, p. 564.

75 Historians such as Ives, *Anne*, and Alison Weir, *The Lady in the Tower: The Fall of Anne Boleyn* (London, 2009) favour the first argument; Warnicke, *Rise and Fall*, believes that the queen miscarried a deformed child, leading to her execution on suspicion of witchcraft and sexual crimes; Bernard, *Fatal Attractions*, contends that she was guilty of the charges of adultery and incest; and others, such as Suzannah Lipscomb, *1536: The Year That Changed Henry VIII* (Oxford, 2009) and Starkey, *Six Queens*, argue that the queen's foolish conversations formed the basis for her downfall.

76 See Starkey, *Six Queens*, pp. 564–66.

77 *Hall's Chronicle*, p. 819.

78 Hamilton, *A Chronicle of England*, I, p. 36.

79 LPX 793.

80 See Elisabeth Wheeler, *Men of Power: Court Intrigue in the Life of Catherine Howard* (Glastonbury, 2008), pp. 110–11.

81 LPX 726.

82 Ibid.

83 See Lyndal Roper, *Oedipus and the Devil: Witchcraft, Sexuality and Religion in Early Modern Europe* (Routledge, 1994), pp. 136–38, 188.

84 Warnicke, *Rise and Fall*, p. 216.

85 Brenan and Statham, *House of Howard*, I, p. 185.

86 Gilbert Burnet, *The History of the Reformation of the Church of England* (ed. Nicholas Pocock, 7 vols, 1865), I, p. 316.

87 LPX 876.

88 LPX 843.

89 Hamilton, *A Chronicle of England*, I, p. 37.

90 Ibid., pp. 37–38.

91 *Hall's Chronicle*, p. 819.

92 Chapuys reported that 'nobody thinks that she [Jane] has much beauty. Her complexion is so white that she may be called rather pale … the said Semel is not very intelligent, and is said to be rather haughty'; LPX 901.

93 See, for instance, Strickland, *Memoirs*.

Chapter 3

1 TNA SP1/107, fol. 127, cited by Clark, 'Dynastic Politics', p. 242.

2 Her birthday may have fallen at the end of the year. See onthetudortrail.com/Blog/2014/08/01/katherine-howards-birthday-a-guest-post-by-conor-byrne, and Appendix II of this book.

3 Baldassarre Castiglione, *The Book of the Courtier* (trans. Leonard Eckstein Opdycke, New York, 1903), p. 65.

4 Lancelot de Carles, cited by Linda Phyllis Austen, 'Women's Musical Voices in Sixteenth-Century England', *Early Modern Women: An Interdisciplinary Journal* 3 (2008), pp. 137–38.

5 Byrne, *Lisle*, III, p. 133.

6 Lawrence Stone, *Broken Lives: Separation and Divorce in England 1660–1857* (Oxford, 1993), p. 22.

7 Elizabeth Foyster, *Manhood in Early Modern England: Honour, Sex, and Marriage* (London, 1999), pp. 13–14, 172.

8 Baldwin Smith, *A Tudor Tragedy*, p. 146.

9 Parts of this are informed by my initial research: C. Byrne, 'The Fall of Katherine Howard: Sexual Politics and the Role of Sexual Deviance in the Tudor Court' (2012), which was submitted to St Hugh's College, Oxford. I wish to thank that college for their support of this work.

10 Heinrich Kramer and James Sprenger, *Malleus Maleficarum* (1486, trans. Montague Summers, London, 1928), pp. 41–66, 109–22, 140–44, 227–30.

11 Cited by Denny, *Katherine Howard*, p. 227.

12 Roper, *Oedipus and the Devil*, p. 53.

13 Ibid., p. 55.

14 *The Catechism of Thomas Becon* (ed. John Ayre, Cambridge, 1844), p. 367.

15 Cited by Barstow, *Witchcraze*, p. 136.

16 Linda A. Pollock, 'Honor, Gender, and Reconciliation in Elite Culture, 1570–1700', *Journal of British Studies* 46 (2007).

17 Warnicke, *Wicked Women*, p. 52.

18 Joy Schroeder, *Dinah's Lament: The Biblical Legacy of Sexual Violence in Christian Interpretations* (Minneapolis, 2007), pp. 51, 63, 67, 95–96.

19 PRO, SP I, vol. 167, f. 139.

20 Ibid., f. 138.

21 G. Steinman Steinman, *Althorp Memoirs*, or *Biographical Notices of Lady Denham, the Countess of Shrewsbury, the Countess of Falmouth, Mrs. Jenyns, the Duchess of Tyrconnel, and Lucy Walter, Six Ladies Whose Portraits are to be Found in the Picture Gallery of His Excellency Earl Spencer, K.G., K.P.* (1869), p. 56.

22 Harris, 'My Lady's Chamber', p. 247; see also Chapter 1.

23 PRO, SP, I, vol. 167, f. 129; LP XVI 1320.

24 Ibid.

25 Ibid., f. 130.

26 Ibid., vol. 168, f. 158; LPXVI 1461.

27 Martin Ingram, 'Child Abuse in Early Modern England', in Michael Braddick and John Walter (eds), *Negotiating Power in Early Modern Society: Order, Hierarchy and Subordination in Britain and Ireland* (Cambridge, 2001), p. 63.

28 Jeremy Goldberg, 'The Right to Choose: Women, Consent and Marriage in Late Medieval England', *History Today* 58.2 (2008).

29 Cited by Barbara J. Harris, 'Power, Profit, and Passion: Mary Tudor, Charles Brandon, and the Arranged Marriage in Early Tudor England', *Feminist Studies* 15 (1989), p. 85.

30 Wilkinson, *Katherine Howard*, p. 41.

31 See Byrne, 'Sexual Deviance'.

32 Wilkinson, *Katherine Howard*. For Worsley, see Lucy Worsley, 'Was Katherine Howard, Henry VIII's "wanton" fifth wife, actually a victim of child sex abuse?', *The Telegraph* (2016); accessed online at www.telegraph.co.uk/women/life/katherine-howard-henry-viiis-wanton-fifth-wife-actually-victim/.

33 Gilbert Burnet, *The History of the Reformation of the Church of England* (A. Rhanes for R. Gunne, J. Smith and W. Bruce, 3 vols, 168,), IV, 71, p. 505.

34 LPXVI 1426.

35 Burnet, *Reformation*, III, 72, p. 130.

36 Roper, *Oedipus and the Devil*, p. 68.

37 PRO, SP, I, vol. 167, f. 130; LPXVI 1320.

38 Roper, *Oedipus and the Devil*, p. 55.

39 PRO, SP, I, vol. 167, f. 136–37; LPXVI 1321. See also LPXVI 1400.

40 Angus McLaren, *Reproductive Rituals: Perceptions of Fertility in Britain from the 16th Century to the 19th Century* (New York, 1984), p. 81; Keith Thomas, *Man and the Natural World: Changing Attitudes in England 1500–1800* (London, 1983), p. 39.

41 Annie Tock, 'Literary Law Enforcement: Gender in Crime Ballads in Early Modern England', Eastern Illinois University (2006); available at www.eiu.edu/~historia/2004/Literary2.pdf.

42 Breitenberg, 'Anxious Masculinity', pp. 378, 389.

43 PRO, SP, I, vol. 167, f. 137; LPXVI 1321.

44 *The Calendar of the Manuscripts of the Marquis of Bath Preserved at Longleat, Wiltshire* (Dublin, 1907), II, pp. 8–9.

45 Ibid., pp. 8–9.

46 *The Remains of Thomas Cranmer, D.D., Archbishop of Canterbury* (ed. Henry Jenkyns, 2 vols, Oxford, 1883), I, pp. 307–10.

47 NA SP 1/167, f. 155.

48 Baldwin Smith, *A Tudor Tragedy*, p. 54; Denny, *Katherine Howard*, p. 121.

49 S. Mendelson and P. Crawford, *Women in Early Modern England 1550–1720* (Oxford, 1998), p. 65.

50 Warnicke, *Wicked Women*, p. 56.

51 Roper, *Oedipus and the Devil*, p. 61. See also Barstow, *Witchcraze*, p. 136.

52 See Garthine Walker, 'Rereading Rape and Sexual Violence in Early Modern England', *Gender & History* 10 (2002), p. 4.

53 Burnet, *Reformation*, IV, p. 505.

54 Ibid.

55 Ibid., p. 504.

56 Eric Carlson, 'Courtship in Tudor England', *History Today* 43.8 (1993).

57 Goldberg, 'Right to Choose'.

58 Ibid.

59 Henry Swinburne, *A Treatise of Spousals, or Matrimonial Contracts* (New York, 1985), pp. 51, 70–73.

60 Walker, 'Rereading Rape', p. 5.

61 James A. Brundage, *Law, Sex and Christian Society in Medieval Europe* (Chicago, 1987), p. 531.

62 Manon van der Heijden, 'Women as Victims of Sexual and Domestic Violence in Seventeenth-Century Holland: Criminal Cases of Rape, Incest, and Maltreatment in Rotterdam and Delft', *Journal of Social History* 33 (2000), pp. 624–25.

63 Barstow, *Witchcraze*, p. 132.

64 See www.aifs.gov.au/acssa/pubs/seets/rs2/.

65 Burnet, *Reformation*, IV, 71, p. 505.

66 Baldwin Smith, *A Tudor Tragedy*, pp. 56–57.

67 Cited by Denny, *Katherine Howard*, p. 220.

68 Walker, 'Rereading Rape', p. 6.

69 Sarah Toulalan, 'Child Victims of Rape and Sexual Assault: Compromised Chastity, Marginalized Lives?', in Andrew Spicer and Jane L. Stevens Crawshaw (eds), *The Place of the Social Margins, 1350–1750* (New York, 2017), p. 181.

70 Ingram, 'Child Sexual Abuse', p. 63.

71 Ibid., pp. 77, 83.

72 Russell, *Young and Damned and Fair*, p. 313.

73 Carolyn Harris, 'Category Archives: The Tudors Books I've Read This Week: Kings and Queens' (2018); accessed online at www.royalhistorian.com/category/the-tudors/.

Chapter 4

1 Henry Ellis (ed.), *Hall's Chronicle; Containing the History of England, during the Reign of Henry the Fourth, and the Succeeding Monarchs, to the End of the Reign of Henry the Eighth, in Which are Particularly Described the Manners and Customs of Those Periods* (London, 1809), p. 819.

2 Hume, *Chronicle of Henry VIII*, pp. 72–73.

3 Holinshed, *Chronicle*.

4 *Statutes of the Realm, 28 Henry VIII*; James Anthony Froude, *History of England: From the Fall of Wolsey to the Death of Elizabeth* (New York, 1868), II, pp. 497–8.

5 *Hall's Chronicle*, p. 819; Holinshed, *Chronicle*.

6 *Statutes of the Realm, 28 Henry VIII*; Froude, *History of England*, II, p. 489.

7 Hamilton, *A Chronicle of England*, I, p. 70.

8 Roger Merriman Bigelow (ed.), *Life and Letters of Thomas Cromwell* (Oxford, 1902), p. 19.

9 Hamilton, *A Chronicle of England*, I, p. 48.

10 LPX 1021; XI 7.

11 Hamilton, *A Chronicle of England*, I, p. 50.

12 Ibid., pp. 53–54.

13 Cottonian MSS., Vespasian, F. xiii, f. 75.

14 Brenan and Statham, *House of Howard*, p. 188.

15 Hamilton, *A Chronicle of England*, I, p. 55.

16 Ibid., p. 51.

17 *Hall's Chronicle*, p. 820.

18 Hamilton, *A Chronicle of England*, I, pp. 56–58.

19 Ibid., pp. 57–58; *Hall's Chronicle*, p. 823.

20 SP, Hen. VIII, I, p. 494.

21 Cited by Denny, *Katherine Howard*, p. 104.

22 *Hall's Chronicle*, p. 824.

23 Hamilton, *A Chronicle of England*, I, p. 60.

24 Ibid., pp. 64–65.

25 SP, Hen. VIII, V, p. 9.

26 Brenan and Statham, *House of Howard*, pp. 226–28.

27 SP, Hen. VIII, V, p. 325.

28 Brenan and Statham, *House of Howard*, pp. 229–30.

29 Hamilton, *A Chronicle of England*, I, p. 64.

30 LPXI 9.

31 LPX 901, 908.

32 Wheeler, *Men of Power*, pp. 224, 236–37.

33 *Hall's Chronicle*, p. 825.

34 Hamilton, *A Chronicle of England*, I, p. 67.

35 Ibid., pp. 68–69.

36 LPXII 1060.

37 *Hall's Chronicle*, p. 825.

38 Ibid.

39 LP XIII 995.

40 Hamilton, *A Chronicle of England*, I, p. 74.

41 Ibid.

42 Ibid., pp. 85–86.

43 Brenan and Statham, *House of Howard*, pp. 236–37.

44 Ibid., p. 238.

45 Ibid., p. 245.

46 Ibid., p. 246.

47 Hamilton, *A Chronicle of England*, I, p. 88.

48 *Hall's Chronicle*, p. 827.

49 Ibid., p. 826.

50 R. McEntegart, 'Fatal Matrimony: Henry VIII and the Marriage of Anne of Cleves', in D. Starkey (ed.), *Henry VIII: A European Court* (London, 1991), p. 140.

51 *Hall's Chronicle*, p. 826.

52 LPXIV 62. See also Retha M. Warnicke, *The Marrying of Anne of Cleves: Royal Protocol in Tudor England* (Cambridge, 2000).

53 Retha M. Warnicke, 'Anne of Cleves, Queen of England', *History Review* (2005).

54 A.G. Dickens, *Thomas Cromwell and the English Reformation*, V, pp. 166–67.

55 See Chapter 2.

56 St. P. I, pp. 604–05; LPXIV 552.

57 LPXIV 33; Strickland, *Memoirs*, p. 239.

58 Warnicke, *Anne of Cleves*.

59 Barbara J. Harris, 'Women and Politics in Early Tudor England', *The Historical Journal* 33 (1990), p. 274.

60 Ellis, *Original Letters*, II, p. 41.

61 LPXV 229; Strickland, *Queens of England*, III, p. 63.

62 Byrne, *Lisle Letters*, IV, p. 895; VI, p. 10.

63 See Wheeler, *Men of Power*, p. 170.

64 Alison Wall, 'Baynton Family (per. 1508–1716), gentry', *Oxford Dictionary of National Biography*; Stanton, 'Sir Thomas Arundell'.

65 See www.tudorplace.com.ar/NORREYS.htm; Appendix II for Katherine's age; Alison Weir, *Mary Boleyn: 'The Great and Infamous Whore'* (London, 2011), pp. 147–49 for Katherine Carey's birth.

66 Hastings Robinson (ed.) *Original Letters Relative to the English Reformation Written During the Reigns of King Henry VIII, King Edward VI and Queen Mary, Chiefly from the Archives of Zurich* (Cambridge, 2 vols, 1847), I, pp. 201–02.

67 Hume, *Chronicle of Henry VIII*, p. 75.

68 Nicola Clark, *Gender, Family, and Politics: The Howard Women, 1485–1558* (Oxford, 2018), p. 38.

69 Warnicke, *Wicked Women*, p. 59.

70 Ibid., p. 58.

71 Burnet, *Reformation*, IV, 71, p. 505.

72 Ibid., III, 7, p. 130.

73 Quoted by Laura Gowing, 'Women, Status and the Popular Culture of Dishonour', *Transactions of the Royal Historical Society*, Sixth Series 6 (1996), p. 225; Mark Breitenberg, 'Anxious Masculinity: Sexual Jealousy in Early Modern England', *Feminist Studies* 19 (1993), pp. 382–83.

74 LPXIV II 388.

75 St. P. VII, pp. 212–13.

76 LPXIV II, 754.

77 *Hall's Chronicle*, p. 833.

78 Retha M. Warnicke, 'Henry VIII's Greeting of Anne of Cleves and Early Modern Court Protocol', *Albion: A Quarterly Journal Concerned with British Studies* 28 (1996), pp. 570–85.

79 *Hall's Chronicle*, p. 833.

80 Strype, *Ecclesiastical Memorials*, VI, pp. 215–16.

81 F.J. Furnivall (ed.), *Ballads from Manuscripts: Ballads on the Condition of England in Henry VIII's and Edward VI's Reign* (London, 2 vols, 1868–72), I, p. 374.

82 Ibid., I, p. 376.

83 LPXI 7.

Chapter 5

1   Brenan and Statham, *House of Howard*, p. 267.

2   Baldwin Smith, *A Tudor Tragedy*, pp. 94–95.

3   Denny, *Katherine Howard*, chapters 9–12. Weir, *Six Wives*, writes in much the same vein: 'She [Katherine] had been deliberately placed in the Queen's household as a maid of honour with detailed instructions as to how to attract the King's attention', p. 413.

4   Burnet, *Reformation*, III, 7, p. 130.

5   Sir Thomas Wyatt, *Collected Poems* (ed. J. Daalder, Oxford, 1975), CVII, p. 112.

6   Byrne, *Lisle*, IV, p. 887; NA SP 1/168, ff. 64–65.

7   Anne Laurence, *Women in England 1500–1760: A Social History* (London, 2005), p. 66.

8   Robert Cawdry, *A Godlye Form of Household Government* (1598), cited by Breitenberg, 'Anxious Masculinity', p. 388.

9   NA E101/422/15.

10 *Hall's Chronicle*, pp. 833–34.

11 Ibid., p. 835.

12 Ibid., pp. 835–36.

13 Kate Emerson, 'Lists of Women at the Tudor Court' (2013); accessed online at www.kateemersonhistoricals.com/lists.htm.

14 Strype, *Ecclesiastical Memorials*, VI, pp. 214–16.

15 Burnet, *Reformation*, IV, pp. 424–25; LPXV 823.

16 Hamilton, *A Chronicle of England*, I, p. 111.

17 *Hall's Chronicle*, p. 836.

18 Burnet, *Reformation*, IV, p. 427.

19 Warnicke, *Anne of Cleves*, p. 166.

20 Roper, *Oedipus and the Devil*, pp. 138, 188.

21 Warnicke, *Anne of Cleves*.

22 Laura Gowing, 'Women's Bodies and the Making of Sex in Seventeenth-Century England', *Signs* 37 (2012).

23 Strype, *Ecclesiastical Memorials*, VI, pp. 220–21; Burnet, *History of the Reformation*, IV, p. 430.

24 St. P. I, pp. 604–05; LPXVI 552.

25 Warnicke, 'Anne of Cleves'.

26 Strype, *Ecclesiastical Memorials*, VI, pp. 221–22.

27 Warnicke, *Anne of Cleves*, pp. 234–35.

28 Starkey, *Six Wives*, pp. 637–38; Baldwin Smith, *A Tudor Tragedy*, Chapter 5; Denny, *Katherine Howard*, Chapter 11, for example.

29 P.R.O., S.P. I, 168, f.60; LPXVI 1409.

30 As suggested by Warnicke, *Wicked Women*, p. 58.

31 LPXV 901.

32 Cited by Strickland, *Memoirs*, p. 329.

33 George Cavendish, *The Life of Cardinal Wolsey and Metrical Visions*, p. 64; LPXVI 12.

34 Hastings Robinson, *Original Letters*, I, p. 202.

35 LPXV 613, 686.

36 Eric Carlson, 'Courtship in Tudor England', *History Today* 43.8 (1993).

37 *Third Report of the Deputy Keeper*, App. II, pp. 264–65.

38 *Hall's Chronicle*, p. 838.

39 Hastings Robinson, *Original Letters*, I, p. 202.

40 Ibid., p. 205.

41 LPXV 831.

42 Greg Walker, 'Henry VIII and the Invention of the Royal Court', *History Today* 47.2 (1997).

43 Starkey, 'From Feud to Faction'.

44 LPXII 1150; XVI 1366.

45 LPXII 711, 808.

46 LPIX 612.

47 John Stow, *A Survey of London* (ed. Charles Lethbridge, 2 vols, Oxford, 1908), II, pp. 99–100.

48 Tudor PCC Will Transcription, L.L. Duncan, 54, p. 28.

49 Hastings Robinson, *Original Letters*, I, p. 227.

50 Warnicke, *Wicked Women*, p. 68.

51 Denny, *Katherine Howard*, pp. 189–90.

52 Ibid., p. 88.

53 Herbert, *The Life and Raigne of King Henry the Eighth*, p. 456.

54 *Hall's Chronicle*, p. 838.

55 Glyn Redworth, *In Defence of the Church Catholic: The Life of Stephen Gardiner* (Oxford, 1990), pp. 106–07.

56 LPXV 766.

57 LPXV 785.

58 Diarmaid MacCulloch, *Thomas Cranmer* (Yale, 1996), p. 272.

59 LPXV 736.

60 Warnicke, *Anne of Cleves*, p. 183.

61 Ibid., pp. 184–85; LPXV 848.

62 LPXV 850.

63 Warnicke, 'Anne of Cleves'.

64 Lawrence Stone, *Broken Lives: Separation and Divorce in England 1660–1857* (Oxford, 1993), p. 22.

65 Wheeler, *Men of Power*, p. 178.

66 Starkey, *Six Wives*, p. 649.

67 Gowing, 'Women's Bodies'.

68 See Linda A. Pollock, 'Honor, Gender, and Reconciliation in Elite Culture, 1570–1700', *Journal of British Studies* 46 (2007).

69 *Hall's Chronicle*, p. 839.

70 Ellis, *Original Letters*, II, p. 159; LPXV 845.

71 LPXV 908, 925.

72 *Hall's Chronicle*, p. 839.

Chapter 6

1   LP XVIII 873.

2   *Hall's Chronicle*, p. 840; Hamilton, *A Chronicle of England*, I, pp. 121–2; Wheeler, *Men of Power*, p. 181; Starkey, *Six Wives*, p. 649.

3   *Hall's Chronicle*, p. 840.

4   LPXV 902, 916.

5   LPXV 902.

6   Hume, *Chronicle of Henry VIII*, p. 76.

7   LPXVI 12.

8   Strickland, *Memoirs*, p. 294.

9   Starkey, *Six Wives*, p. 810 n. 17.

10 J.L. Laynesmith, *The Last Medieval Queens: English Queenship 1445–1503* (Oxford, 2004), p. 95.

11 Ibid., pp. 97, 82.

12 LPXVI 712.

13 See Chapter 1.

14 'HOWARD, Sir George (1519–80), of London and Kidbrooke, Kent', in S. T. Bindoff (ed.), *The History of Parliament: the House of Commons 1509–1558* (Boydell and Brewer, 1982), pp. 399–400.

15 Hume, *Chronicle of Henry VIII*, p. 76.

16 LPXVI 128.

17 Leanda de Lisle, *The Sisters Who Would Be Queen: The Tragedy of Mary, Katherine and Lady Jane Grey* (London, 2008), pp. 320–21 n. 3.

18 For Katherine's household, see LPXV 21.

19 LPXV 875.

20 Ibid., 21.

21 Ives, *Anne*, p. 205.

22 Maria Dowling, 'A Woman's Place? Learning and the Wives of Henry VIII', *History Today* 41.6 (1991).

23 John Matusiak, 'Faction, Intrigue and Influence at the Mid Tudor Court', *History Review* (2012); accessed online at www.historytoday.com/john-matusiak/faction-intrigue-and-influence-mid Tudor-court.

24 Baldwin Smith, *A Tudor Tragedy*, p. 186.

25 Hume, *Chronicle of Henry VIII*, p. 77.

26 Weir, *Six Wives*, p. 434.

27 Crawford, *Letters*, p. 207.

28 Margaret of Anjou was 15 when she married Henry VI in 1445. Her successor Elizabeth Wydeville was 27, while Anne Neville was also 27 when her husband Richard III became king. Elizabeth of York was 19 when she wed Henry VII in 1486, while Katherine of Aragon was 23 when she became queen in 1509. Anne Boleyn was aged between 26 and 32, Jane Seymour was aged between 25 and 28, and Anne of Cleves was 24, when each married Henry VIII.

29 LPXVI 217.

30 Ibid.

31 Lionel Cust, 'A Portrait of Queen Catherine Howard, by Hans Holbein the Younger', *Burlington Magazine for Connoisseurs* 17 (1910), p. 193.

32 Fraser, *Six Wives of Henry VIII*, believes that the sitter's black dress signifies that she is a widow, and on this basis, identifies the sitter as Elizabeth, sister of Queen Jane, and wife of Gregory Cromwell, p. 386. Roy Strong, *Tudor and Jacobean Portraits* (London, 1969), I, pp. 41–44, agrees, suggesting the sitter is Elizabeth Cromwell. Other historians dispute this; Alison Weir questions whether the daughter of a mere knight (John Seymour) would have been entitled to wear such rich dress and suggests that it is significant that at least three copies of this portrait survive (email to the author).

33 Teri Fitzgerald and Diarmaid MacCulloch, 'Gregory Cromwell: Two Portrait Miniatures by Hans Holbein the Younger', *The Journal of Ecclesiastical History* 67 (2016), pp. 587–601.

34 Cust, 'Portrait of Catherine', p. 194.

35 Ibid.

36 Hume, *Chronicle of Henry VIII*, p. 77.

37 LPXVI 804.

38 For Katherine's inventory, see LP XVI 1389.

39 William Thomas, *The Pilgrim: A Dialogue on the Life and Actions of King Henry the Eighth* (ed. J. Froude, London, 1861), p. 58.

40 See Chapter 1.

41 Cust, 'A Portrait of Catherine', p. 194.

42 Roy Strong, *Tudor and Jacobean Portraits* (London, 1969), p. 41.

43 See, for instance, the 1544 portrait painted by Master John.

44 Rosalind K. Marshall, 'Douglas, Lady Margaret, Countess of Lennox (1515–78), Noblewoman', *Oxford Dictionary of National Biography*.

45 Denny, *Katherine Howard*, p. 98.

46 Russell, *Young and Damned and Fair*, p. 387.

47 Starkey, *Six Wives*, pp. xxv, 651.

48 Susan E. James, 'Lady Margaret Douglas and Sir Thomas Seymour by Holbein: Two Miniatures Re-identified', *Apollo* 147 (1998), pp. 15–16.

49 Ibid., p. 17.

50 Fraser, *Six Wives*, pp. 406–7.

51 LPXVI 217.

52 Nigel Reynolds, 'The True Beauty of Lady Jane Grey', *The Telegraph* (5 March 2007); accessed online at www.telegraph.co.uk/news/uknews/1544576/The-true-beauty-of-Lady-Jane-Grey.html.

53 Russell, *Young and Damned and Fair*, pp. 389–90.

54 Brett Dolman, 'Wishful Thinking: Reading the Portraits of Henry VIII's Queens', in Suzannah Lipscomb and Thomas Betteridge (eds), *Henry VIII and the Court: Art, Politics and Performance* (London, 2016), p. 126.

55 Baldwin Smith, *A Tudor Tragedy*, p. 10.

56 Weir, *Six Wives*, p. 3.

57 Plowden, *Tudor Women*, p. 96.

58 Diarmaid MacCulloch, review of E. W. Ives, *The Life and Death of Anne Boleyn* (2004); accessed online at www.telegraph.co.uk/culture/?xml=/arts/2004/07/18/boive18.xml.

59 Warnicke, *Wicked Women*, p. 183.

60 Sir John Harington, *Nugae Antiquae: Being a Miscellaneous Collection of Original Papers in Prose and Verse* (eds Henry Harington and Thomas Park, New York, 2 vols, 1966), I, pp. 28–29; cited by Warnicke, *Wicked Women*, p. 6.

61 Cal. SP. Span., VI, I, p. 155; accessed online at www.british-history.ac.uk/cal-state-papers/ spain/vol6/no1, pp. 312–15.

62 Ibid.

63 Retha M. Warnicke, *Elizabeth of York and Her Six Daughters-in-Law: Fashioning Tudor Queenship, 1485–1547* (New York, 2017), p. 152.

64 Cal. SP. Span., V, ii, p. 61; accessed online at www.british-history.ac.uk/cal-state-papers/ spain/vol5/no2, pp. 137–62.

65 LPXI 860.

66 LPX 908.

67 Lauren Mackay, 'The Hidden Lives of Henry VIII's Six Wives', *History Extra* (2014); accessed online at www.historyextra.com/period/tudor/the-hidden-lives-of-henry-viiis-six-wives/.

68 Hamilton, *A Chronicle of England*, I, p. 123.

69 LPXVI 60.

70 LPXVI 223.

71 LPXVI 26.

72 Strickland, *Memoirs*, p. 291.

73 Breitenberg, 'Anxious Masculinity', pp. 384–88.

74 See Chapter 5.

Chapter 7

1 Denny, *Katherine Howard*, p. 160.

2 LP VI 351.

3 Ann Weikel, 'Mary I (1516–1558), Queen of England and Ireland', *Oxford Dictionary of National Biography* (2004); accessed online at www.oxforddnb.com/view/10.1093/ ref:odnb/9780198614128.001.0001/odnb-9780198614128-e-18245.

4 See, for example, John Edwards, *Mary I: England's Catholic Queen* (Yale, 2011).

5 LPXVI 314.

6 Baldwin Smith, *A Tudor Tragedy*, p. 141.

7 Edwards, *Mary I*, p. 62.

8 Hume, *Chronicle of Henry VIII*, p. 76.

9 Cal. SP. Span., VI, i, pp. 305–06.

10 LPXVI 835.

11 LPXVI 1389.

12 Ibid.

13 Starkey, *Six Wives*, p. 660.

14 LPXVI 835.

15 SC 6/HEN VIII/6332; 6365; 6397.

16 Ibid., 804.

17 LPXV 21.

18 James Carley, *The Books of King Henry VIII and His Wives* (London, 2004), p. 134.

19 Ibid.

20 Ibid., p. 135.

21 Ibid., p. 136.

22 Olga Hughes, 'Royal Library: Catherine Howard's Books' (2014); accessed online at nerdalicious.com.au/books/royal-library-catherine-howards-books/.

23 LPXVI 316.

24 LPXVI 379 (38); 947 (10).

25 Warnicke, *Elizabeth of York*, p. 103.

26 Richard Jones, *The Byrth of Mankynde, Newly Translated Out of Laten Unto Englysshe* (London, 1540).

27 Cal. SP. Span., VI, i, pp. 305–06.

28 Honeycutt, 'Medieval Queenship'.

29 LPXVI 581.

30 Ibid., 660, 678, 1391 (18).

31 Russell, *Young and Damned and Fair*, pp. 296–97.

32 Harris, 'Women and Politics', p. 260.

33 LPXV 21.

34 Harris, 'View from My Lady's Chamber', pp. 237–38.

35 LPXVI 1389.

36 Baldwin Smith, *A Tudor Tragedy*, p. 146.

37 Harris, 'View from My Lady's Chamber', p. 243.

38 Clark, *Gender*, p. 12.

39 Ibid., p. 39.

40 LPXVI 379 (18).

41 LPXVI 1416 (2).

42 LPXVI 1339; NA, S.P. I, 167, f. 157.

43 Ibid., f. 161.

44 Goldberg, 'Girls Growing Up in Later Medieval England'.

45 LPXVI 589.

46 LPXVI 1328.

47 Hamilton, *A Chronicle of England*, I, p. 124.

48 Ibid., p. 712.

49 Ibid., p. 1332.

50 See Chapter 3.

51 Kathleen Coyne Kelly, *Performing Virginity and Testing Chastity in the Middle Ages* (Routledge, 2002), p. ix.

52 CSP Span, V, i, p. 328.

Chapter 8

1 See, for example, Baldwin Smith, *A Tudor Tragedy*, and Fraser, *Six Wives*.

2 See Starkey, *Six Wives*.

3 See Warnicke, *Wicked Women*.

4 Retha M. Warnicke, 'Queenship: Politics and Gender in Tudor England', *History Compass* 4 (2006), pp. 203–27.

5 Laurence, *Women in England*, p. 61.

6   Gilbert Burnet, *The History of the Reformation of the Church of England* (ed. Nicholas Pocock, Oxford, 1865), VI, pp. 250–52.

7   Wilkinson, *Katherine Howard*, pp. 66–67.

8   LPXVI 1339.

9   LPXVI 712.

10 LPXVI 1339; PRO, SP 1/167, fo. 157.

11 *Bath Manuscripts*, pp. 8–10.

12 Retha M. Warnicke, 'The Fall of Anne Boleyn Revisited', *English Historical Review* 108 (1993), p. 658.

13 Patricia Ellen Thompson, 'Decline and Fall of Courtly Love', MA Dissertation, Kansas University (1964), pp. 4–5.

14 'The Conventions of Courtly Love'; accessed online at www.research.uvu.edu/mcdonald/britquestions/courtlylove.html.

15 'Medieval View of Love: Courtly Love'; accessed online at www.academic.brooklyn.cuny.edu/english/melani/cs6/love.html.

16 Kathleen Forni, 'Literature of Courtly Love: Introduction' (2005); accessed online at www.lib.rochester.edu/camelot/teams/forcrtlvint.htm.

17 Elizabeth Heale, 'Women and the Courtly Love Lyric: the Devonshire MS (BL Additional 17492)', *Modern Language Review* 90 (1995), p. 298.

18 *Book of the Courtier*, p. 191.

19 Heale, 'Women', p. 300.

20 Ibid., pp. 296–315.

21 Johanna Rickman, *Love, Lust, and License in Early Modern England: Illicit Sex and the Nobility* (Ashgate, 2008), p. 29.

22 Harris, 'Arranged Marriage in Early Tudor England', p. 66.

23 Hume, *Chronicle of Henry VIII*.

24 Eric W. Ives, 'Faction at the Court of Henry VIII: The Fall of Anne Boleyn', *Journal of the Historical Association* 57 (1972), p. 170.

25 Hume, *Chronicle of Henry VIII*, pp. 74–75.

26 Warnicke, *Wicked Women*, p. 3.

27 Ibid., p. 4.

28 Hume, *Chronicle of Henry VIII*, p. 82.

29 Ibid.

30 Historians have disagreed about the date of its composition. Warnicke, *Wicked Women*, p. 69, indicated that it was written in July 1541, whereas Denny, *Katherine Howard*, p. 191, argued that Katherine penned the letter in April 1541 when Culpeper fell ill. Baldwin Smith, *A Tudor Tragedy*, p. 155, also thought that the letter was written in April 1541.

31 LPXVI 941; 1011.

32 LPXVI 1338.

33 Wheeler, *Men of Power*, p. 274.

34 NA, S.P. I, vol. 167, f. 14.

35 Warnicke, *Wicked Women*, p. 69.

36 Linda Pollock, 'Anger and the Negotiation of Relationships in Early Modern England', *Historical Journal* 47 (2004), p. 571.

37 Fay Bound, 'Writing the Self? Love and Letter in England, *c.* 1660–1760', *Literature and History* 11 (2002), pp. 1–19. See also James Daybell, *The Material Letter in Early Modern England: Manuscript Letters and the Culture and Practices of Letter-Writing, 1512–1635* (Palgrave Macmillan, 2012).

38 Susan M. Fitzmaurice, *The Familiar Letter in Early Modern English: A Pragmatic Approach* (John Benjamins Publishing Company, 2002), pp. 1–2.

39 Katherine Kong, *Lettering the Self in Medieval and Early Modern France* (Cambridge, 2010), p. 235.

40 Warnicke, *Wicked Women*, p. 70.

41 LPIII 2394.

42 Kong, *Lettering the Self*, p. 235.

43 Hume, *Chronicle of Henry VIII*, p. 82.

44 Denny, *Katherine Howard*, p. 93.

45 Warnicke, *Wicked Women*, p. 70.

46 Kong, *Lettering the Self*, p. 235.

47 James Daybell, *Women Letter-Writers in Tudor England* (Oxford, 2006), p. 46.

48 Conor Byrne, 'Queen Katherine Howard's Letter to Thomas Culpeper', *Tudor Life Magazine* (May 2016), pp. 2–7.

49 Julia Fox, *Jane Boleyn: The Infamous Lady Rochford* (London, 2007), p. 361.

50 For instance, Starkey, *Six Wives*, p. 675.

51 Baldwin Smith, *Tudor Tragedy*, p. 156. But as Fox (*Jane Boleyn*, p. 362) notes, there is no evidence to suggest that Jane's behaviour was 'unbalanced' until she was imprisoned in the Tower in early 1542. See also Elizabeth Norton, *The Boleyn Women: The Tudor Femme Fatales who Changed English History* (Stroud, 2013).

52 Fox, *Jane Boleyn*. Warnicke, *Rise and Fall*, pp. 216–17, 302, also recognises that Lady Rochford's association with Anne Boleyn's downfall was much more minimal than it has usually been assumed to be.

53 Denny, *Katherine Howard*, p. 194.

54 Helen E. Maurer, *Margaret of Anjou: Queenship and Power in Late Medieval England* (Woodbridge, 2003), p. 88.

55 Ives, 'Marrying for Love'.

56 Retha M. Warnicke, 'Katherine [Catherine] [née Katherine Howard] (1518–42), Queen of England and Ireland, Fifth Consort of Henry VIII', *Oxford Dictionary of National Biography* (2004); accessed online at www.oxforddnb.com/view/10.1093/ref:odnb/9780198614128.001.0001/odnb-9780198614128-e-4892.

57 LPXVI 1339.

58 LPXVI 1336.

59 Baldwin Smith, *A Tudor Tragedy*, p. 146, comments that 'if the testimony purporting to prove the Queen's carnal desires and activities demonstrates anything, it indicates that imagination largely supplemented memory and that almost everyone concerned lied like a trooper'. Despite this, he accepts Katherine's guilt and validates the claim that she engaged in adultery with Culpeper, assisted by the 'insane' Lady Rochford.

60 LPXVI 1339.

61 Roper, *Oedipus and the Devil*, pp. 138, 188.

62 Warnicke, 'Fall of Anne Boleyn', p. 658.

63 Heale, 'Women and the Courtly Love Lyric', p. 298.

64 Fox, *Jane Boleyn*, p. 364.

65 *Bath Manuscripts*, p. 9; NA SP 1/167, ff. 149, 160.

66 LPXVI 1339.

67 NA SP 1/167 f. 153.

68 *Bath Manuscripts*, pp. 9–10.

69 Hume, *Chronicle of Henry VIII*, pp. 82–84.

70 *Bath Manuscripts*, p. 9; NA SP 1/167, f. 158.

71 *Hall's Chronicle*, p. 842.

72 LPXVI 1088.

73 Ibid.

74 Ibid.
75 LPX 1134/4; XVI, 678 (13), XVI 1339; NA SP 1/167 f. 158–59.
76 NA SP 1/167, f. 160.
77 NA SP 1/167, f. 158–59.
78 *Bath Manuscripts*, pp. 8–10.
79 *Hall's Chronicle*, p. 842.
80 LPXVI 1208.
81 *Bath Manuscripts*, p. 9.
82 Ibid.
83 Ibid., p. 10.
84 Ibid., p. 10.
85 LPXVI 1183.

Chapter 9

1   LPXVI 1297.
2   LPXVI 1334.
3   NA SP 1/163 fol. 46r.
4   LPXVI 101.
5   Wilson, *The Queen and the Heretic*, p. 64.
6   LPXVI 1320.
7   Ibid.; NA SP 1/167 f. 129.
8   Ibid.; fs. 138–138v.
9   LPXVI 1339.
10 Walker, 'Rereading Rape', pp. 4–6.
11 Barstow, *Witchcraze*, p. 138.
12 LPXVI 1332.
13 LPXVI 1325.
14 LPXVI 1334.
15 Burnet, *Reformation*, VI, p. 250.
16 Ibid., pp. 250–52.
17 *Bath Manuscripts*, pp. 8–9.
18 LPXVI 1328.
19 LPXVI 1332.
20 Warnicke, *Wicked Women*, p. 73.
21 LPXVI 1332.
22 Baldwin Smith, *A Tudor Tragedy*, pp. 171–72.
23 LPXVI 1331.
24 Maria Hayward, '"We Should Dress Us Fairly for Our End": The Significance of the Clothing Worn at Elite Executions in England in the Long Sixteenth Century,' *History* 101 (2016), p. 228.
25 LPXVI 1332.
26 Heijden, 'Women as Victims', p. 625.
27 Roper, *Oedipus and the Devil*, pp. 136, 188.
28 Elizabeth Foyster, *Manhood in Early Modern England: Honour, Sex, and Marriage* (London, 1999), p. 60.
29 Breitenberg, 'Anxious Masculinity', pp. 377–98.
30 LPXVI 1334.
31 LPXVI 1426.
32 LPXVI 1339.

33 LPXVI 1337, 1338.

34 Lacey Baldwin Smith, 'English Treason Trials and Confessions in the Sixteenth Century', *Journal of the History of Ideas* 15 (1954), p. 478.

35 LPXVI 1457, 1454.

36 Alec Ryrie, 'John Lassells [Lascelles] (*d*. 1546), Courtier and Religious Activist', *Oxford Dictionary of National Biography* (2004–13); accessed online at www.oxforddnb.com/view/10.1093/ref:odnb/9780198614128.001.0001/odnb-9780198614128-e-68897.

37 Gowing, 'Women, Status and Dishonour', p. 234.

38 Fletcher, 'Men's Dilemma', p. 67.

39 Pollock, 'Honor, Gender, and Reconciliation'.

40 LPXVI 1395.

41 LPXVI 1401.

42 Harris, 'Women and Politics', p. 276; Harris, 'My Lady's Chamber', p. 243.

43 LPXVI 1394.

44 LPXVI 1400.

45 *St. Papers* I, ii, 180, pp. 722–23.

46 Ibid., 1461.

47 Baldwin Smith, *A Tudor Tragedy*, p. 175.

48 LPXVI 1403.

49 Baldwin Smith, *A Tudor Tragedy*, pp. 177–78.

50 LPXV 1471.

51 LPXVI 1426.

52 Heijden, 'Women as Victims', pp. 624–25.

53 LPXVI 578.

54 Cited by Denny, *Katherine Howard*, p. 242; LPXVI 1470.

55 Fox, *Jane Boleyn*, p. 363.

56 LPXVII 415; 568; 1258; LPXVIII, i, 415.

57 Brenan and Statham, *House of Howard*, I, p. 307.

58 LPXVI 1426.

59 LPXVII 28 (21).

60 *Lords' Journal*, I, p. 171.

61 Cited by Alison Weir, *Mary, Queen of Scots and the Murder of Lord Darnley* (London, 2003), p. 447.

62 Strickland, *Memoirs*, p. 325.

63 Calendar of State Papers, Spain, Volume 6 Part 1, 1538–42, p. 228.

64 Ibid., 232.

65 Ibid. See also Fox, *Jane Boleyn*.

66 Frances E. Dolan, '"Gentlemen, I Have One Thing More to Say": Women on Scaffolds in England, 1563–1680', *Modern Philology* 92 (1994) makes the point (p. 164) that beheading was the method of execution reserved for aristocrats and queens in this era because it was thought to be both quick and dignified.

67 Cited by Strickland, *Memoirs*, p. 325.

68 Ibid.

69 Speed, 1030; Carte; Burnet, cited by Strickland, *Memoirs*, p. 324.

70 Cal. SP. Span., VI, i, p. 232.

71 LPXVII 124.

72 *Hall's Chronicle*, p. 843.

73 Ellis (ed.), *Original Letters*, II, pp. 128–29.

74 LPXVII 100.

75 Doyne Bell, *Notices of the Historic Persons Buried in the Tower of London* (London, 1877).

76 Warnicke, *Wicked Women*, pp. 188–89.

77 Hume, *Chronicle of Henry VIII*, p. 86.

78 *Hall's Chronicle*, p. 843; Hamilton, *A Chronicle of England*, I, p. 134; LPXVII 124.
79 See my article, 'The Misconceptions of Katherine Howard' (2013), available online at conorbyrnex.blogspot.co.uk/2013/10/misconceptions-of-katherine-howard.html.
80 LPXVII 100.

Appendix II

1 Baldwin, *A Tudor Tragedy*; Fraser, *The Wives of Henry VIII*; Starkey, *Six Wives*.
2 Weir, *Six Wives*; Denny, *Katherine Howard*; Wilkinson, *Katherine Howard*.
3 Warnicke, *Rise and Fall*, p. 35.
4 Warnicke, *Wicked Women*, pp. 27–28; Gareth Russell, 'The Age of Anne Boleyn' (2010); accessed online at garethrussellcidevant.blogspot.co.uk/2010/04/age-of-anne-boleyn.html.
5 Joseph Stevenson (ed.), *The Life of Jane Dormer Duchess of Feria by Henry Clifford* (London, 1887), p. 80.
6 LPX 901.
7 Ibid.
8 Russell, *Young and Damned and Fair*, p. 423 n. 11.
9 LPXVI 1426.
10 Warnicke, *Wicked Women*, p. 48.
11 Wilkinson, *Katherine Howard*; Russell, *Young and Damned and Fair*.
12 Conor Byrne, 'Katherine Howard's Birthday' (2014); accessed online at onthetudortrail.com/Blog/2014/08/01/katherine-howards-birthday-a-guest-post-by-conor-byrne/.

BIBLIOGRAPHY

Primary Sources

Archaeologia Cantiana: Being the Transactions of the Kent Archaeological Society (London, 1861, 1917).

Ayre, John (ed.), *The Catechism of Thomas Becon* (Cambridge, 1844).

Bergenroth, G.A., de Goyangos, P., Mattingley, G., Tyler, R. et al. (eds), *Calendar of Letters, Despatches and State Papers Relating to Negotiations between England and Spain, Preserved in the Archives at Simancas and Elsewhere* (London, 17 vols, 1862–1965).

Bigelow, Roger Merriman (ed.), *Life and Letters of Thomas Cromwell* (Oxford, 1902).

Brewer, J.S. and Brodie, R.H. (eds), *Letters and Papers, Foreign and Domestic, of the Reign of Henry VIII. Preserved in the Public Record Office, the British Museum, and Elsewhere in England* (London, 21 vols, 1862–1932).

Burnet, Gilbert, *The History of the Reformation of the Church of England* (A. Rhanes for R. Gunne, J. Smith and W. Bruce, 3 vols, 1683).

Byrne, Muriel St. Clare (ed.), *The Lisle Letters* (Chicago, 6 vols, 1981).

Carles, Lancelot de, *La Grande Bretagne devant L'Opinion Francaise* (ed. G. Ascoli, Paris, 1927).

Castiglione, B., *The Book of the Courtier* (trans. T. Hoby, 1946).

Cavendish, George, *The Life of Cardinal Wolsey and Metrical Visions* (ed. Samuel Weller Singer, London, 1825).

Cavendish, George, *Thomas Wolsey Late Cardinal his Life and Death* (ed. Roger Lockyer, 1962).

Cockayne, G.E., *The Complete Peerage* (eds V. Gibbs, H. A. Doubleday, D. Warrand, T. Lord Howard de Walden and G. White, London, 13 vols, 1910–59).

Ellis, Henry (ed.), *Hall's Chronicle; Containing the History of England, during the Reign of Henry the Fourth, and the Succeeding Monarchs, to the End of the Reign of Henry the Eighth, in Which are Particularly Described the Manners and Customs of Those Periods* (London, 1809).

Ellis, Henry (ed.), *Original Letters Illustrative of English History,* third series (London, 4 vols, 1846).

Forest, William, *The History of Grisild the Second: A Narrative in Verse of the Divorce of Queen Katherine of Aragon* (ed. M.D. Macray, London, 1875).

Foxe, John, *The Acts and Monuments of John Foxe* (ed. G. Townsend, London, 8 vols, 1965).

Furnivall, F. J., *Ballads from Manuscripts: Ballads on the Condition of England in Henry VIII's and Edward VI's Reign* (London, 2 vols, 1868–72).

Guistinian, Sebastian, *Four Years at the Court of Henry VIII* (trans. R. Brown, 2 vols, London, 1854).

Harpsfield, Nicholas, *A Treatise on the Pretended Divorce between Henry VIII and Catharine of Aragon* (ed. Nicholas Pocock, London, 1878).

Herbert, E., *The Life and Raigne of King Henry the Eighth* (London, 1649).

Holinshed, Raphael, *Chronicles of England, Scotland and Ireland* (London, 1807–8).

Hume, Martin (ed.), *The Chronicle of King Henry VIII of England. Being a Contemporary Record of Some of the Principal Events of the Reigns of Henry VIII and Edward VI* (London, 1889).

Jones, Richard, *The Byrthe of Mankynde, Newly Translated Out of Laten Unto Englysshe* (London, 1540).

Journal of the House of Lords (1846).

Kramer, Heinrich and Sprenger, James, *Malleus Maleficarum* (trans. Montague Summers, London, 1928).

Luce, J.W. (ed.), *The Love Letters of Henry VIII to Anne Boleyn: With Notes* (London, 1906).

Rawdon Brown, L., Bentnick, C. et al. (eds), *Calendar of State Papers Relating to English Affairs in the Archives of Venice and in the other Libraries of Northern Italy* (London, 7 vols, 1864–1947).

Robinson, Hastings (ed.), *Original Letters Relative to the English Reformation Written During the Reigns of King Henry VIII, King Edward VI and Queen Mary, Chiefly from the Archives of Zurich* (Cambridge, 2 vols, 1847).

Sander, Nicholas, *Rise and Growth of the Anglican Schism* (trans. David Lewis, London, 1877).

Stevenson, Joseph (ed.), *The Life of Jane Dormer Duchess of Feria by Henry Clifford* (London, 1887).

Stow, John, *A Survey of London* (ed. Charles Lethbridge, Oxford, 2 vols, 1908).

Strype, John, *Ecclesiastical Memorials* (Clarendon Press, 1822).

Surrey Archaeological Collections, LI.

The Calendar of the Manuscripts of the Marquis of Bath Preserved at Longleat, Wiltshire (Dublin, 1907).

The Remains of Thomas Cranmer, D.D, Archbishop of Canterbury (ed. Henry Jenkyns, Oxford, 2 vols, 1883).

Thomas, William, *The Pilgrim: A Dialogue on the Life and Actions of King Henry the Eighth* (ed. J. Froude, London, 1861).

Wriothesley, Charles, *A Chronicle of England During the Reign of the Tudors* (ed. William Douglas Hamilton, 2 vols, 1875–7).

Wyatt, Thomas, *Collected Poems* (ed. J. Daalder, Oxford, 1975).

Secondary Sources

Achinstein, Sharon, 'Romance of the Spirit: Female Sexuality and Religious Desire in Early Modern England', *ELH* 69 (2002), pp. 413–38.

Austen, Linda Phyllis, 'Women's Musical Voices in Sixteenth-Century England', *Early Modern Women: An Interdisciplinary Journal* 3 (2008), pp. 127–52.

Baldwin Smith, Lacey, 'English Treason Trials and Confessions in the Sixteenth Century', *Journal of the History of Ideas* 15 (1954), pp. 471–98.

Baldwin Smith, Lacey, *A Tudor Tragedy: The Life and Times of Catherine Howard* (London, 1961).

Barstow, Anne L., *Witchcraze: A New History of the European Witch-Hunts* (San Francisco, 1994).

Bell, Doyne, *Notices of the Historic Persons Buried in the Tower of London* (London, 1877).

Bernard, G.W. *Anne Boleyn: Fatal Attractions* (London, 2010).

Biller, Peter, 'Childbirth in the Middle Ages', *History Today* 36.8 (1986).

Bindoff, S.T. (ed.), *The History of Parliament: the House of Commons 1509–1558* (London, 1982).

Borman, Tracy, *Elizabeth's Women: The Hidden Story of the Virgin Queen* (London, 2010).

Bound, Fay, 'Writing the Self? Love and Letter in England, c. 1660-c. 1760', *Literature and History* 11 (2002), pp. 1–19.

Breitenberg, Mark, 'Anxious Masculinity: Sexual Jealousy in Early Modern England', *Feminist Studies* 19 (1993), pp. 377–98.

Brenan, Gerald and Statham, Edward, *The House of Howard* (New York, 2 vols, 1907).

Brundage, James, *Law, Sex, and Christian Society in Medieval Europe* (Chicago, 1987).

Byrne, Conor, 'The Birth Date and Childhood of Katherine Howard, Queen of England' (2012), unpublished research.

Byrne, Conor, 'The Fall of Katherine Howard: Sexual Deviance at the Tudor Court' (2012), unpublished research.

Byrne, Conor, 'Queen Katherine Howard's Letter to Thomas Culpeper', *Tudor Life Magazine* (May 2016), pp. 2–7.

Byrne, Conor, 'Katherine Howard's Age' (2017), published online at conorbyrnex.blogspot. co.uk/2017/06/katherine-howards-age.html.

Byrne, Conor, 'The Wanton and the Nurse: Katherine Howard and Katherine Parr in Film', *Tudor Life Magazine* (April 2017), pp. 20–6.

Byrne, Conor, 'The Portraiture of Katherine Howard', *Tudor Life Magazine* (October 2017), pp. 54–8.

Capp, Bernard, 'The Double Standard Revisited: Plebeian Women and Male Sexual Reputation in Early Modern England', *Past & Present* 162 (1999), pp. 70–100.

Carley, James P., *The Books of King Henry VIII and His Wives* (London, 2004).

Carlson, Eric, 'Courtship in Tudor England', *History Today* 43.8 (1993).

Clark, Nicola, 'Dynastic Politics: Five Women of the Howard Family During the Reign of Henry VIII, 1509–1547'. PhD Thesis, Royal Holloway College, University of London (2013).

Clark, Nicola, *Gender, Family, and Politics: The Howard Women, 1485–1558* (Oxford, 2018).

Crawford, Patricia, 'Attitudes to Menstruation in Seventeenth-Century England', *Past & Present* 91 (1981), pp. 47–73.

Cust, Lionel, 'A Portrait of Queen Catherine Howard, by Hans Holbein the Younger', *Burlington Magazine for Connoisseurs* 17 (1910), pp. 192–9.

Davies, Catharine, 'Howard, Agnes [née Tilney], Duchess of Norfolk (*b.* in or before 1477, *d.* 1545), Noblewoman', *Oxford Dictionary of National Biography* (2004); accessed online at www.oxforddnb.com/view/10.1093/ref:odnb/9780198614128.001.0001/ odnb-9780198614128-e-70806.

Daybell, James, *Women Letter-Writers in Tudor England* (Oxford, 2006).

Daybell, James, *The Material Letter in Early Modern England: Manuscript Letters and the Culture and Practices of Letter-Writing, 1512–1635* (Basingstoke, 2012).

De Lisle, Leanda, *The Sisters Who Would Be Queen: The Tragedy of Mary, Katherine and Lady Jane Grey* (London, 2008).

Denny, Joanna, *Anne Boleyn: A New History of England's Tragic Queen* (London, 2004).

Denny, Joanna, *Katherine Howard: A Tudor Conspiracy* (London, 2005).

Dolan, Frances E., '"Gentlemen, I Have One More Thing to Say": Women on Scaffolds in England, 1563–1680', *Modern Philology* 92 (1994), pp. 157–78.

Dolman, Brett, 'Wishful Thinking: Reading the Portraits of Henry VIII's Queens', in Suzannah Lipscomb and Thomas Betteridge (eds), *Henry VIII and the Court: Art, Politics and Performance* (London, 2016), pp. 115–31.

Dowling, Maria, 'A Woman's Place? Learning and the Wives of Henry VIII', *History Today* 41.6 (1991).

Edwards, John, *Mary I: England's Catholic Queen* (Yale, 2011).

Elton, G.R., 'Thomas Cromwell's Decline and Fall', *Cambridge Historical Journal* 10 (1951), pp. 150–85.

Emerson, Kate, 'Lists of Women at the Tudor Court' (2013); accessed online at www.kateemersonhistoricals.com/lists.htm.

Fischer-Yinon, Yochi, 'The Original Bundlers: Boaz and Ruth, and Seventeenth-Century English Courtship Practices', *Journal of Social History* 35 (2002), pp. 683–705.

Fitzgerald, Teri and MacCulloch, Diarmaid, 'Gregory Cromwell: Two Portrait Miniatures by Hans Holbein the Younger', *The Journal of Ecclesiastical History* 67 (2016), pp. 587–601.

Fitzmaurice, Susan M., *The Familiar Letter in Early Modern English: A Pragmatic Approach* (Philadelphia, 2002).

Fletcher, Anthony, 'Men's Dilemma: The Future of Patriarchy in England 1560–1660', *Transactions of the Royal Historical Society* 4 (1994), pp. 61–81.

Forni, Kathleen, 'Literature of Courtly Love: Introduction' (2005), accessed online at www. lib.rochester.edu/camelot/teams/forcrtlvint.htm.

Fox, Julia, *Jane Boleyn: the Infamous Lady Rochford* (London, 2007).

Foyster, Elizabeth, *Manhood in Early Modern England: Honour, Sex, and Marriage* (London, 1999).

Fraser, Antonia, *The Six Wives of Henry VIII* (London, 1992).

Froude, James Anthony, *History of England: From the Fall of Wolsey to the Death of Elizabeth* (New York, 1868), Volume II.

Froude, James Anthony, *History of England from the Fall of Wolsey to the Death of Elizabeth* (New York, 1870), Volume III.

Gil, Daniel Juan, 'Before Intimacy: Modernity and Emotion in the Early Modern Discourse of Sexuality', *ELH* 69 (2002), pp. 861–87.

Goldberg, Jeremy, 'Girls Growing Up in Later Medieval England', *History Today* 45.6 (1995).

Goldberg, Jeremy, 'The Right to Choose: Women, Consent and Marriage in Late Medieval England', *History Today* 58.2 (2008).

Gowing, Laura, 'Women, Status and the Popular Culture of Dishonour', *Transactions of the Royal Historical Society* 6 (1996), pp. 225–34.

Gowing, Laura, 'Women's Bodies and the Making of Sex in Seventeenth-Century England', *Signs* 37 (2012).

Graves, Michael A.R., 'Thomas Howard, Third Duke of Norfolk (1473–1554)', *Oxford Dictionary of National Biography* (2004); accessed online at www.oxforddnb.com/view/10.1093/ref:odnb/9780198614128.001.0001/odnb-9780198614128-e-13940.

Gunn, Steven, 'Tournaments and Early Tudor Chivalry', *History Today* 41.6 (1991).

Harris, Barbara J., 'Power, Profit, and Passion: Mary Tudor, Charles Brandon, and the Arranged Marriage in Early Tudor England', *Feminist Studies* 15 (1989), pp. 59–88.

Harris, Barbara J., 'Women and Politics in Early Tudor England', *The Historical Journal* 33 (1990), pp. 259–81.

Harris, Barbara J., 'The View from My Lady's Chamber: New Perspectives on the Early Tudor Monarchy', *Huntingdon Library Quarterly* 60 (1997), pp. 215–47.

Harris, Barbara J., *English Aristocratic Women, 1450–1550: Marriage and Family, Property and Careers* (Oxford, 2002).

Harris, Carolyn. 'Category Archives: The Tudors Books I've Read This Week: Kings and Queens' (2018); accessed online at www.royalhistorian.com/category/the-tudors/.

Hayward, Maria, '"We Should Dress us Fairly for Our End": The Significance of the Clothing Worn at Elite Executions in England in the Long Sixteenth Century,' *History* 101 (2016), pp. 222–45.

Head, D., 'The Life and Career of Thomas Howard, Third Duke of Norfolk: The Anatomy of Tudor Politics', PhD Dissertation, Florida State University (1978).

Heale, Elizabeth, 'Women and the Courtly Love Lyric: the Devonshire MS (BL Additional 17492)', *Modern Language Review* 90 (1995), pp. 296–313.

Heijden, Manon van der, 'Women as Victims of Sexual and Domestic Violence in Seventeenth-Century Holland: Criminal Cases of Rape, Incest, and Maltreatment in Rotterdam and Delft', *Journal of Social History* 33 (2000).

Herbert, Henry, *Memoirs of Henry the Eighth of England: With the Fortunes, Fates and Characters of His Six Wives* (New York, 1860).

Hufton, Olwen, 'Women in History. Early Modern Europe', *Past & Present* 101 (1983), pp. 125–41.

Hufton, Olwen, 'What is Women's History?', *History Today* 35.6 (1985).

Hughes, Olga, 'Royal Library: Catherine Howard's Books' (2014); accessed online at nerdalicious.com.au/books/royal-library-catherine-howards-books/.

Hume, Martin, *The Wives of Henry the Eighth and the Parts They Played in History* (New York, 1905).

Huneycutt, Lois, 'Medieval Queenship', *History Today* 39.6 (1989).

Ingram, Martin, 'Child Abuse in Early Modern England', in Michael Braddick and John Walter (eds), *Negotiating Power in Early Modern Society: Order, Hierarchy and Subordination in Britain and Ireland* (Cambridge, 2001), pp. 63–85.

Ives, E.W., 'Faction at the Court of Henry VIII: The Fall of Anne Boleyn', *Journal of the Historical Association* 57 (1972), pp. 169–88.

Ives, Eric, 'Marrying for Love: The Experience of Edward IV and Henry VIII', *History Today* 50.12 (2000).

Ives, Eric, *The Life and Death of Anne Boleyn* (Oxford, 2005).

James, Susan E., 'Lady Margaret Douglas and Sir Thomas Seymour by Holbein: Two Miniatures Re-identified', *Apollo* 147 (1998), pp. 15–20.

Kelly, Kathleen Coyne, *Performing Virginity and Testing Chastity in the Middle Ages* (London, 2000).

Kizewski, Holly K., 'Jewel of Womanhood: A Feminist Reinterpretation of Queen Katherine Howard', Lincoln Masters Thesis, University of Nebraska (2014); accessed online at digitalcommons.unl.edu/cgi/viewcontent.cgi?article=1073&context=historydiss.

Kong, Katherine, *Lettering the Self in Medieval and Early Modern France* (Cambridge, 2010).

Lane, Joan, 'Obstetrics and Gynaecology in Tudor and Stuart England', *History Today* (1983).

Laurence, Anne, *Women in England 1500–1760: A Social History* (London, 2005).

Laynesmith, J.L., *The Last Medieval Queens: English Queenship 1445–1503* (Oxford, 2004).

Lechnar, M. J., 'Henry VIII's Bastard: Henry Fitzroy, Duke of Richmond', PhD Dissertation, West Virginia University (1977).

Leneman, L., '"A Tyrant and Tormentor": Violence Against Wives in Eighteenth- and Early Nineteenth-Century Scotland', *Continuity and Change* 12 (1997).

Lindsey, Karen, *Divorced, Beheaded, Survived: A Feminist Reinterpretation of the Wives of Henry VIII* (Cambridge, MA, 1996).

Loades, David, *The Tudor Queens of England* (London, 2009).

Loades, David, *Catherine Howard: The Adulterous Wife of Henry VIII* (Stroud, 2012).

MacCulloch, Diarmaid, review of E.W. Ives, *The Life and Death of Anne Boleyn* (2004); accessed online at www.telegraph.co.uk/culture/?xml=/arts/2004/07/18/boive18.xml.

Mack, Phyllis, 'Women and Gender in Early Modern England', *The Journal of Modern History* 73 (2001).

Mackay, Lauren, *Inside the Tudor Court* (Stroud, 2014).

Mackay, Lauren, 'The Hidden Lives of Henry VIII's Six Wives', *History Extra* (2014); accessed online at www.historyextra.com/period/tudor/the-hidden-lives-of-henry-viiis-six-wives/.

Marshall, Rosalind K., 'Douglas, Lady Margaret, Countess of Lennox (1515–1578), Noblewoman', *Oxford Dictionary of National Biography* (2004–13); accessed online at www.oxforddnb.com/view/10.1093/ref:odnb/9780198614128.001.0001/odnb-9780198614128-e-7911.

Matusiak, John, 'Faction, Intrigue and Influence at the Mid Tudor Court', *History Review* (2012).

McEntegart, R., 'Fatal Matrimony: Henry VIII and the Marriage of Anne of Cleves', in D. Starkey (ed.), *Henry VIII: A European Court* (London, 1991).

McLaren, Angus, *Reproductive Rituals: Perceptions of Fertility in Britain from the 16th Century to the 19th Century* (New York, 1984).

McNabb, Jennifer, 'Ceremony versus Consent: Courtship, Illegitimacy, and Reputation in Northwest England, 1560–1610', *The Sixteenth Century Journal* 37 (2006), pp. 59–81.

'Medieval View of Love: Courtly Love', accessed at www.academic.brooklyn.cuny.edu/english/melani/cs6/love.html.

Mendelson, S. and Crawford, P., *Women in Early Modern England 1550–1720* (Oxford, 1998).

Nichols, J.G. (ed.), *Inventories of the Wardrobes, Plate, Chapel Stuff, etc., of Henry Fitzroy, Duke of Richmond and of the Wardrobe Stuff at Baynard's Castle of Katharine, Princess Dowager*, Camden Society, vol. LXI (London, 1855).

Peakman, Julie, 'Medieval Desire: Poise and Passion in the Middle Ages', *History Today* 61.8 (2011).

Peters, Christine, 'Gender, Sacrament and Ritual: The Making and Meaning of Marriage in Late Medieval and Early Modern England', *Past & Present* 169 (2000), pp. 63–96.

Phillips, Julia, 'Women and Society', *History Today* 33.2 (1984).

Plowden, Alison, *Tudor Women: Queens and Commoners* (Stroud, 2002).

Pollock, Linda, 'Anger and the Negotiation of Relationships in Early Modern England', *Historical Journal* 47 (2004), pp. 567–90.

Pollock, Linda A., 'Childbearing and Female Bonding in Early Modern England', *Social History* 22 (1997), pp. 286–306.

Pollock, Linda A., 'Honor, Gender, and Reconciliation in Elite Culture, 1570–1700', *Journal of British Studies* 46 (2007).

Reynolds, Nigel, 'The true beauty of Lady Jane Grey' (2007); accessed online at www.telegraph.co.uk/news/uknews/1544576/The-true-beauty-of-Lady-Jane-Grey.html.

Richardson, Douglas, *Magna Carta Ancestry: A Study in Colonial and Medieval Families* (ed. Kimball G. Everingham I, Salt Lake City, 2011).

Rickman, Johanna, *Love, Lust, and License in Early Modern England: Illicit Sex and the Nobility* (Abingdon, 2008).

Roper, Lyndal, *Oedipus and the Devil: Witchcraft, Sexuality and Religion in Early Modern Europe* (London, 1994).

Rublack, Ulinka, 'Pregnancy, Childbirth and the Female Body in Early Modern Germany', *Past & Present* 150 (1996), pp. 84–110.

Russell, Gareth, *Young and Damned and Fair: The Life and Tragedy of Catherine Howard at the Court of Henry VIII* (London, 2017).

Ryrie, Alec, 'Lassells [Lascelles], John (d.1546), Courtier and Religious Activist', *Oxford Dictionary of National Biography* (2004–13); accessed online at www.oxforddnb.com/view/10.1093/ref:odnb/9780198614128.001.0001/odnb-9780198614128-e-68897;jsessionid=E574A74795646B305DD3A5357D6D67B1.

Schroeder, Joy, *Dinah's Lament: the Biblical Legacy of Sexual Violence in Christian Interpretations* (Minneapolis, 2007).

Somerset, Anne, *Ladies in Waiting: From the Tudors to the Present Day* (London, 1984).

Stanton, Pamela Y., 'Arundell, Sir Thomas (c.1502–1552),' *Oxford Dictionary of National Biography* (2004); accessed online at www.oxforddnb.com/view/10.1093/ref:odnb/9780198614128.001.0001/odnb-9780198614128-e-725?rskey=TTPaja&result=3.

Starkey, David, 'From Feud to Faction: English Politics 1450–1550', *History Today* 32.11 (1982).

Starkey, David, *Six Wives: The Queens of Henry VIII* (London, 2004).

Steinman, G., *Althorp Memoirs, or Biographical Notices of Lady Denham, the Countess of Shrewsbury, the Countess of Falmouth, Mrs. Jenyns, the Duchess of Tyrconnel, and Lucy Walter, Six Ladies Whose Portraits are to be Found in the Picture Gallery of His Excellency Earl Spencer, K.G., K.P.* (1869).

Stone, Lawrence, *Broken Lives: Separation and Divorce in England 1660–1857* (Oxford, 1993).

Strickland, Agnes, *Memoirs of the Queens of Henry VIII., And of His Mother, Elizabeth of York* (Philadelphia, 1853).

Strong, Roy, *Tudor and Jacobean Portraits* (London, 1969).

Swinburne, Henry, *A Treatise of Spousals, Or Matrimonial Contracts* (New York, 1985).

'The Conventions of Courtly Love', accessed online at www.research.uvu.edu/mcdonald/britquestions/courtlylove.html.

Thomas, Keith, *Man and the Natural World: Changing Attitudes in England 1500–1800* (London, 1983).

Thompson, Patricia Ellen, 'The Decline and Fall of Courtly Love', MA dissertation, Kansas State University (1964).

Thurley, Simon, *Houses of Power: The Places That Shaped the Tudor World* (London, 2017).

Tock, Annie, 'Literary Law Enforcement: Gender in Crime Ballads in Early Modern England', Eastern Illinois University (2006); accessed online at www.eiu.edu/~historia/2004/Literary2.pdf.

Toulalan, Sarah, 'Child Victims of Rape and Sexual Assault: Compromised Chastity, Marginalized Lives?', in Andrew Spicer and Jane L. Stevens Crawshaw (eds), *The Place of the Social Margins, 1350–1750* (New York, 2017), pp. 181–203.

Tucker, M.J., *The Life of Thomas Howard, Earl of Surrey and Second Duke of Norfolk, 1443–1524* (London, 1964).

Virgoe, R., 'The Recovery of the Howards in East Anglia, 1485–1529', in E.W. Ives, R.J. Knecht and J.J. Scarisbrick (eds), *Wealth and Power in Tudor England* (London, 1978), pp. 5–16.

Walker, Garthine, 'Rereading Rape and Sexual Violence in Early Modern England', *Gender & History* 10 (2002).

Walker, Greg, 'Henry VIII and the Invention of the Royal Court', *History Today* 47.2 (1997).

Wall, Alison, 'Baynton Family (per. 1508–1716), gentry', *Oxford Dictionary of National Biography* (2004–13); accessed online at www.oxforddnb.com/view/10.1093/ref:odnb/9780198614128.001.0001/odnb-9780198614128-e-71877.

Warnicke, Retha M., *The Rise and Fall of Anne Boleyn: Family Politics at the Court of Henry VIII* (Cambridge, 1989).

Warnicke, Retha M., 'The Fall of Anne Boleyn Revisited', *English Historical Review* 108 (1993), pp. 653–65.

Warnicke, Retha M., 'Henry VIII's Greeting of Anne of Cleves and Early Modern Court Protocol', *Albion: A Quarterly Journal Concerned with British Studies* 28 (1996), pp. 565–85.

Warnicke, Retha M., 'Anne of Cleves, Queen of England', *History Review* (2005).

Warnicke, Retha M., 'Queenship: Politics and Gender in Tudor England', *History Compass* 4 (2006), pp. 203–27.

Warnicke, Retha M., *Wicked Women of Tudor England: Queens, Aristocrats, Commoners* (New York, 2012).

Warnicke, Retha M., *Elizabeth of York and Her Six Daughters-in-Law: Fashioning Tudor Queenship, 1485–1547* (New York, 2017).

Weikel, Ann, 'Mary I (1516–1558), Queen of England and Ireland', *Oxford Dictionary of National Biography* (2004); accessed online at www.oxforddnb.com/view/10.1093/ref:odnb/9780198614128.001.0001/odnb-9780198614128-e-18245.

Weir, Alison, *The Six Wives of Henry VIII* (London, 1991).

Weir, Alison, *The Lady in the Tower: The Fall of Anne Boleyn* (London, 2009).

Weir, Alison, *Mary Boleyn: 'The Great and Infamous Whore'* (London, 2011).

Wheeler, Elisabeth, *Men of Power: Court Intrigue in the Life of Catherine Howard* (Glastonbury, 2008).

Wilkinson, Josephine, *Katherine Howard: The Tragic Story of Henry VIII's Fifth Queen* (London, 2016).

Wilson, Derek, *The Queen and the Heretic: How Two Women Changed the Religion of England* (Oxford, 2018).

Worsley, Lucy, 'Was Katherine Howard, Henry VIII's "Wanton" Fifth Wife, Actually a Victim of Child Sex Abuse?', *The Telegraph* (2016); accessed online at www.telegraph.co.uk/women/life/katherine-howard-henry-viiis-wanton-fifth-wife-actually-victim/.

INDEX

If you enjoyed this title, you might enjoy ...

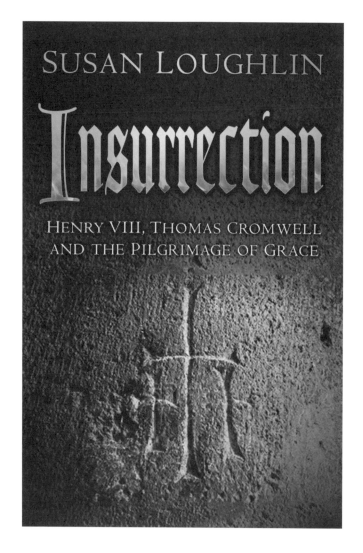

SUSAN LOUGHLIN

Insurrection

HENRY VIII, THOMAS CROMWELL
AND THE PILGRIMAGE OF GRACE

978 0 7509 6733 4